THE DISCOVERY OF KING ARTHUR

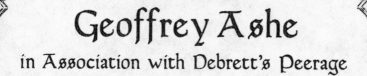

Geoffrey Ashe
in Association with Debrett's Peerage

THE DISCOVERY OF KING ARTHUR

Anchor Press/Doubleday, Garden City, New York
1985

Library of Congress Cataloging in Publication Data

Ashe, Geoffrey.
   The discovery of King Arthur.

   Bibliography: p. 211
   Includes index.
   1. Arthur, King. 2. Geoffrey, of Monmouth, Bishop of
St. Asaph, 1100?–1154. Historia Britonum. 3. Arthurian
romances. 4. Great Britain—Kings and rulers—Biography.
I. Title.
DA152.5.A7A793 1985   942.01′4   [B]   83-45168
ISBN 0-385-19032-8

Designed by Virginia M. Soulé

Anchor Press Edition 1985
Copyright © 1985 text by Geoffrey Ashe
Copyright © 1985 illustrations and captions
by Debrett's Peerage Ltd.

Contents

As a British monarch with a supposedly authentic career, Arthur is the creation of one man, Geoffrey of Monmouth. Writing in the twelfth century, Geoffrey portrays him as a great warrior and ruler, reigning in the period after Britain's severance from the Roman Empire. How was Geoffrey's narrative meant to be taken? Did Geoffrey's readers, and the romancers who followed him, regard it as truth or fiction? And what is special about King Arthur? Does his legend look like a medieval invention, or does it seem to belong in the age when he is said to have lived?

The later Roman Empire, plagued by barbarian incursions and civil strife, cherished a dream of a World-Restorer—a Restitutor Orbis. He was pictured as an Emperor who would turn back the destructive forces and renovate Roman civilization, with some sort of divine aid. The hope could persist because it had been fulfilled, to a certain extent, by a series of able emperors. Even amid disasters after their impact waned, the Roman ideal stayed powerful, and a Restitutor was still a thinkable figure. One result of the disasters was that Britain, alone among Roman lands, attained independence. Arthur's legend is fundamentally the legend of a Restitutor in Britain.

8

MAJESTY   164

In the Middle Ages the rise of a powerful monarchy under the kings of England encouraged the growth of Arthurian romance. Furnished with a "historical" framework by Geoffrey, this gave new life to traditions from the Celtic past, and combined them with medieval themes. Arthur supplied a mystique for English royalty; a mystique which sometimes carried political weight, and was still significant in the revival of his legend by Tennyson.

9

THE MODERN QUEST   184

In the twentieth century the work of archaeologists and historians has given the theme fresh vitality and helped to create a new Arthurian literature. Profound questions arise about the reasons for the perennial spell.

Introduction

Mention King Arthur, and the name conjures up a romantic image. The image is richly complex, comprising not merely a single character but a group, and a constellation of themes. Beside the King stand his Queen, Guinevere, and his enchanter, Merlin. Their home is Camelot, the royal city of a mysterious, wonderful Britain. It houses the Round Table, where Arthur presides over a company of knights headed by Lancelot, devoted to the noblest ideals. In war he quells his enemies with a magical sword, Excalibur. If we explore the scene more deeply, we see a brooding tragedy overhanging it. The King's reign is only a "brief shining moment"; he is doomed to be plotted against, betrayed, and brought down. Camelot must fall.

Common sense would say that this is all remote, irrelevant, medieval; a daydream of romancers in a past age and an obsolete society. Yet since the middle of the twentieth century the spell has strengthened, not weakened. Arthur's legend has inspired musicals, bestselling novels, successful films. It has even been re-created politically. In the eyes of many President Kennedy's Washington was a new Camelot, Kennedy himself a new Arthur. Twenty years after his passing a commemorative feature in *Newsweek* magazine could take this notion for granted, and comment that all presidential candidates since 1960 have "had to run against the myth of Camelot."

There is more to this than a vague sense of charisma in high places. King Arthur is a figure of a specific kind. People saw Kennedy, with however little precise awareness, as a figure of a similar kind. In this book I try to show what that statement implies, and why the vision is so perennially powerful. I also try to show where the vision came from, who the original Arthur was, what he did to be immortalized.

Attempts to find the truth about him, the man (if any) behind the legend, have been going on for some years. The search has disclosed interesting facts, and it has also led to sharp disagreements. By the early 1980s, among professional scholars, it seemed to have reached a dead end. I believe I have been lucky enough to find a way through, and press on to a fruitful outcome. Anyone who has followed the search (and I am endlessly surprised to find how many have) will notice that the view of Arthur which I am offering modifies views which have been offered before, by others and by myself. However, the change is not a total reversal. Rather, it defines, clarifies, enlarges. It not only gives Arthur a firmer status in history, it makes him more interesting—more like his legend—than appeared probable a few years ago. It reveals why he became the kind of figure he did, what shaped the image which had so strange a rebirth in a President. It also reveals how he embodied a more general hope, familiar in the world where he reigned, and not wholly unfamiliar today.

The long delay in running Arthur to earth has been due to the nature of the problem he poses. Medieval authors who gave him his literary grandeur fitted him, loosely, into what they claimed was the history of Britain some centuries earlier. Not much of this history as they tell it stands up in the light of present knowledge. It is mostly legend, as Arthur himself is. So the few historians who have looked for him have swept the medieval accounts aside, and searched in other and older records. But that search can take us only so far. A convincing answer calls for a different approach. Arthur's legend itself must be brought back into the investigation and taken seriously. It must be sifted for clues. The right questions to ask are not the direct ones Who was Arthur? or Did he exist? but Where did the legend come from? and What facts is it rooted in? If we line up the legend side by side with history, as we know it today, the problem can be solved. It almost solves itself.

Oddly, after working out my case, I found that the crucial point was made nearly two centuries ago. It was the fleeting, forgotten insight of an almost forgotten historian, long before his

modern successors began disputing. On the basic issue of Arthur's identity, there need never have been any mystery at all.

I should make it clear that the main thesis has been published elsewhere, with the fullness of detail which scholars rightly
demand. Several have shown a generous interest and carried it
further. The first academic article was in *Speculum,* the journal of
the Medieval Academy of America, in April 1981. I have presented the essentials in a paper read at the Thirteenth International Arthurian Congress, held at the University of Glasgow in
1981; in lectures at Keele University and Oxford, and under the
auspices of American and Canadian universities; in a course
given at the University of Bath; and as a visiting professor at the
University of Southern Mississippi, and at Union College, Sche-
nectady, New York.

Some of the arguments have been left out of the text, as
appealing only to readers with specialized interests, but any such
reader can find them in the notes at the end.

In 1982, on the advice of Professor Charles Moorman, I drew
up some proposals for further research. One result was the formation of Debrett's Arthurian Committee, which I have the
honor to chair. I would like to express my special thanks to three
members of it who have given specific help with this book: Sir
Iain Moncreiffe of That Ilk, Professor Léon Fleuriot, and Professor Barbara Moorman. I must also thank Professor A. O. H.
Jarman, Mr. Charles Evans-Günther, and Dr. Mildred Day, especially the last, who devoted much time and trouble to discussing
the implications of a medieval text. None of them should be held
responsible for more than the points they gave me themselves.

THE DISCOVERY OF KING ARTHUR

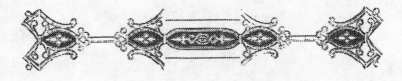

Part 1
A LEGEND AND ITS ROOTS

1

The Kingmaker

The Tale as It Was Told

Arthur is one among many mythological heroes, yet most people would agree that he stands out from the crowd. If asked why, they might speak of the haunting mystery that surrounds him, or the evergreen stories inspired by the legend of his reign. These are good reasons, but not the only ones. A third marks him off from the majority even more clearly.

He has an official history. This is not the earliest setting where he appears; it follows on from centuries of growing renown, but it gives that renown a fully articulated form, with a rare completeness. Arthur's history is more than just a medley of yarns, more than just a saga in the "dream time" of myth. It puts him within a definite period. It names definite places, and takes him to definite countries. All the further legend-weaving presupposes this history. Romancers add to it and enlarge it; they change its emphasis and the order of events; they draw in matter from other sources, sometimes to a point where they lose sight of it. But in substance they accept it. Their own stories assume it as a backdrop, and fit, more or less, into the scene structure it creates.

This is not to say that the official history is true. As it stands, it isn't. But its fullness and firmness, and its power of shaping a consensus, justify a search for realities behind it.

One wayward genius carries almost the whole responsibility for this official history. He lived in the first half of the twelfth century and was known as Geoffrey of Monmouth, after a town on the southeastern fringe of Wales. While his family may have been Welsh, it may possibly have been Breton. Brittany, in the Atlantic corner of France, is so called because it was colonized from Britain in early times. Shortly before Geoffrey's time the shifting fortunes of war and conquest brought many Bretons back to the island of their ancestors. His parents or grandparents may have been among them.

Geoffrey himself is elusive. From 1129 to 1151 he was living at Oxford, certainly as a cleric and almost certainly as a teacher, though the university was unborn as yet. Afterward he moved to London and was made bishop of St. Asaph in Wales, although the turmoil of that country prevented him from ever taking up his appointment. He died in or about 1155. His masterpiece, defining, among much else, the career of Arthur, is a so-called *History of the Kings of Britain* in Latin. He composed it while at Oxford and finished it about 1136. There are grounds for suspecting that he revised it, and that the text we have is a second edition. European literature has nothing else like it. It is one of the great books of the Middle Ages, and the source of a number of famous stories besides Arthur's.

The *History* (to use Geoffrey's misnomer) begins about 1200 B.C. in the world of Greek and Roman epic. After the fall of Troy one of its princes, Aeneas, is said to have migrated to Italy with a party of refugees. Geoffrey tells us that Aeneas's great-grandson Brutus led a later group of Trojans to Britain. The island, then called Albion, was uninhabited, except for a few giants. The Trojans took possession of the island and killed off the giants, and Albion was renamed Britain after their leader Brutus—a nice example of medieval etymology. The settlers and their descendants were henceforth "Britons," and Brutus became their first King and founded the capital city by the River Thames. This was New Troy, later called London.

Geoffrey goes on to describe the reigns of seventy-five kings; nearly all of them were products of his imagination. One of them is Bladud, who made himself a pair of wings, and came to grief over New Troy in the first flying accident. After Bladud comes his son Leir, or Lear, whose troubles with his own offspring became a theme for Shakespeare, and who flourished, we are told, in the eighth century B.C. At last Geoffrey reaches the conquest of Britain by the Romans. Since he can now be checked against real history, he has to be somewhat more factual. Still, he makes out patriotically that it wasn't a conquest at all, in the full sense, since British kings went on reigning by agreement with the Empire, as tributary rulers.

Toward the close of the Roman phase Geoffrey takes up several pages with an account of the way Brittany began. One of the reasons for thinking he was of Breton stock is his interest in the subject. He adopts—and improves—a Welsh tradition that Brittany began late in the fourth century A.D., when the Emperor Maximus, whose army included a strong contingent of Britons, allowed them to settle in this area. Geoffrey inflates the colony of veterans into a full-blown and important kingdom.

Geoffrey then goes on to paint a dramatic picture of the near conquest of Britain by the barbarians and its subsequent resurgence. The glories of Arthur arise from this resurgence. This is one of the principal things about him; the prior disaster is part of Arthur's legend and vital to appreciating its nature. Geoffrey relates how Britain was harassed by marauding barbarians, especially the Picts—fierce, unconquered tribesmen who raided out of what is now Scotland. After one Roman rescue operation, and a plea for another, all aid from the Empire came to an end. The Britons had lost the habit of self-reliance and were unequal to defending themselves, so the Archbishop of London took a radical step. He went to the offshoot kingdom of Brittany, and offered the crown of Britain to its ruler, Aldroenus, if he would come over and take charge of defense. Aldroenus declined the risky honor, but put forward his brother Constantine instead. Constantine took an army to the island and temporarily scattered its enemies, aided by the Britons, whose fighting qualities revived under his leadership. They crowned him at the Roman-built city of Silchester. He married and had three sons. The firstborn was Constans, who became a monk. The second was Aurelius Ambrosius. The third was Uther, destined to become the father of Arthur.

We are now in the fifth century A.D. and an independent Britain, with the Roman connection at an end. Constantine reigned in peace for ten years, until he was finally murdered by a Pictish assassin. The succession was disputed. A solution was devised by an ambitious noble, Vortigern. In Geoffrey's imagination

Vortigern is the central figure of a grandiose tragedy, sinister yet pitiable. Shakespeare might well have taken it up, as he did take up Geoffrey's account of Lear. (Samuel Ireland, an eighteenth-century forger, faked a Shakespeare tragedy on this theme in the belief that it was a play Shakespeare ought to have written.)

Vortigern (says Geoffrey) visited the youth Constans in his monastery and advised him, as the eldest son of Constantine, to come out and be King. Constans agreed to this and, as intended, became a puppet in Vortigern's hands. Vortigern took control of the treasury, promoted his supporters to key positions, and re-cruited a force of Pictish guards. In response to some crafty prompting, the Picts assassinated Constans. Vortigern had the killers beheaded, but everything was going as he had planned, and soon he had the crown himself. The guardians of the two junior princes, Aurelius Ambrosius and Uther, took them away to safety in Brittany.

Vortigern's execution of the Pictish guards annoyed their compatriots, who began raiding again. At this juncture two Saxon chieftains, the brothers Hengist and Horsa, landed in Kent with three shiploads of followers. They told Vortigern they were exiles from their German homeland, and offered him their services. Vortigern was glad to employ these newcomers as auxiliaries against the Picts. After a successful campaign he rewarded Hengist with lands in Lincolnshire, facing the North Sea. With Vortigern's compliance, Hengist brought more Saxons into Brit-ain. The British King banqueted with the leaders as their guest. During the banquet Hengist's beautiful daughter, Renwein (or, as others spell it, Rowena), came in. She carried a golden goblet of wine, and offered it to Vortigern, who was smitten with desire for her. Hengist was quick to exploit Vortigern's desire and con-sented to the King's marrying Renwein, in exchange for Kent. Vortigern ceded the territory and married her, to the disgust of most of his subjects, and especially his sons by a previous mar-riage. The eldest of these was Vortimer.

Alien settlement in Britain grew rapidly. To the horror of male Britons, the heathen Saxons began to cohabit with British women. Fearing that the new race would become dominant, the Britons' leaders protested to Vortigern. But he was now commit-tedly pro-Saxon because of his wife. When he refused to listen to them they proclaimed Prince Vortimer King instead. Vortimer attacked the Saxons in Kent and routed them in four battles. Many, including Hengist himself, withdrew to Germany. But Vortimer's Saxon stepmother contrived to have him poisoned. Before dying he directed that his body should be entombed in a bronze pyramid by the Kentish coast, as a warning to the Saxons if they approached again. His wishes, however, were ignored.

Vortigern resumed his usurped kingship and arranged for the Saxons to return. Hengist landed with a huge army and protestations of peace. At a conference of British and Saxon nobles, convened to draw up a treaty, the Saxons whipped out daggers at a signal from Hengist and massacred the unarmed Britons. Vortigern was spared, but he was abjectly in Hengist's power, and had to allow the Saxons to occupy London, York, and other cities, where they afflicted the inhabitants and destroyed the churches. Vortigern fled to Wales and tried to build himself a fortress in the remote mountainous region of Snowdonia, but even this went wrong—the walls kept sinking into the ground. His soothsayers told him the only solution was to find a boy who had no father, kill him, and sprinkle his blood upon the stones.

Messengers went out through Wales to look for this human sacrifice. At Carmarthen, in the South, they found a lad whose mother claimed to have had intercourse with no mortal man. Her son had been begotten by a spirit companion who used to appear and disappear. This son was Merlin—thus Geoffrey ushers the enchanter onto the stage of literature. At the site of the would-be fortress Merlin saved his life by revealing what Vortigern's soothsayers had failed to detect. The instability of the walls was due to a subterranean pool with two dragons in it.

When the pool was drained the dragons emerged. One was white, the other red. They fought, and the white one drove the red to the edge of the pool. Then the red recovered and beat back the white. Merlin interpreted: the red dragon stood for the Britons, the white for the Saxons. Thanks to Vortigern's crimes and blunders the Saxons were winning now, but in time they would be repelled.

At this point in the *History* Geoffrey has a digression. He puts in a note explaining that he had collected some prophecies by Merlin about events in Britain. A bishop asked him to publish them, and he did. Having done so, he went on with the *History* and copied the prophecies into it, saying Merlin uttered them during his meeting with Vortigern. There is no serious doubt that Geoffrey invented most of them. They are very obscure, but near the beginning Merlin is made to foretell Arthur, calling him "the Boar of Cornwall"—the first hint of his coming. Further on he promises that in a distant future the reversal of fortune will be complete: "The foreigners shall be slaughtered. . . . The island shall be called by the name of Brutus and the title given to it by the foreigners [that is, England] shall be done away with."

After the prophecies the story resumes. Geoffrey says Merlin warned Vortigern that his doom was near. Merlin spoke truly; the rightful princes, Aurelius Ambrosius and Uther, had grown up and were on their way from Brittany to depose him. They landed, and Aurelius was crowned King. Vortigern moved down through Wales, and when an army led by Aurelius approached he took refuge in a castle near Monmouth. Aurelius laid siege, his troops managed to set the castle on fire, and the usurper perished. Then Aurelius attacked the Saxons, using cavalry he had brought from Brittany, and drove them back toward the North Sea. Hengist was captured and put to death.

Aurelius rebuilt the churches which the Saxons had destroyed, and planned to raise a monument over the mass grave of the Britons who had been murdered at the conference. He was doubtful what form it ought to take until Merlin told him of a hill in Ireland where, in ancient times, giants had brought huge stones from Africa and arranged them in a magic circle. The King resolved to transplant them to the grave, so Uther went over to Ireland, taking Merlin with him. His workmen were unable to shift the stones, but Merlin dismantled the circle by his secret arts, and the stones were shipped to Britain. Merlin set them up in the same formation on Salisbury Plain, where the dead were buried. And that is how Stonehenge came to be there.

Aurelius's reign was a short one. A surviving son of Vortigern bribed a Saxon assassin who posed as a doctor when the King was lying sick, and gave him poison instead of medicine. He was succeeded by his brother Uther Pendragon, as he was called. Geoffrey says Pendragon means "dragon's head," and explains it by a celestial portent. More likely it means "head dragon," that is, "foremost leader." Uther had to cope with a Saxon revival. After victory in a close-run campaign he held court in London at Easter.

Here the history of Arthur himself begins. Geoffrey has set the stage carefully. He has depicted Britain going through a fearful crisis, almost a dissolution, due to invading barbarians and an unprincipled ruler. With Vortigern's death and the return of the rightful princes, the pendulum has swung back. It has not, however, swung completely. The kingdom is still in peril from the Saxons and from feuding among the Britons. The accession of Uther opens the way to the red dragon's promised recovery. Yet even Uther cannot be the agent of this in person. His only real function is to launch Arthur, with the aid of Merlin, the skillfully planted wonder-worker. This happens through a second royal amour, undoing the effects of Vortigern's infatuation.

At the Easter gathering (says Geoffrey) Uther was seized with an obsessive lust for Ygerna, the beautiful wife of Gorlois, Duke of Cornwall. His advances to her were obvious. Gorlois withdrew from the court, taking his wife with him. The King treated this action as an insult. He sent Gorlois an ultimatum ordering him to return, and, when this was rejected, marched to Cornwall to ravage the ducal lands. Gorlois put Ygerna in Tintagel Castle, on a coastal headland which could only be approached along a narrow, easily guarded ridge. Having stowed her beyond Uther's presumed reach, he led a force to oppose the royal army, making his base at a fort some distance off.

Uther surrounded Gorlois's weaker force and prevented its escape. Then, on a friend's advice, he sent for Merlin. The magician gave him a potion which turned him into an exact replica of Gorlois. Thus, effectively disguised, Uther passed the guards at Tintagel and found his way to Ygerna. Supposing him to be her husband, she caused no difficulties, and as a result of this encounter she conceived Arthur. Meanwhile, the real Gorlois had been killed in a sortie. Uther reverted to his own shape and married the lady.

He reigned another fifteen years after Arthur's birth. His health gradually failed, and it became evident that the Saxons were still not cowed. They brought over reinforcements, kept up a troublesome warfare, and at last disposed of Uther by poison, like Vortimer and Aurelius. However, they could not prevent the coronation of Arthur at Silchester as the Britons' new sovereign. Young as he was, he took the offensive against the Saxons in Britain, first simply to plunder them, then to crush them. Their field army put up a fierce resistance, aided by Pictish and Scottish allies. But Arthur was already an able leader. Three battles—one by the "River Douglas," one near Lincoln, and one in the Caledon Wood in Scotland—ended with the Saxons handing over their treasures and promising to leave Britain.

The promise was broken. They changed course at sea and tried to take Arthur by surprise, sailing round into the Channel and coming ashore in Devon. He checked their advance at the ancient city of Bath and won a decisive victory on a hill nearby. In the battle he carried a shield with a picture of the Virgin Mary, affirming his role as a Christian champion. His sword Caliburn had been forged in the Isle of Avalon, an enchanted place. The remaining Saxons in Britain were dispersed and reduced to powerlessness. Arthur completed his success by a pursuit of the Picts and Scots. They took refuge on islands in Loch Lomond, where he starved them into submission.

Victory in the North brought the first phase of his reign to an end. He had restored Britain to peace, to stable government, to the dignity of its traditions. A further rebuilding of churches was undertaken, and dispossessed landowners were restored to their estates. Arthur's "outstanding courage and generosity," his "inborn goodness," as Geoffrey puts it, won him the love of the vast majority of his subjects. After marrying a Roman-descended lady, Guinevere, he began to carry his kingdom to new heights of eminence. First he led an expedition abroad. Since the Irish had helped the Picts and Scots, he invaded Ireland and conquered it. He went on from there to conquer Iceland (which would not have been difficult, because in those days Iceland was uninhabited). Twelve years of peace ensued. This part of the story is the basis of the Round Table theme. Says Geoffrey:

> Arthur began to increase his personal entourage by inviting very distinguished men from far-distant kingdoms to join it. In this way he developed such a code of courtliness in his household that he inspired peoples living far away to imitate him. The result was that even the man of noblest birth, once he was roused to rivalry, thought nothing at all of himself unless he wore his arms and dressed in the same way as Arthur's knights. At last the fame of Arthur's generosity and bravery

spread to the very ends of the earth; and the kings of countries far across the sea trembled at the thought that they might be attacked and invaded by him.

The awe he caused did in fact give him the notion of conquering Europe. He began with Norway and Denmark. So far none of his forays had taken him into Roman territory. But the Roman Empire still held the western part of the Continent, and when Arthur invaded Gaul (now France) he confronted the tribune Frollo, who governed it for the Emperor. The imperial hold was feeble. Arthur slew Frollo in single combat, cleaving his head in two with the sword Caliburn, and took possession. Nine years passed, partly taken up with consolidation, partly with a second peace in which he organized his Gallic conquests. He put his cupbearer, Bedevere, in charge of Normandy, his seneschal, Kay, in charge of Anjou.

Arthur held a Whitsun court at the former Roman garrison town of Caerleon. The occasion was marked by field sports and a tournament. Knights and prelates, nobles and subject monarchs from overseas came to pay homage. In a solemn church ritual the King and Queen ceremoniously wore their crowns, attended by archbishops and other clergy. Geoffrey's sketch of the splendors of the court, and the loves and exploits of those who came to it, prepares the ground in more detail for the cycle of chivalric romance.

Britain had reached such a standard of sophistication that it excelled all other kingdoms in its general affluence, the richness of its decorations, and the courteous behaviour of its inhabitants. Every knight in the country who was in any way famed for his bravery wore livery and arms showing his own distinctive colour; and women of fashion often displayed the same colours. They scorned to give their love to any man who had not proved himself three times in battle. In this way the womenfolk became chaste and more virtuous and for their love the knights were ever more daring.

While the court was still in session envoys arrived from Rome, sent by Lucius Hiberius, Procurator of the Republic. They brought a letter from this oddly styled dignitary condemning Arthur's conduct. The British King had not paid the tribute which the Britons usually had paid; instead, he had seized Roman lands in Gaul. Lucius demanded his submission and threatened a war of reconquest if it were refused.

Arthur conferred with his subkings and principal nobles, who agreed that Lucius must be defied. On the strength of various precedents (invented and planted earlier in the *History*), Arthur could claim to rule in Rome himself. He took the offensive. He put his nephew Modred in charge at home, jointly with the Queen, and assembled an immense army in Gaul. After turning aside to kill a cannibal giant on the isle of Mont-Saint-Michel, he marched into the country southeast of Paris. There Lucius opposed him with forces drawn from all over the Roman world. In a terrific struggle Arthur's other nephew, Gawain, played an impressive part. At last the Britons routed the imperial host on the fringes of Burgundy. Lucius fell, and Arthur sent his corpse to Rome, telling the Senate they would get no other tribute from Britain.

During the ensuing winter, Arthur was active in the land of the pro-Roman Burgundians—Geoffrey calls them Allobroges, but there is no doubt who he means—"subduing their cities." He prepared to cross the Alps and march on to Rome, with the ultimate aim of attacking the Emperor who ruled the Roman East from Constantinople. Thus he would have completed his long-meditated conquest of Europe. But news came from Britain that his deputy ruler, Modred, had turned traitor, setting himself up as King and persuading the Queen to live in adultery with him. Arthur headed for home. Modred, it transpired, had made an agreement with the Saxon leader Cheldric, securing Saxon support in return for the cession of parts of Britain. Arthur drove Modred's army westward, routing him by the River Camel in Cornwall. The traitor was killed, but Arthur was severely wounded; mortally, according to Geoffrey. Nevertheless, he was "carried off to the Isle of Avalon so that his wounds might be attended to," handing over the crown to a cousin.

That is as far as Geoffrey takes him. He leaves it an open question where Avalon was, and whether the King died of his wounds or, in some supernatural way, recovered. In a poem which he wrote later, *The Life of Merlin*, he speaks of Avalon as a paradisal "island of apples" over western waters, where Arthur was nursed by the enchantress Morgen.

After Arthur the *History* goes on, but it drifts off into anticlimax. Five more kings of Britain follow him. The Saxons are still contained until the last of these reigns. The fifth is a "fomenter of civil discords" who exposes the island to renewed onslaughts. The Saxons get help from a surprising ally, Gormund, King of the Africans. Thanks to the African Army, they swiftly occupy most of the country. The remaining Britons are hemmed in in Wales and Cornwall, though overseas, Brittany carries on. The Saxons are left in possession of most of the country now called England.

Truth or Lies or What?

In 1155 a native of the island of Jersey, Wace, published a paraphrase of Geoffrey's *History* in French verse, which he called the *Roman de Brut,* or Romance of Brutus, referring, of course, to the legacy of Britain's Trojan founder. To the description of Arthur's knighthood in the twelve-year peace, Wace added the Round Table, thus introducing another of the famous themes. He also added a passage referring to tales about the King and his knights which had become popular. Many of these came from Breton and Welsh storytellers and were not directly inspired by Geoffrey, though they could fit into his scheme. Wace says of them:

> During the long peace of which I speak—I know not whether you have heard of it—the wonders were demonstrated and the adventures were found which are so often related of Arthur that they have been turned into a fable. The tales of Arthur are not all lies nor all true. So much have the story-tellers told and so much have the makers of fables fabled to embellish their stories that they have made everything seem a fable.

These cautious words raise the issue we must now begin to approach: what Arthur's amazing "history" is based on. The texts of Geoffrey's book give what looks like a link with real history, namely, a date for his passing—542. To the very end of the reign, however, the Roman Empire is portrayed as still struggling on in western Europe, whereas in 542 it had been defunct in the West for more than sixty years. Therefore the date is almost certainly a mistake, and useless. Wace, in fact, betrays its flimsiness by changing it to 642. The whole structure of the narrative confirms the Roman clue. Not only the Western Empire's continuance, but Arthur's family relationships and numerous other details put him firmly in the fifth century.

However, it would be premature to look for him there without first deciding how much point there may be in looking. Geoffrey certainly did not invent him. As we shall see, there are earlier Welsh references to a hero called Arthur. But they are not early enough to prove that he lived in the fifth century, or indeed at any other time. Nor do they account for much of the tale which Geoffrey tells. It could be that the tale is rooted in the realities of post-Roman Britain, so that if we search in that milieu in some other way, we may trace it to its beginnings. But it could also be that the whole thing is a medieval fiction which Geoffrey has falsely planted there.

In view of what Wace says, it is worth asking what people thought who lived closer to the reputed time of Arthur than we do. As Arthurian stories spread during the Middle Ages, how did readers regard them? Did most think of Arthur and his court as grounded on fact, or as pure fantasy?

The question is tricky. Medieval ideas about authenticity were unlike our own. A modern historical novelist is frankly writing fiction, yet even so, such a novelist will try to get the period right: to find out how the characters would have lived, how they would have dressed, what they would have eaten, what their interests and customs would have been. In the Middle Ages authors did not do this, since authenticity did not matter to them in the same way. When they handled an ancient story they medievalized it, making the characters very much like their own contemporaries. Legends of Greece and Rome became medieval tales, with only such differences as could not be ignored, such as the worship of pagan gods. So the Arthurian adventures, whatever their date was supposed to be, were handled in medieval terms and expressed medieval interests. Geoffrey began the process and romancers after him carried it much further. That is why the knights of the Round Table wear elaborate armor, engage in jousts, observe the rules of chivalry, and have courtly love affairs.

They are not like post-Roman British warriors and they are not meant to be, since the realities of post-Roman Britain were not thought to be important.

Yet they were not thought to be illusory either. "Realities" was accepted to be the right word. Readers of medieval romance thought of the Arthurian realm somewhat as we, today, think of the Wild West. The Wild West of fiction and films is a country of the imagination, created by novelists like Zane Grey and by Hollywood. All the same, we know in a hazy way that realities underlie it. For thirty or forty years the American West *was* wild, or a good deal of it was. Sheriffs and marshals flourished; persons such as Billy the Kid and Calamity Jane existed, however unlike their fictitious guises they may have been. Unless we have a special interest in Western history, it doesn't matter much, but we understand that the history is there. So it was, on the whole, with medieval views of King Arthur. For the purposes of romance his existence didn't matter much. Still, like Billy the Kid, he had existed, and more or less when Geoffrey said. Among serious chroniclers, many were doubtful and one or two were hostile, but quite a number succumbed to popular belief by including him in their histories.

So the consensus in Geoffrey's own time, and for some centuries after him, was in favor to that extent. Among readers who considered the matter at all, hardly anyone took the tale of Arthur as a pure fiction, given a bogus setting in an earlier age. Almost everyone took it as genuinely belonging to that earlier age, however flamboyantly it had been expanded, altered, and updated in spirit and in detail. Today, knowing history more accurately, we can see that those readers were at least more right than wrong. Whatever Arthur may actually have been, he does belong where Geoffrey puts him. That is where his legend began; that is where the initial facts are. In that setting we can look for illumination, and for the man himself. Despite all the medieval veneer, Geoffrey's King is authentically a figure from late antiquity, from the last stormy vicissitudes of the Roman order in western Europe.

We can make that basic judgment if we simply try to define what is special about him, what kind of a hero his "history" makes him out to be. Different ages imagine outstanding qualities, and fine or adventurous achievement, in different ways. Hence, confronted with a story, we can sometimes say that its sources of inspiration lie in the ideals or enthusiasms of a particular period. A medieval romance about a Christian knight going to the Holy Land to fight Saracens would obviously have been inspired by the actual Crusades. It could not have anything to do with events a thousand years earlier. Sherlock Holmes belongs to the nineteenth century, James Bond to the twentieth. While there are countless stories of London detectives and wide-roaming secret agents, they all belong to comparatively modern times; no one would think them contemporary with Julius Caesar. The same applies to fictionalized history. If, in some future era, no record remained of Admiral Nelson but a woolly romantic treatment of his affair with Lady Hamilton and his victories over French fleets, readers could at least be sure that it was derived from the saga of Britain's greatness at sea, the naval wars with France, and the popular hero worship of sailors. They could add that if Nelson lived at all, he lived when all this was happening.

Geoffrey's placing of King Arthur can be confirmed in much the same way. Behind all the fantasy he embodies a myth, an ideal, a need, which can be recognized in the age when he is supposed to have lived.

Lewis Thorpe, Geoffrey's modern translator, asks what sets Arthur apart from his other kings. The first quality Thorpe picks out is "the air of other-worldliness and mystery attached to his person from before his birth"; the last is "the fact that he did not die, but was carried away to the Isle of Avalon." In other words, he is a mystical figure. Yet his mystical quality is related to a special mission. Merlin's magic brings Arthur into a land that has been divided and ravaged, sapped by internal conflict and usurpation, partly occupied by barbarians. Britain has an ancient and august civilization, but Vortigern and his heathen friends have brought it low. Something of profound value is at desperate risk, and Arthur's uncle and father have only stemmed the tide. Arthur arrives with his unorthodox background, his youth, his freshness, and with supreme military flair he smashes Britain's tormentors and brings order out of chaos. He restores, and builds on the restoration. He seizes his heritage and propels it into a golden age, where everything Britain has ever stood for is raised to a higher degree. At the end the strangeness of his passing echoes the strangeness of his coming. He is the vessel of a higher calling and a more-than-human mystique, related, nevertheless, to this world and not the next.

The pattern persists in the later versions, through many variations in detail. In Malory's fifteenth-century work, *Morte d'Arthur,* the best-known Arthurian book in English, the supernatural parts reappear and others are added. Arthur is a deliverer from local despots who are tearing the land to pieces, but he is still a deliverer, a bringer of order out of chaos, here chiefly through Merlin's magical aid. He then creates a sort of chivalric Utopia centered on the Round Table.

Victoria's poet laureate Tennyson, in his *Idylls of the King,* suppresses Uther's disreputable exploit but still gives Arthur a marvelous origin, even inventing a wholly new one. Arthur enters the human world at Tintagel, as before, but not by a normal process of birth. The witnesses are Merlin and a companion, who

> . . . from the castle gateway by the chasm
> Descending thro' the dismal night—a night
> In which the bounds of heaven and earth were lost—
> Beheld, so high upon the dreary deeps
> It seem'd in heaven, a ship, the shape thereof
> A dragon wing'd, and all from stem to stern
> Bright with a shining people on the decks,
> And gone as soon as seen. And then the two
> Dropt to the cove, and watch'd the great sea fall,
> Wave after wave, each mightier than the last,
> Till last, a ninth one, gathering half the deep
> And full of voices, slowly rose and plunged
> Roaring, and all the wave was in a flame:
> And down the wave and in the flame was borne
> A naked babe, and rode to Merlin's feet,
> Who stoopt and caught the babe, and cried "The King!
> Here is an heir for Uther!" And the fringe
> Of that great breaker, sweeping up the strand,
> Lash'd at the wizard as he spake the word,
> And all at once all round him rose in fire,
> So that the child and he were cloth'd in fire.
> And presently thereafter follow'd calm,
> Free sky and stars.

When the child grows up and is enthroned his primary achievement is much the same as before.

Arthur and his knighthood for a space
Were all one will, and thro' that strength the King
Drew in the petty princedoms under him,
Fought, and in twelve great battles overcame
The heathen hordes, and made a realm and reign'd.

The special pattern of Arthur's life singles him out as a type of hero whose image haunted the world of late antiquity. He is the British version of that hero. How the legend of such a person could have been handed down, all the way through six or seven centuries to Geoffrey of Monmouth, is a topic to explore later. What matters is that Arthur, as shaped by imagination, *is* such a person and therefore plainly belongs in that milieu, or at any rate makes better sense in it than anywhere else.

It is time to step from the realm of Geoffrey's imagination into genuine history, and start appraising the relationship of one to the other. In the realities of the late-Roman world we can grasp what the underlying conception was and how it took shape. We can also assess that world's great issues, so as to understand the Britain which was a part of it, and see what Geoffrey found there to work upon. Somehow, apparently, he found King Arthur there. Maybe we cannot get to Arthur directly. But we can hope to close in on him.

2

The
Unextinguished Light

Troublers and Rescuers of the Empire

On August 24, 410, an army of Goths marched into Rome and
looted it. To the city's inhabitants the world seemed to be coming
to an end. Throughout western Europe there was ample reason
for feeling the same. From the Atlantic to the Adriatic the Roman
Empire was crumbling. Predatory barbarians were in Gaul and
Spain as well as in Italy. They were not conquerors, not yet, for no
territory had been signed away to them. But there they were,
unassimilated and menacing: not only the Goths but other alien
peoples—Franks, Vandals, Alans, Suevi. Saxons and Burgundians
were on the move. From over the eastern plains came the most
alarming barbarians of all, the Huns, who had pushed some of the
Goths across the frontier and were soon to push across it themselves.

   On the face of it a battered society was dying. Of despair, in
the words of one modern diagnosis. The despair was real enough,
and yet it seems another feature of that age was a stubborn,
defiant hope. With the Empire's swaying fortunes, the oscillation
of darkness and light had long since become a breeder of myth.
Emperor might succeed Emperor in more or less disillusion, yet
the next could always be different. He could be the one who
would pull the Empire together in a lasting peace, a harmony of
the nations, a reign of law. Although no ruler had ever achieved

this for long, the vision of the ruler who would, or could, refused to die.

In spite of the Empire's oppressions, failures, and crimes, no other world order was conceivable. Because of that, it could still cast its spell over its citizens. The spell extended to barbarians too. Even Gothic chiefs who planned to destroy it had changed their minds and preferred to uphold it; on their own terms, perhaps, but to uphold it all the same. The days were long past when Rome had been an engine of dominance by an Italian master race. Now, all free men were imperial citizens, and nationality nowhere debarred from power. *Romanitas* meant civilization, and while that word can be awkwardly translated as "Roman-ness," it is best left in its Latin majesty. From the Stoic philosophy of the Greeks had come the ideal of a cosmopolis, a world unity. In the eyes of the more thoughtful Romans, Rome was not so much unity's creator as its custodian. *Romanitas* was a mystique, a trust. The vision of a possible savior was therefore spiritually charged. It came and went, and in 410 it was at a low ebb, but it still had powers of recuperation. The role of the World-Restorer, the *Restitutor Orbis* (again the Latin is best), was still there for a ruler to fill.

Imagery of disaster and rescue had been planted in Roman minds as far back as the third century, when the Empire had passed through a previous crisis. With no fixed rule of succession, it had been rent apart for decades by the unscrupulous bids of rival pretenders, and barbarian invaders had exploited the confusion. After many false hopes a *Restitutor* appeared, and was voted such by the Senate. He was Aurelian, a soldier who rose from the ranks, was chosen Emperor by the army, repulsed the barbarians, and pacified the Roman world. Aurelian was assassinated, but one of his own soldiers, Diocletian, became Emperor in 284 and continued the restoration on a grand scale, building on Aurelian's work. The Empire of 410 was still largely of his making, and because of the restoration which had actually happened, it remained possible to dream of another.

Diocletian aimed to stabilize things. His further antibarbarian campaigns brought peace within the borders, and he tried to regulate the succession by a scheme of adoption and marriages of state. He enormously expanded and strengthened the government, providing for regional emperors associated with himself, so that all things should be properly attended to. Already there was much more to this than politics or economics. The cosmopolis had been taking on its mystical tinge for many years. Worship of the Emperor was an established practice, sometimes in a style borrowed from Asian solar cults. Diocletian's absolutism confirmed the mystique.

All gods were held to be aspects or deputies of a single Godhead watching over the Empire. The Emperor was his earthly representative, the focus of unity, divinely appointed and divine in his own person. Diocletian surrounded himself with pomp and ritual. The civilization centered upon him was "the eternal light." The local administrators who made it work were expected to "remain in the bosom of their native place" to "guard the eternal mystery," which they "could not abandon without impiety." As a religious duty and loyalty test, everyone could be required to pay homage at the Emperor's altars. Nearly everyone was willing to do so, but the Christians refused, and their refusal convicted them of treason. Furthermore, the Church was a self-contained, well-organized body which Diocletian's system could not control. He therefore launched an annihilating persecution.

Diocletian retired in 305 with the religious discord unresolved. It was soon clear that his plans for stabilization had failed. After years of war between several competing rulers another *Restitutor* arose, Constantine the Great. He retained most of the state machinery, and strengthened the mystique, laying new stress on the solar divinity that the Emperor represented. Then he had second thoughts: he was right about the Supreme Being, but wrong about his nature and preferences. The persecution of Christians was a mistake which had offended heaven. So Constantine called it off, explaining that at a crucial moment during the wars he had seen a vision, a cross of light in the sky. Eventually he became sole Emperor and made Christianity the official cult. Christians were a minority, but the persecution had proved their conviction and cohesion. With lavish patronage, Constantine tried to annex the Church as the spiritual arm of the state.

The change which he envisaged was not very sweeping. As Emperor he could not be divine any longer, but he could be God's viceroy, the focus of a mystical unity still, superior to all priests. Most of the priests responded, and his biographer, Bishop Eusebius, concurred with him in the notion of "One God, one ruler." Meanwhile, the Emperor's mother, Helena, won the hearts of Christians by miraculously finding the True Cross on which Jesus was crucified. Though Constantine put off his own baptism to the last moment, he was hailed as "equal to the apostles." Through statecraft rather than conversion he had come as close to being an earthly messiah as any Emperor ever had. Such a reign was not going to be forgotten.

After Constantine's death in 337 his sons shared the Empire. For a time the fresh moral energy kept up an impression of renewal. "The Age of Restoration" was a frequent motto on coins and in inscriptions. It was not too ironic. Most of the men who had saved the Empire from its crisis, and carried through its renovation, had been soldiers of humble birth and miscellaneous background, so that a plentiful crop of new talent had sprung up beside the old aristocracy. Shared education helped to weld the elite together. Classical culture, Greek as well as Roman, was a prized aspect of *Romanitas*.

But after a time the barbarians began encroaching again. Within the Empire, meanwhile, Christianity had not cemented unity. For one thing, it was split itself by the Arian heresy, which denied the full divinity of Christ. Several emperors favored the heresy and consequently clashed with Catholic subjects. Orthodoxy triumphed at last under Theodosius, who was briefly sole Emperor in 395 and tried to reestablish a state-Church concord. Christians, nominal Christians at any rate, were by then a majority through most of the Empire. However, the barbaric peoples who had been Christianized were Arian heretics. As they moved in among the Catholic masses—who vastly outnumbered them, but were unarmed—the rift meant that a common religion did not reconcile.

Nor was the Catholic faith itself as useful as Constantine had expected. It insisted on drawing a distinction, unknown to paganism, between the things which were Caesar's and the things which were God's. In addition to this, a move Constantine had made in 330 unleashed forces beyond his understanding. Having enlarged the city of Byzantium, on the Bosporus, he turned it into a new capital, which in his honor was called Constantinople. Rome then ceased to be a center of government in the Empire (even when the West had separate emperors again, they usually preferred Milan or Ravenna), but the great city's ancient prestige could never be blotted out or replaced. In the absence of an Emperor, some of this began to pass to its bishop. As successors to St. Peter the bishops of Rome held a special place. Their see was revered as the fountainhead of orthodoxy. Now they were no longer overshadowed by an imperial neighbor, and they lived in the impressive quarters which Constantine had allotted to them. Increasingly they were looked to for authority; increasingly they were known by the title of Pope.

Since orthodoxy involved communion with the Roman see, the Church was a vehicle for *Romanitas.* But this religious *Romanitas* had a life of its own; it was not always in step with the political kind. At Constantinople the Emperor might manage, sometimes, to dictate to the Church. In large parts of the Empire, and more particularly the West, he could not.

This division had practical effects. The Empire was still well provided with public-spirited citizens, willing to affirm civilized ways through service or teaching or leadership. There were, however, two competing paths for them. Once they would have devoted their abilities to the state; now they could choose between state and Church. Often they opted for the Church. Some, such as St. Ambrose of Milan, went over from civic to ecclesiastical office. The state inspired a dwindling enthusiasm; the drain of talent lowered its quality; and so it tended to drift downhill.

Pagans of equal caliber might have filled the gaps, but by the beginning of the fifth century they were too few, and the emperors' sponsorship of the other religion had estranged them. In 410, when the Gothic blow fell, pagans said Rome was being punished for deserting the old gods. The Church found its defender in St. Augustine. His brilliant, passionate mind outclassed anything paganism could offer. Yet his answer seemed to confirm disunion. There were two communities, he said, the city of this world—in effect, of fallen and unregenerate man—and the City of God. The former committed and suffered evil. The latter could influence it for good, but was primarily concerned with eternal things. While the City of Man was not exactly the state, and the City of God was not exactly the Church, Augustine's argument forbade seeing the two as one.

A strong and respected Emperor might still have forged a

working alliance. After Theodosius the emperors for a number of crucial decades were practicing Christians, sometimes devout, but they were neither strong nor respected. In a cosmopolitan world, the seriousness and dedication of the old Roman upper class were no longer found. Most of the rich betrayed their outlook in colorful clothes and colorless talk. When it came to warfare, the solid line of the legions, which had once unnerved Rome's enemies, was a thing of the past. The imperial army was a patchwork. Swarms of barbaric auxiliaries variegated the battlefront; mailed cavalry and mounted bowmen rode among a babel of foot soldiers hired by the treasury.

The mystique of *Romanitas* survived. In the late fourth century and the first few years of the fifth, rhetoric about Eternal Rome, as an ideal or symbol, was louder than ever. But the mystique survived in a tangle of divided wills, unsolved problems, heavy and growing pressures from within and without. A *Restitutor* to pull everything together and reaffirm the ideal could still be dreamed of, and with more yearning because of the needs of the time. No one could tell where he might come from, or how he might act if he ever came.

Britain Alone

We can now see better what kind of a hero Geoffrey's Arthur is. He is a regional *Restitutor,* fulfilling the dream—for a time—in one fragment of the imperial world. He has the blessing of supernatural agencies. He saves a battered realm from the results of crime and strife in high places. He drives back the barbarians who have been let in. He recruits new men, men of ability and integrity, without distinction as to their origins. He champions the Christian faith, and associates the Church with his rule, but not in the otherworldly style of royal saints admired in the Middle Ages. He proves himself a master of warfare, yet he gives his subjects a long spell of peace. He carries a rescued civilization to fresh heights. He has a magnificent court. He even builds something like a new empire.

Most of these things applied, not entirely in rose-tinted retrospect, to the real restorers in past times: less strikingly to any one of the three, Aurelian, Diocletian, Constantine, but very strikingly indeed to the series together and the net achievement.

King Arthur, within his limits, incarnates the sort of vision which that achievement did so much to perpetuate. Even the fact that he fights against the Romans can be taken to mean that the vitality and ideals of the effete Empire have passed to Britain. Geoffrey's details are mostly medieval fancy. His basic concept is not medieval; it is a product of late antiquity. Somehow a legend sprouting out of that soil reached him in the twelfth century, to be distorted and fantasized in the medieval manner, but not wrested from its original nature.

The natural explanation is that there actually was a *Restitutor* for Britain. Perhaps only briefly, perhaps only sketchily, but with enough of an impact to be cast in that role by a people who had been Roman citizens and remembered *Romanitas*. If he existed, he was surely the original Arthur. That, however, would imply that Geoffrey's account has a factual foundation. He tells of a fifth-century Britain separated from Rome, having its own rulers; and of a catastrophe, in a form recalling the troubles of the Empire, with its usurpers and barbarians; and of a resurgence, in which Arthur the King can play the *Restitutor*'s part. This is all very well as literature, and aptly matched to the period. But does it reflect anything that really happened?

As we edge closer to Geoffrey's mighty riddle, we need to be clear what sort of author we have to deal with. Whatever he may pretend, he is not giving us history. Even apart from the giants, dragons, and so forth, we can never believe anything he says merely because he says it. Primarily Geoffrey is a writer of fiction, concocting a pseudohistory, and with propagandist objects in view. He wants to glorify the Britons of old, ancestors of the Welsh and Bretons, so that his own Welsh and Breton kinsfolk can bask in ancestral splendors and the future Merlin foretells for them. Also (though we need not go into this now) parts of his narrative are angled so as to please important men in his own day, and win their favor.

Yet we cannot stop there and forget about a real Arthur. In weaving his fiction, Geoffrey uses facts. In his invented history, he culls people and events from real history. His coverage of the Roman period brings in Julius Caesar, the Emperor Claudius, who invaded Britain, and others from the real world. What he says they did usually has a contorted likeness to what they actually did. Sometimes the resemblance between a Geoffrey character and the original is very slight, but it is there. When Merlin prophesies the foreigners' final downfall, Geoffrey is echoing an actual "prophecy of Merlin" recorded centuries earlier. Further on, after Arthur, the *History* shows the same quality. Several of the rulers he mentions are authentic.

To quote his translator, Lewis Thorpe, again:

> The list of proper names and place-names given at the back of this volume includes 871 head-words. A large proportion of these are the names of historical people and of places actually on the map. Much of this background material is twisted almost beyond recognition; but in earliest essence it has some element of truth. Geoffrey did not invent it.

What this amounts to is that we can follow up Geoffrey's story rather as we might follow up a historical novel. A novel is not history, and should never be relied on for facts, however accurate the novelist has tried to make it. That is true even with such a learned writer as Robert Graves, in his two novels of the Emperor Claudius, memorably serialized on television. But a reader or viewer who became interested could read around in that phase of history, find out the facts the novels are grounded on, make connections, confirm Claudius's reality, assess Graves's portrayal of him. Likewise with Geoffrey of Monmouth. He begins the Arthur part of his book in an independent Britain in the fifth century, separated from Rome. If we turn to genuine history, and look at Britain in the fifth century, what do we find?

We find, in the first place, that Britain *was* independent, with a legacy of civilization from the Empire yet also a character of its own, and a past of which a good deal is relevant to understanding not only Arthur but Merlin, Guinevere, and other characters and motifs.

Britain had been a latecomer to the Roman system. The Britons were a Celtic people, one branch of a powerful nation which had spread through central and western Europe during the last centuries B.C. The Celtic complex embraced a variety of groupings and cultures. It included the Gauls, who were in the Empire, and the Irish, who never were. Britons spoke a language which is now dead, but has a living descendant in Welsh. In the last century or two B.C. the outside world still knew little about the Britons, although it did know about their Druid intelligentsia. The Druids were a close-knit, highly trained religious order, an immensely influential elite. They were priests, scholars, bards, royal counselors, and seers. They flourished in Ireland and Gaul as well, but their advanced colleges were in Britain. Their religion was a mixture of the sophisticated and the savage. Greek observers took an interest in their doctrine of immortality; Romans were more struck by their subversiveness and their practice of human sacrifice. Druidism reflected a special feature of Celtic society, the unusually high status of women. Members of both sexes could be Druids. Similarly, members of both sexes could hold royal power. Celtic queens ruled over tribal coalitions in their own right. In sexual morality at that level, the double standard was far from absolute. A Queen could take a lover without being condemned any more than a King who took a mistress.

Julius Caesar made two incursions into the island, but the Romans did not begin its conquest till A.D. 43. After decades of struggle against resistance leaders—such as the heroic Boudicca, Queen of the Iceni, who rebelled in A.D. 60 and temporarily recaptured London—Roman Britain, or Britannia, comprised roughly the present England and Wales. The country beyond, as far as the narrow waist of Scotland, was garrisoned in places but never completely taken over. Farther north again were tribes whom the Romans fought and beat a few times but left unconquered; in view of later events, an occupation of the whole island might have been wise. As it was, the permanent frontier was a fortified wall set up by the Emperor Hadrian, across the northern angle of England. (Parts of it are still there.)

South of the wall, Romanization was the watchword, as it was everywhere else. Towns were built with roads linking them. The provincial governor and senior officials came from outside, but most of the country was parceled out into *civitates*, "cantons," with councils made up of wealthy Britons and descendants of former chiefs and nobility. These, and the councilors of the towns, sent delegates to an all-British provincial council which could advise the governor.

From the early third century on, all free male Britons were imperial citizens equal to any other. The upper classes received a Roman-type education and were bilingual, using Latin as a written and business language. Often they gave their children Roman names. Many of the wealthier lived in villas—luxurious country houses with farmlands and workshops and staffs of slaves. Anyone from the household of George Washington or Thomas Jefferson, in old Virginia, would probably have felt at home there. The Romanized, villa-rich society was strongest in parts of the South, such as the present county of Gloucestershire.

Throughout the third century and some of the fourth, Roman Britain was more peaceful than most of the Continent. Its population was two million or so, perhaps more. Light industry and mining prospered. Agriculture produced grain surpluses which could be exported, though sometimes the exporting was compulsory, a cause of resentment. In the reigns of Diocletian and Constantine an awareness dawned that Britain was no longer passive. It was a country where things could happen, initiatives could be taken.

In 286 an admiral named Carausius made himself independent ruler for a few years. When Britain was reconquered a commemorative medallion portrayed London greeting the Roman commander as REDDITOR LUCIS AETERNAE, "Restorer of the Eternal Light." But the commander's son was the great Constantine himself, who was proclaimed Emperor at York, thus beginning the messianic career that took him clean across Europe. Britain was growing in stature as an imperial member, and with the rest of the Empire it became officially Christian. British bishops attended councils in Gaul and Italy. But even after Constantine, Christians were few. There was even a short revival of Celtic paganism. New temples were built, including a large one dedicated to the god Nodons, not far from Geoffrey's Monmouth.

In 367 the imperial structure in Britain began to crack. Here real history meshes more closely with Geoffrey, who, in principle, gives a true picture of the way things went. For some decades the Britons had been suffering from barbarian raids. From the North came the Picts, whose aggressions Geoffrey makes so much of. They streamed out of their homeland beyond the Firth of Forth: small, bearded, tattooed warriors who fought with slings and spears. From the West came the Irish. Many of them were confusingly known as Scots (it was a later migration of "Scots" to northern Britain which gave it the name Scotland). Geoffrey mentions these also. They crossed the sea in light, seaworthy boats called curraghs, made from animal hides stretched over wooden frames. They carried spears and swords and round shields. When they were ashore their leaders summoned them with blasts on immense war horns. Lastly, there were Saxons from the coastlands of Germany, destined to be Geoffrey's arch-villains. They had appeared first as pirates preying on shipping, but were now coming ashore and probing inland. Their chief weapon was a short sword, or seax, from which they took their name. They also wielded eight-foot lances and powerful bows.

For a long time these assailants had raided piecemeal and separately. Then the Picts and Scots had begun to aid each other, and in 367 all three nations pounced together, helped by disaf-fected Britons and reinforced by slaves who deserted the villas. Britain was briefly torn from the Empire. After a muddled and panicky campaign it was won back, but the restoration of peace was not a restoration of all that had been. Too many estates had been plundered; too many slaves had escaped in the confusion. The villa life-style began to decline, and most of the towns began to deteriorate. These changes did not bring a sharp fall in stan-dards of living. Large numbers of Britons were at least as well off as they had ever been. The Empire, however, could be viewed with a more critical eye. There was more scope for unease about the central authority and Britain's dependence on it.

In 383 another Emperor was proclaimed in Britain as Con-stantine had been and attracted popular support. He was an army commander of Spanish birth, Magnus Clemens Maximus, and he is said to have married a British wife. With an army including many Britons, he gained control of western Europe and even captured Rome. Theodosius, who held the East, finally defeated him. But again someone in Britain had taken a major initiative; again someone in Britain had made his mark on the Continent. Maximus left a curious lingering impression on the island where he began his adventure. Legends among the Britons' descendants, in Wales and Cornwall, were to turn him into a noble sovereign and an honorary Briton by marriage. Princes traced their pedigrees to him. This was the Maximus whose British soldiers were said to have settled in northwestern Gaul, then called Armorica, thus launching the transformation of part of it into "Brittany."

Maximus's main effect at the time was to revive Britain's

difficulties. He had taken too many of the troops out of the country. Soon the barbarians returned, and now the Irish were not only raiding but seizing land in Wales. At first the Empire did very little. Theodosius died in 395 and was succeeded in the West by his son Honorius. The boy was only ten years old and was never to mature into an Emperor of character. A Roman expedition saved Britain again for a while, but the rescue was strictly temporary.

In 406 the last convulsion began. Three barbarian tribes from Germany, the Vandals, Alans, and Suevi, crossed the Rhine and surged across Gaul, plundering all the way. Britain was practically cut off. The soldiers tried to set up an Emperor of their own to take charge and, after two false starts, picked a comrade named Constantine in 407, who may have been a Briton. He was of low rank and no great talent, but his name was auspicious. He called himself Constantine III (there had been a Constantine II). His son Constans left a monastery to join him. At this point, history coincides more closely with Geoffrey's imagination, and his prelude to Arthur. His "King Constantine," with a son Constans who is a monk and leaves his monastery, is based on this pretender. Geoffrey's Constantine and Constans are not like their originals, and he gives them both very different careers. Nevertheless, they are based on these two men, father and son.

Constantine asserted his claim by taking nearly all the remaining troops to Gaul, and negotiating with the recognized Emperor, Honorius. Constans assumed control of Spain with support from a force of auxiliaries of mixed nationality, called the Honoriaci because they had first been recruited under Honorius's auspices. However, in 409 one of the pretender's commanders turned against him, let the Vandals into Spain, and stirred up rebels in Gaul. Constantine did not last much longer. He was crushed by an imperial general and murdered. The general was rewarded with the hand of Honorius's sister. Their son presently became Emperor as Valentinian III.

Meanwhile, during the chaos of the West, Britain had done an unprecedented thing, broken away from the Roman Empire. In 410 the seaborne Saxons made a fresh and terrible assault. Very little stood in their way, because the army, apart from a few garrisons, had gone abroad with Constantine. The councilors of the *civitates* threw out his officials and got in touch with

Honorius. If they asked for help, none came. What did come was momentous: a message authorizing the Britons to look after themselves, with permission to take up arms. It had always been illegal to form an armed band without special leave, which was never given on a large scale like this. Now it was. A self-armed Britain would be a self-governing Britain. Whatever Honorius's wishes, he had to acknowledge that Britain must be independent, at least for a while. That, after all, was the year when the Goths sacked Rome. The Emperor was at Ravenna, keeping chickens.

Britain's destiny was unique, and remained so. The notion that Rome pulled the legions out and left the island defenseless is quite mistaken. The legions went away because Constantine took them to the Continent. The result in Britain was active, not passive: the creation of a new state by citizens of a Roman territory. While it may not have been their first intention, it became a fact. British militia fought the barbarians with success, and government, on the imperial model, carried on. The *civitates* survived with the municipalities. Britain, for the moment, still counted as a "Roman" land by tradition and culture, in contrast with "barbarian" lands. But external rule never returned.

Arthur's Forerunners

For all of that century after 410 Britain was on its own as Geoffrey claims. He knows, or elects to say, hardly anything factual as to the way this came about. But at least the setting of his story, from here on, looks right. The next question is whether anything else does. He gives his postimperial Britain a series of kings succeeding Constantine and Constans—Vortigern, Aurelius Ambrosius, Uther, and, finally, Arthur. On the face of it, the series might not inspire much confidence. Most of his earlier "British kings" are fabricated; some are imaginary, some are grossly misplaced in time, and some are emperors falsely made out to have been British.

The Britons' history after their severance from Rome is very obscure. Parts of the country were finding leaders of a more masterful kind than local administrators and town councilors. The word "tyrant," *tyrannus*, appears in the few writers overseas who take any notice. It does not imply tyranny so much as doubt-

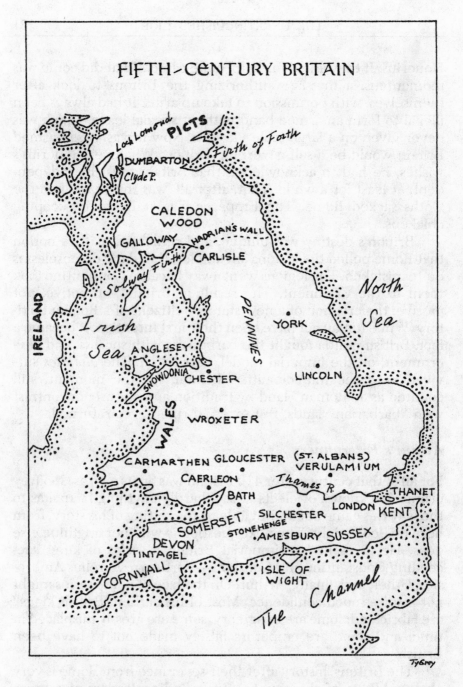

FIFTH-CENTURY BRITAIN

Showing the principal real locations which occur in Geoffrey's *History*, and also illustrating the actual history. Most of the names are given in modern forms.

ful legitimacy, power with no constitutional basis. The new leaders were military bosses who rose by way of the fight against the barbarians.

Welsh tradition about them, centuries later, comes up with the term *gwledig*, "landholder." In its basic sense this means a military chief with regional power, though it tends to acquire a more polite sense as, simply, a prince. Behind some of these figures there may have been improvised defensive structures dating from the twilight of imperial rule. The most famous of the Britons called a landholder is Cunedda. The modern form of his name is Kenneth. He is reputed to have come from the North near Edinburgh to take charge in Wales and expel or subdue the Irish squatters. Many Welsh kings and princes in later times trace their ancestry to him. Skeptics have argued that he is a mythical patriarch, invented to give pedigrees for Welsh families, and to account for Welsh places supposedly named after descendants. But Cunedda is most likely real, because another of the border landholders undoubtedly is, Ceredig, who governed the country around the Clyde in western Scotland.

A third "tyrant" of the same type, though not actually given the landholder label, is Coel. He was active in the mountainous Pennine region of north-central England. Legend was to transform him into the Old King Cole of nursery-rhyme fame and make him the father of Helena, she who became the mother of Constantine the Great, and discovered the Cross. Since she was born well over a hundred years earlier, this was a fearful twisting of dates, but it converted the saintly lady into a true-born Briton. A fourth regional ruler, who does get called a landholder, is Ambrosius Aurelianus. This Roman-named leader flourished in southern England. We shall be meeting him again. He is the first proof that Geoffrey's series of post-Roman kings is not out of touch with facts. Aurelius Ambrosius, Arthur's uncle, is based on him, though the family relations which Geoffrey contrives are unlikely to be real.

Border despots like Cunedda were probably only lightly Romanized. They were more like the Celtic chieftains of ancient times. Yet even Cunedda, according to his pedigree, had a father, grandfather, and great-grandfather with Roman names. Ambrosius, in the deeply civilized South, certainly belonged to the more Romanized element and helped to keep *Romanitas* glowing. His power may have been founded on some civilian office as well as military force. We can form a notion of the way such a British ruler might have been conditioned and educated by looking across the sea to a better-documented Gaul.

One Gallo-Roman gentleman of that age has left himself very fully on record, and we can eke out his evidence with what is known of a number of others. He is Sidonius Apollinaris, a landed aristocrat who lived in the Auvergne, in the south-central part of the country. He married the daughter of another rich Gaul named Avitus, who was briefly Emperor in the West. Later Sidonius was city prefect of Rome, and somewhere about 470 he became bishop of Clermont. He had so many important contacts that his writings are of high value for all this period. He has several special points of interest. One is that he wrote letters to prominent Britons, and copies have survived. Another is that he proves the vitality of the *Restitutor* idea: even when the Empire was plainly falling to pieces, he composed poems hailing each of three emperors (including his father-in-law) as the desired savior, in tones of unquenchable optimism and flattery.

The education that formed him, and many other well-off gentlemen in the West, was in some ways impressive. A boy was taken through standard Greek authors, Homer being the chief, and standard Latin ones, mainly Virgil, Horace, Cicero. He spent a good deal of time on mythology. Later he passed to "rhetoric," meaning, primarily, a training in speech-making and debate on set subjects. Along with this went "philosophy," which included the thought of Plato and Aristotle, but also geometry, arithmetic, and perhaps astrology. Sports and games, indoor and outdoor, were encouraged.

Most of this education was sound, yet it covered the past only. *Romanitas* as absorbed by the pupil meant lingering over the products of a creative era centuries earlier, supplemented by Greek matter that was earlier still, to the neglect of the present. Fixed classical models fostered an imitative spirit, a stress on the technique of oratory or prose-writing or verse-writing, rather than on having anything to say. In the words of Sidonius's modern biographer, "fifth-century educational principles set more store on the training of the intellect than on the intellect itself." The Latin of that age could be elegant. However, outside of religious writing, where it broke new ground magnificently un-

der a different impulse, "elegant" was usually the highest praise
it deserved. Surviving specimens by Britons are very refined
indeed.

Culture tended to be a closed system. In Sidonius's time Gaul
had suffered fearfully from barbarian marches and counter-
marches, brigandage, and violence by rebellious slaves. But
whatever he was saying in conversation, he ignored it in his
writing; most of his letters and poems are curiously untroubled.
He might almost be living in the Roman peace his ancestors
knew. Such serenity may seem complacent, yet it could be a
source of strength. It was an insulation. During a large part of
Sidonius's life the Gallic economy was, in fact, recovering, yet he
hardly discusses that either. There is just a tacit assumption that
fortunes may ebb and flow, but the strength of the land is fundamentally "there," and possibilities for the future remain intact.
That frame of mind did not outlive Sidonius, nor did the education. Everything did change, radically. But fifth-century Britons
like Ambrosius Aurelianus may well have thought in much the
same way, as long as circumstances allowed.

As for their Christianity, it tended to be less than fervent. Yet
it was genuine. Sidonius became not only a bishop but, in the
Church's roll of honor, a saint. Geoffrey's kings who give priority
to rebuilding churches, and bear Christian emblems into battle,
are not at odds with reality. Britain, in fact, had begun to be
rather notable for producing men of religious enterprise. Thus
far they came from the higher ranks of society, if not the highest;
the effective conversion of the masses was to be a slow process.
Christian loyalties, however, were now frequently more than
official.

Nor were they a matter of unthinking and passive orthodoxy.
Even before the break with the Empire, Britain had given Europe the heretic Pelagius. A well-read amateur of theology, possibly a doctor, he settled in Rome and was busy in 405 writing
books and teaching. His version of Christianity credited human
nature with more self-determination than the Church cared to
admit. He stressed freedom and moral responsibility, and denied
original sin, insisting that human beings were not born tainted.
His social outlook was left of center, and he discussed topics more
familiar today than they were then, such as the layperson's voca-
tion in the Church.

Pelagius was big, easygoing, reluctant to dogmatize. Unfortunately, he attracted disciples who did. Their arguments drew retorts which were not all strictly concerned with his doctrine. One opponent described him as "heavy with Scots porridge" (an early gibe at the British breakfast?). The Briton came under fire from the great Augustine, that somber thinker who expounded the concept of the City of God. In 418, under pressure from the Emperor Honorius, the Pope ruled that Pelagianism was heresy. Three years later Honorius forbade its advocates to approach nearer Rome than the hundredth milestone.

In most of the Christian world, Pelagianism faded out as a doctrine, though it survived as an attitude, as it does to this day. But it took fresh hold in the heretic's native Britain, which, being independent, was beyond the reach of orthodox emperors. In 429 two bishops arrived to counter the trend, Germanus of Auxerre and Lupus of Troyes. Germanus staged a public debate, perhaps near London at Verulamium, afterward St. Albans.

The bishops' visit supplies us with one of the few chronological fixes in Geoffrey's history. When telling of King Vortigern's marriage to Hengist's daughter, Geoffrey says: "It was at this time that St Germanus, Bishop of Auxerre, came, and Lupus, Bishop of Troyes, with him, to preach the word of God to the Britons: for their Christian faith had been corrupted not only by the pagans but by the Pelagian heresy." In other words, the marriage took place in 429. Geoffrey has little more to tell of Germanus, but the bishop's biographer records an event showing how Christianity did go hand in hand with a recurrent struggle against the barbarians. While Germanus was in Britain a combined force of Saxons and Picts came raiding inland. A British army was stationed to oppose them. Germanus, who had held military posts in Gaul, was invited to join it. The camp was in hilly country. Easter was approaching, and the bishop improvised a chapel with boughs and baptized many of the soldiers. As the barbarians approached, he posted the army in a valley. The Picts and Saxons entered it. He gave a signal, a shout of "Hallelujah!" The Britons roared "Hallelujah!" three times, and the enemy bolted. Having made his impact in both religious and military affairs, Germanus went back to Gaul. About 446 he paid Britain a second visit. By then Pelagianism, as an organized movement, was much reduced. On his advice some persistent preachers were banished—an approved measure in an age when Christians, unhappily, were beginning to practice persecution themselves. Henceforth the Church in Britain was solidly Catholic.

Christian energy was not confined to stirring up controversy —it also took missionary forms. One of the pioneers was St. Ninian, who is said to have been born near the Solway Firth, the deep inlet of the Irish Sea between England and Scotland, and to have studied in Rome in the 390s. On his way back through Gaul he met St. Martin of Tours, who had been friendly with Maximus, the British-backed Emperor proclaimed a few years before. Martin was an enthusiast for missions, going out to the rustic folk who were still pagan when most prelates were content with the Empire's being "officially" Christian. Returning to his native North, Ninian built a church at Whithorn in Galloway near the modern Wigtown, called the *Candida Casa*, "White House," because it was made of whitewashed stones. Then he journeyed on into central Scotland as a missionary to the Picts. He is commemorated by church dedications and place names as far afield as the Shetland Islands. His traditional date of death is 432.

A Briton of kindred interests and greater fame was Patricius, otherwise known as St. Patrick. The son of a town councilor whose family had been Christian for two or three generations, he was born about 390, somewhere near the west coast of Roman Britain. Irish raiders carried him off at the age of sixteen. After six years of slavery he escaped and found his way to Gaul. Convinced that he should go back to evangelize the Irish, he took holy orders and studied for a long time without any chance offering itself. By the 420s a significant number of Irish had become Christian. They were scattered, unorganized, and probably under Pelagian influence. In 432, with Germanus's backing, Patrick was chosen to reconstruct a papal mission which had gone astray.

Knowing the country and the language, and being resolute without arrogance, he made a good impression. The unpolished Latin of his writings shows a straightforward, nonintellectual character. Ireland still had Druids, who were hostile, but he succeeded in putting the Church on a firm basis. His mission lasted for nearly thirty years. He regarded his converts as Romans. The word has no political meaning. To be Roman meant to belong to what was still the worldwide civilization. The Church was becoming the custodian of a great deal that was durable in it. In other places besides Ireland the Church's *Romanitas* was on the way to being the strongest kind; even the only kind.

That, however, was far from being the case in Britain. Its Christianity was still an ambience for rulers who carried on from the Empire and claimed to be the heirs of its authority. By now, though, it was an inescapable ambience. Here Geoffrey's insight is correct, not only in his portrayal of "good" kings, but in his portrayal of the "bad" one, Vortigern. When the Saxon chiefs Hengist and Horsa land in Britain, Vortigern questions them as to their religion. They name their deities—Woden, Freya, and so forth—and the King replies, "I am greatly grieved by your belief, which, indeed, can better be called unbelief; but all the same I am delighted that you have come, for either God himself, or someone else, has brought you here to help me at a most convenient moment." Heathenism does not deter Vortigern from hiring Saxons to fight for him, but he is enough of a Christian to ask, and regret the answer.

So far we have found only regional "tyrants," but Geoffrey makes Vortigern the ruler of all Britain except the far North, the Pictland, which Rome never absorbed. Did this higher sovereign, Vortigern, really exist?

Once again, the history of the times is obscure. But there are hints of a breathing space somewhere between the break with the Empire in 410 and the visit of Germanus in 429. Britain had a respite from raiding, and was showing signs of renewed agrarian prosperity, which was to go on and increase for a generation. At this point, the idea of a "supreme authority" began to assert itself among the Britons. We can see its shape better among their fellow Celts in Ireland, who for some centuries had regional kings but also a High King over them. The Britons too accepted a High King—in Latin their *superbus tyrannus*, "preeminent ruler," above the lesser *tyranni*. Judging from Ireland, his power was restricted. He certainly governed with a council, which may have been an adaptation of the former provincial council. One such ruler is spoken of in detail long before Geoffrey; and he is called Vortigern. However fictionalized, the royal traitor was real.

His personal name is not known. Vortigern means simply "overking." It is a Celtic form of the supreme title. Welshmen who tell what purports to be his story transform it into

Gwrtheyrn and treat it as, in effect, his name. They dub him Gwrtheyrn the Thin: perhaps because he was, or perhaps metaphorically, because they regard him as lacking in substance. His family is said to have been connected with Gloucestershire, which was strongly Romanized, villa-rich country. A short way out of Llangollen in northern Wales there is a monument that mentions him, a weather-beaten stone shaft on top of a mound near Valle Crucis Abbey. The inscription, now too worn to be read, traced the genealogy of a Welsh prince and apparently claimed Vortigern as his ancestor. According to this, Vortigern's wife (his first wife, if he also married the Saxon) was a daughter of the Emperor Maximus. Other clues point in the same direction. After Maximus's downfall his young daughters became imperial wards. The marriage of one of them to a British noble would have been in keeping with late-Roman policy, as part of an agreement devolving power. Vortigern could have exploited it as giving him rights over the whole ex-Roman territory.

Whatever his credentials, he was probably the first High King whom the Britons acknowledged. His reign began in or about 425, so Geoffrey's indication of date for him, making him out to have been King when Germanus came, is not out of line. Some believe that there is a link, and Vortigern favored the Pelagian doctrine, which Germanus came to combat. The heretics whom Germanus met were socially prominent and may have been under royal patronage. There are legends of a violent conflict, with the bishop anathematizing the King. These could go back to a pro-Pelagian stance on Vortigern's part.

But his real biography is almost effaced by the tradition of that disaster which marks the point of Arthur's rise. Long before Geoffrey, Vortigern is blamed for the major event of the fifth century: the coming of the Saxons, no longer merely as raiders or squatters, but as armed settlers in intimidating numbers.

3

Arthur's Context

Devastation

Geoffrey tells his tale of catastrophe and resurgence, placing Arthur in the resurgence. The last preliminary step in the quest for Arthur is to trace the events on which Geoffrey based his scenario. We cannot be as sure about them as he is, or rather as he pretends to be. But the landscape does fitfully light up and figures do begin to loom through the mist.

The Saxons did come. The term covers several Germanic groups: some were Saxons proper and some were differentiated as Angles and Jutes. From these, mingled with the stock of the Britons themselves, the "English" nation was to emerge, inhabiting "England"—Angle-land—but that was a very long way off. In Vortigern's day the Saxons were still ruthless pirates, dreaded on the Continent as well as in Britain. Unlike the Goths and other barbarians, they were pagan and practiced human sacrifice. They had been spreading from Germany along what is now the Dutch littoral, then called Frisia, and mixing with the Frisians. It was a poor, damp, comfortless country, where much of the population kept above water by living on mounds of mud and refuse. The Saxons were bold seafarers, and they spread farther afield in search of better things.

Some cruised around Gaul and seized land in several areas, especially on the lower reaches of the River Loire. Others looked to Britain. Early in the fifth century a fair number were already squatting in widely scattered parts of the country, mainly near the North Sea coast and up the Thames Valley. A few may have arrived as auxiliary troops before British independence. Germanus's victory in 429 shows that besides piratical raiders, there were uncontrolled Saxons inland, harassing the country in alliance with Picts.

The Picts—who were based out of reach in their northern fastnesses, and had been mounting campaigns for decades—still seemed to be the worst enemies. On that premise the Britons adopted a Roman course of action. They hired one set of barbarians to oppose another. Organized Saxon units were allowed to live on British soil, and subsidized, in return for military service. They had to forswear friendship with the Picts and defend Britain against them. Those who occupied land on such a basis were *foederati*, "federates." The western Goths, known as Visigoths, had settled in southwestern Gaul in 418 on the understanding that they would deal with the Vandals who were loose in Spain. (Eventually they took over Spain themselves.)

Some at least of the Saxon federates in Britain were employed through a decision at top level, by a High King with his council. Allegedly Vortigern was the King concerned, and there is no good reason to doubt it. Since the policy turned out badly, the Britons' Welsh descendants made him a villain and scapegoat. On that view of him Geoffrey builds his story. Really we have no way of knowing how far he was responsible. Regional rulers may have hired Saxons on their own, and started doing it before Vortigern did. Nor perhaps was he quite as culpable as wisdom-after-the-event made him out to be. He was not launching into any wild novelty; he was following imperial precedent. The flaw, not an obvious one, was that he lacked imperial resources. To keep his Saxons satisfied and under control, ample supplies would be needed, and in the long run these might be hard to find.

The time-hallowed tradition which Geoffrey enlarges on is that the first federates were led by Hengist and Horsa, brothers who landed with three shiploads of warriors and were posted by Vortigern on Thanet at the tip of Kent. A schoolbook date for their arrival used to be 449. This is out of the question for the first settlement, and is due to an error in the reckoning by early historians. Other information points to 428. If that is correct, when Germanus was routing hostile Saxons, friendly ones had been installed somewhere else. It is perfectly possible. There had long been pro-Roman and anti-Roman Goths. Germanus's action crushed the Saxons who remained hostile, ended a ragged situation, and allowed the program to proceed.

It proceeded. It also got out of hand. More Saxons were settled, in areas stretching inland from the east coast. What the Britons had not provided for was that they would be followed by an influx of their kinsfolk, bringing wives and families. By the early 440s the reinforced federates were dominating parts of the country. Pressure was building up as the growing horde presented growing demands. During that decade fighting broke out again. In 446 we have an authentic document, or at least, extracts from it. A group of prominent Britons addressed an appeal to the general and consul Aëtius. Last of the great Roman soldiers, he was struggling to maintain the West for its unprepossessing Emperor Valentinian III. Aëtius was embroiled with a variety of enemies, and still a few years away from the crowning victory he was to gain over Attila's Huns. The British message was desperate:

> To Aëtius, three times consul: the groans of the Britons.
> . . . The barbarians push us back to the sea, the sea
> pushes us back to the barbarians; between these two
> kinds of death, we are either drowned or slaughtered.

Aëtius was in no position to help, and the Britons were abandoned to the barbarians.

Which ones? An opinion based on the earliest authors is that they were Picts, and Picts only, resuming their aggressions. But the Saxons were now established in Britain and had been there for years; the Picts could never have campaigned without their connivance. The 440s seem to have brought a gradual and spreading loss of control. Frustrated in their demands for more supplies, which could not be met, many of the federates mutinied. The Angles in the North of the settled zone broke their undertakings and revived the Pictish alliance. Britain slid into a nightmare period of revolt, raiding, and looting. The British forces could win isolated successes, and did. Mostly, however, they were swept aside. By this time the notorious Hengist was in Kent playing an active role.

In the anguished words of a Briton:

> A fire heaped up and nurtured by the hand of the impious easterners spread from sea to sea. It devastated town and country round about, and, once it was alight, it did not die down until it had burned almost the whole surface of the island and was licking the western ocean with its fierce red tongue. . . . All the major towns were laid low by the repeated battering of enemy rams; laid low, too, all the inhabitants—church leaders, priests and people alike, as the swords glinted all around and the flames crackled. It was a sad sight. In the middle of the squares the foundation-stones of high walls and towers that had been torn from their lofty base, holy altars, fragments of corpses, covered (as it were) with a purple crust of congealed blood, looked as though they had been mixed up in some dreadful winepress. . . . A number of the wretched survivors were caught in the mountains and butchered wholesale. Others, their spirit broken by hunger, went to surrender to the enemy; they were fated to be slaves for ever, if indeed they were not killed straight away.

Lurid as all this sounds, it is probably rather nearer truth than falsehood. But something which is not said needs to be stressed: the Saxons' onslaught was not an attempt to conquer Britain or even to expand their holdings. They were still far too few for that. Their war bands roamed the country at will, and doubtless camped and wintered a long way across it. Their forays, as reported, spread to the western sea, and the Picts aided them. But they were sacking, not occupying. Neither history nor archaeology indicates any new settlements. The basic enclaves remained; here and there the chiefs may have extended them slightly as opportunity served, but throughout the ordeal the Saxon territory was one thing and the much larger British territory another.

Raiding continued for years, well into the 450s, possibly even longer in places. As ever, life went on with more normality than the cries of the horrified would suggest. Germanus's second visit was Saxon-free, and the government could enforce sentences of exile on Pelagian diehards. In 455, when the Pope revised the method of fixing Easter, the British Church was informed of the change and adopted it. But whether or not "all the major towns" were raided, urban society sank into a deeper decay. The remnants of the villa economy faded out.

Centuries after, when the Saxons had become literate, a compilation known as the *Anglo-Saxon Chronicle* put a few of their early exploits on record. Scraps of royal eulogy and the balladry of war, handed down by minstrels, were written with dates alongside. The entries for the first upheaval suffer from the error which put the Saxon advent too late, but references to fighting southeast of London may have something in them. The *Chronicle* mentions Vortigern as still living in 455. Nothing is said about him later than that, anywhere. He would probably have been in his sixties or seventies. Legend gives ugly and conflicting accounts of his end. The most prosaic is that amid general hate, he "wandered from place to place until at last his heart broke, and he died without honour."

No son of his succeeded to the High Kingship. But members of his family can be traced, arguably, in Gaul. A son named Faustus is mentioned as entering the Church, and an early Welsh family tree includes a grandson called Riagath. These are interesting names. An ecclesiastical Faustus is well attested abroad. He was born between 405 and 410, a little early for a son of Vortigern, but possible. Whatever his parentage, he was British. At about the age of thirty he became abbot of Lérins, an important community on an island off the Mediterranean coast. Such advancement hints at exalted connections. Later he was made bishop of Riez in southern Gaul. Books written by him survive. What gives him his special interest here is that we find him linked with another Briton called Riocatus. This is simply a Latin form of the name given to Vortigern's grandson in the family tree. If that is right, Riocatus was Faustus's nephew; and the two of them do make an appearance together.

The person who links them is Sidonius. One of his poems and two of his letters are addressed to Faustus. The second letter, written when Sidonius was bishop of Clermont, tells of an intercepted package. Riocatus had been staying with Faustus, and called on Sidonius on the way home. In his baggage he had a copy of a book Faustus had written. Though he paused for some time in Clermont, he never mentioned that he had it. Sidonius only found out after he left. Anxious to read the book, he set off in pursuit.

> I chased the runaway with swift horses, easily capable of catching up on the one day's start he had . . . stopped the horses, tied up their bridles, undid his baggage, and, finding the book I sought, drew it forth, read and re-read it, and made excerpts, picking out the greatest of those great chapters. I also secured some saving of time by the speed of the scribes in following my rapid dictation and denoting by signs what they did not compass by letters.

Sidonius wrote this when the country around was overrun by Goths and in chaos. Under such conditions the literary idyll is refreshing. Life did go on. Vortigern's son and grandson, if that is what they were, had chosen a more tranquil path. As we shall see, Faustus was not the only Briton whom Sidonius corresponded with, nor the most important.

Recovery

Back in Britain, by 460 or thereabouts, the worst was over and things seemed to be on the mend. The resurgence was as real as the catastrophe had been. Meanwhile, the Empire was at last truly breaking up in the West. Viewed from Rome, the process was disaster unmitigated; viewed from other angles, it was by no means so.

In 455, the year when we last hear of Vortigern, the Emperor Valentinian III was murdered. His death was masterminded as an act of revenge by a senator whose wife he had raped. The senator replaced him as Emperor, and then, the rape victim having died, married Valentinian's widow, Eudoxia. Any doubts she might have had over the killing of her first husband were dispelled by the second, who was perfectly frank about it. She sent a message to Gaiseric, the King of the Vandals, who had moved from Spain into northern Africa. Would he come over and

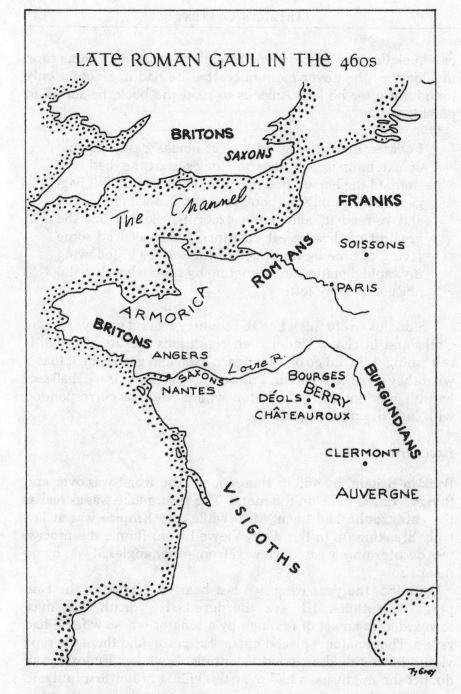

LATE ROMAN GAUL IN THE 460s
Illustrating events in that decade.

rescue her? Gaiseric responded. He appeared in the mouth of the Tiber with a sea-commanding fleet, and put an army ashore.

The Emperor was stoned to death by rioting Romans. The Vandals sacked the city as the Goths had in 410, if not quite so ruinously, thanks to a plea from Pope Leo. He was qualified in this kind of intercession, having turned back Attila the Hun a few years previously. In two weeks of pillage the Vandals robbed the Capitol of its gilt statues and stripped its roof; removed the Jews' sacred treasures, which Roman soldiers had taken from the Temple when Jerusalem fell; and extracted most of the objects of value from the palace Eudoxia was occupying. Though she had got rid of her husband, she was a loser in other respects. The Vandals seized her jewelry and carried her home to Africa, together with thousands of prisoners of lower rank.

The Western emperorship, however, was not finished. Sidonius's father-in-law, Avitus, became Emperor, and Sidonius composed a flattering poem commemorating the event which he read before the Senate. Even in the aftermath of assassination and ruin Sidonius could still believe in a *Restitutor Orbis,* and hail the prospect of his wife's father's reign. His poem runs to 602 lines, and takes the form of a plea to Jupiter by a distracted Rome, and Jupiter's response in the shape of the new Augustus, at whose very name the Goths falter and even the Saxons desist from raiding. Jupiter perorates:

> "This man I have given thee, Rome, while Gaul throughout her wide plains thunders with plaudits for Augustus, and the north, now stronger, carries the auspicious clamour to the pale-cheeked south. . . . How he shall, time and again, bring nations under thy yoke, dashing his eagles against them! . . . Be of good cheer with such a man for emperor, O Rome, ancient mother of gods; lift up thine eyes and cast off thine unseemly gloom. Lo! a prince of riper years shall bring back youth to thee, whom child-princes [such as the luckless Honorius] have made old."

> The great Father had scarce ended his utterance when the gods clapped their hands and a shout of applause rang through the council. The fateful Sisters spun out a happy time for thy rule, Augustus, and for

thy consular year they drew out with their whirling spindles a golden age.

Within months Avitus was deposed, to be succeeded by Majorian. The undaunted Sidonius addressed a poem to him too. Personified Rome is trotted out again; Majorian's feats in war are recalled. And now: "Jubilant Europe shouts a 'bravo' for thee, echoing through sky and countryside and cities and waters, since thou who wert a conqueror art now greeted as ruler." Majorian did not last long either and, unlike Avitus, he was a real loss. Character and intentions were not enough, however. The Western emperors, now back in Rome for most of the time, were increasingly at the mercy of Count Ricimer, an unscrupulous noble of barbarian parentage who commanded the troops there.

Outside of Italy disenchantment was giving birth to a new development, the rise of men loyal to *Romanitas* but not to the Emperor. Marcellinus, a general whose authority Ricimer was trying to sap, set up a domain of his own on the opposite coast of the Adriatic. In Gaul another general, Aegidius, established himself at Soissons about 457. The Franks who were settled in that area happened to be at odds with their King, Childeric. They banished him and accepted Aegidius as overlord. In 461 Ricimer installed an Emperor who was blatantly a puppet. Even Sidonius did not address a poem to this one. Aegidius ignored him and ruled over northern Gaul independently.

The detached *Romanitas* of these rebel patriots was paralleled in Britain. There the tide of destruction had ebbed. The worst raiding was past. New leaders were emerging, and their presence was felt in Aegidius's Gallic domain. One effect of the Saxon forays had been an exodus of Britons to Armorica, in northwestern Gaul. Archaeology suggests that small British communities may have been there for some time. Geoffrey exploits the legend that they were founded in the fourth century by veterans of the Emperor Maximus. Whatever the truth about that, settlement was certainly going on in the late 450s, beginning the conversion of a part of Armorica into Brittany. It had begun as a flight of refugees, but its character altered as it gathered momentum.

Many colonists were drawn from the better-educated and better-off—they are said to have taken numerous books with them—and came from Cornwall and Devon, where the Saxons were not a very terrible menace. They may simply have been depressed by the prospects, but some probably went to Gaul in a more positive spirit, with Aegidius's aid and under his auspices. He and they very possibly had plans for a new regional system, with benefits on both sides of the Channel. Two new Armorican cities came into being about this time. Aegidius, or his son Syagrius, who succeeded him, may have put the Britons in charge of coastal defense and sponsored these settlements.

One reason for doubting that the migration was merely an escape from Saxons is that colonists went to areas which were already occupied by Saxons, in possession along the Loire and on islands in the river. For a while coexistence may have been the norm. Presently, however, fighting developed there too, and the Saxons wasted a tract of country where Britons were settling. The colonists held their own and rooted themselves in their new homes. In 461 a "bishop of the Britons" attended a council at Tours. Though his flock was still small, the creation of a lesser overseas Britain had started.

About this time Ambrosius Aurelianus comes into view, the man on whom Geoffrey bases his successor to Vortigern, Aurelius Ambrosius. He is spoken of vaguely as a surviving Roman, and as the son of parents who had worn the purple and died in the devastation. "Wearing the purple" could mean that his father was of senatorial rank. As for his being Roman, that has nothing to do with ethnic origins. It refers to his allegiance, his pro-Roman leanings in independence; his resemblance, in fact, to Aegidius in Gaul. Traditions of the Welsh call him Emrys, the Welsh form of Ambrosius, and, as already noted, make him a landholder or army chief with regional power. He is on record as having fought a rival at a place called Guoloph in 437. If that is correct, he was middle-aged during his rise as a "Roman" leader in the late 450s and 460s. Guoloph is Wallop in Hampshire. Ambrosius's sphere of influence was in southern Britain, where the magnates of the villa society, or rather their sons and grandsons, would not have been an extinct species.

The fresh impulse to the Britons' *Romanitas* was minor, but tangible. For a while some Britons continued to give their children Roman names. For almost another century, some were to think of themselves as "citizens" and of Latin as "our language."

Meanwhile, something more solid was happening, a genuine recovery. The Picts faded beyond the horizon. The Saxons themselves drew back. They returned finally to their enclaves in the East and Southeast, where more of their kinsfolk were streaming in from the Continent. How much their withdrawal was due to British action and how much to their having had enough of roving and ravaging is hard to tell.

During the 460s Ambrosius is assembling forces, organizing counterattacks, pressing forward to contain the barbarians. With no known help from overseas, the Britons are regaining control. Clues begin to slip through from the other side. While the *Anglo-Saxon Chronicle* records no defeats—Germanic minstrels preferred not to sing about them—it drops unintended hints by the tailing-off of victories. Its early entries, though unreliable as to date, show a trend. In 455 the Saxons are in the full tide of revolt. Hengist fights the Britons and begins calling himself King of Kent. In 457 he fights them again and they flee in terror to London. But an eight-year silence follows. A battle in 465 is not claimed as a victory. Its outcome is glossed over by boasting about the enemy casualties. Then there is silence for another eight years. We can picture Ambrosius taking command in the 460s and hemming the Saxons in.

A few place names may commemorate him. One is Amesbury. The "bury" part is Saxon, the first part is originally "Ambr." This town near Salisbury Plain is the site of an early monastery, and according to one guess, Ambrosius founded it. More likely he stationed troops there. In the later Empire military forces were sometimes named after their heads or nominal heads. Hence the Honoriaci, "Honorius's men," who defected to the pretender Constantine. Ambrosius's men would have been Ambrosiaci or Ambrosiani. Their presence could have given his name to a base they used, so that eventually it became his "bury," his "fort" or "town." The same might be true of Ambrosden in Oxfordshire, which is "Ambr's Hill."

A High King and a Birth of Nations

Professor Leslie Alcock, after writing of the High King who brought in the Saxons, suggests that Ambrosius was "probably responsible to this same king or his successor." Ambrosius might have been responsible to Vortigern, at some previous stage, but to a successor certainly, since the rally Ambrosius led came after Vortigern's death. Despite Geoffrey, Ambrosius is not called a King himself except in legend. If he was not, who was? To what High King was he responsible?

Affairs were in flux. Britons had accepted monarchical rule, with the limits implied by the High King's council. Meanwhile, there had been territorial changes, the most important of which was due to the Saxons. Several fair-sized areas were securely theirs. Many of their children were born in the settlements and were incipiently English, though the use of that word was still far in the future. The British-held portion of the island remained much larger, and contained nine tenths of the population. But it was no longer united from end to end, even tenuously.

By the River Clyde the regional chief Ceredig (in Latin, Coroticus) ruled independently from a stronghold on the rock of Dumbarton, the "Fort of the Britons." During the 450s a crew of his warriors had crossed the sea and fallen on an assembly of Irish, including newly baptized converts of St. Patrick. They massacred some and carried others away as slaves. For the converts it was discouraging; their assailants were nominally Christians. Patrick wrote a letter of protest and then another, of which a copy has survived, giving Ceredig an unsavory immortality. These Britons of the far North had seceded into a barbarism of their own, counterraiding against the Irish. The Britons of the far South, in Armorica, were beginning to build a mini-Britain across the Channel. Their children were incipient Bretons, as the Saxons' children were incipient English, though with them also the term was still unborn.

The net result of these changes was that there could no longer be a King of Britain, even to Vortigern's dubious extent. But apart from Ceredig, no regional boss had yet set up on his own. There could still be a ruler paramount over most of the British people, a "King of the Britons" at least in name; just as there were kings of the Visigoths and Vandals, called after their subjects and not their ill-defined territories. This period in the 450s and 460s was the only time when such a man could have existed, when the British High Kingship could have taken this shape. And it did. The phrase "King of the Britons" is on record, and the man did exist, whether or not his paramountcy extended as far as it might have done. He was the hero of an episode underlining the Britons' recovery, when their partly revived *Romanitas* gave them a sudden meteoric importance.

In 465 there was once again an imperial vacancy at Rome. For over a year the West had no separate Emperor. At last Leo I, the Emperor at Constantinople, intervened. In 467 he appointed a Western colleague himself. The choice was Anthemius, a Greek noble of admired character and respected family. He marched to Rome with a splendid retinue and was accepted by the Senate. Predictably, Sidonius addressed a poem to him, and read it before the assembled senators.

> When nature established the young Jupiter above the stars and the new god was entering upon an ancient sovereignty, all the deities vied in paying worship to their deity, and uttered in diverse measures the same "bravo." . . . In like manner, O Caesar, chiefest hope of our time, I come after great lords and offer thee humble incense. . . .
>
> This, my lords, is the man for whom Rome's brave spirit and your love did yearn, the man to whom our commonwealth, like a ship overcome by tempests and without a pilot, hath committed her broken frame, to be more deftly guided by a worthy steersman, that she may no more fear storm or pirate. . . .
>
> Forward, then, Father of thy Country, blest of fortune.

Sidonius's third *Restitutor* faced a pressing problem in Gaul. Though still part of the Empire, it had been subjected to many inroads and much land seizure, and was in a complicated condition. Aegidius had died and his son Syagrius dominated the North, at some point, interestingly, adopting the title "King of the Romans." Within his sphere of influence lived the Franks, whose own King had returned from exile. For the present they and Syagrius were on good terms. The emigrant Britons confronted Saxons along the Loire. Part of Gaul stretching south from Syagrius's domain was held by pro-Roman Burgundians. The danger came from the Visigoths. Their new King, Euric, was master of much of Spain. He had schemes of conquest in Gaul too, which he was putting into effect. The Visigoths were Arian heretics, and the religious difference was no quibble. Euric was not a systematic persecutor, but in parts of Gaul which he over-ran, church doorways were blocked, priests were jailed, bishops were exiled. Faustus, that possible son of Vortigern, was among the exiles.

In 468 the Emperor Anthemius took a most original step. He sought a British alliance. It is a measure of the Britons' revival, and the strengthening of their Roman sympathies, that he should have tried it. Moreover, he succeeded. An account of these happenings was set down in a *Gothic History* by a certain Jordanes, summarized in 551 from an earlier work now lost. The account begins as follows:

> Leo . . . chose as emperor [in the West] his patrician Anthemius and sent him to Rome. . . .
>
> Now Euric, king of the Visigoths, perceived the frequent changes of Roman emperors and strove to hold Gaul in his own right. The emperor Anthemius heard of it and asked the Britons for aid. Their king Riotimus came with twelve thousand men into the state of the Bituriges by the way of Ocean, and was received as he disembarked from his ships.

Here is a King of the Britons, pointing at a 460s version of the High Kingship. Further on, Jordanes uses the phrase in plain terms. One reason for historians' taking little notice of this affair has been a notion that the Britons were Bretons—settlers in Armorica—and the King merely a local chief. But the British soldiers came "by the way of Ocean," which can only mean sailing over from Britain, as the settlers would not have done, being on the spot already. They came in greater numbers than the infant colonies could have produced. Twelve thousand may be an exaggeration, but the force was strong enough to hold out a hope of checking Euric. Professor James Campbell, in a recent discussion, has moved back toward the natural reading. In his eyes the King is acceptable as "a British ruler having authority on both sides of the Channel."

On the face of it he was Vortigern's successor, to whom Ambrosius was answerable, as a regional ruler in charge of containment of the Saxons in Britain. He may have begun to reign in the 450s through some unrecorded coup, or marriage to a daughter of Vortigern, though all such guesses are guesses only. A King taking British troops abroad may strike us as irresponsible, if we think of the Saxons as a continued menace at home. At the time it may well have seemed that the danger was past, that Ambrosius had contained them. It may even have seemed that the main Saxon threat to Britons was now on the Continent. Since 464 a Saxon chief named Odovacar had been making his aggressive mark in the Loire Valley, raiding the city of Angers.

Jordanes's summary telescopes the campaign. The "state of the Bituriges" which the Britons entered was Berry, in the heart of Gaul. They had to traverse intermediate country to get there. No doubt they sailed into the mouth of the Loire, where the unidentified person who "received" them could have been Syagrius, self-styled King of the Romans in northern Gaul. They marched along the north side of the river, close to the Saxon zone, and paused. About this time the "Roman" forces smashed the Saxons near Angers. Franks took part in the war, capturing islands in the river which the Saxons had held, and so did Britons, helping to destroy their ships. The Saxons' power hereabouts was broken, though the Frankish King, Childeric, saved them from total ruin by a deal enlisting some of them in his own service.

Hopes were surely high on both sides of the Channel. The Britons advanced up the Loire, crossed into Berry, and occupied Bourges. At this point, or about this point, we have a surprising piece of evidence: nothing less than a letter to their King. Its writer is the invaluable Sidonius. He addresses the King as Riothamus, using a Latin spelling which would be closer to the British original than Jordanes's. The letter introduces its bearer, a landowner who complains that the Britons have been enticing his slaves away. Sidonius refers back to a previous contact. If there is anything in the linkage of the clerics Faustus and Riocatus with Vortigern, Sidonius was on friendly terms with three royal Britons, and may have come to know this one through the others. He says:

> I am a direct witness of the conscientiousness which
> weighs on you so heavily, and which has always been of

such delicacy as to make you blush for the wrongdoing of others.

He goes on to explain the landowner's grievance, but is uncertain of the reception he is likely to get.

I fancy that this poor fellow is likely to make good his plaint, that is, if amid a crowd of noisy, armed and disorderly men who are emboldened at once by their courage, their number, and their comradeship, there is any possibility for a solitary unarmed man, a humble rustic, a stranger of small means, to gain a fair and equitable hearing.

Whether he did or not is not recorded.

There is disagreement about the date and circumstances. However, the British soldiers seem to be in a lively mood, and we should surely picture them in Berry, buoyed by a feeling of success. Any landowner living near Sidonius is more likely to have had trouble with them in that phase of their movements, and Sidonius speaks elsewhere of his many Berry acquaintances. His earlier contact with the King suggests a passage of time, putting the letter in late 469, even early 470.

It was a dizzy moment. After all the Britons' losses, they had recovered to a point where their principal King was courted by an Emperor, and had the power to respond. He had grown in stature till he was Rome's last hope beyond the Alps, the last Western prop of the tottering cosmopolis. This was fully realized by those who plotted to undermine it: while Riothamus awaited Euric's advance, treachery had begun to work.

Gaul still had an imperial prefect, the Emperor's deputy ruler there. His name was Arvandus. He had had a good first term in office and a bad second term, marked by bitter unpopularity and the use of public funds to pay private debts. Soon after Riothamus's arrival in Gaul he had written Euric a treasonable letter, urging the Visigoth not to come to terms with the "Greek emperor" (a sneer at Anthemius) but to crush "the Britons posted north of the Loire," as they then were. Again some historians have minimized these Britons as being merely "Bretons." But Euric would have achieved nothing by overrunning the small, out-of-the-way colonies. The whole point was that the British King's imported army was central to the situation, the only obstacle in the way of Euric's plans. Once it was gone, Arvandus continued, Euric could detach the Burgundians from their Roman alliance and carve up Gaul with them.

The letter was intercepted, and Arvandus was recalled to Rome and impeached by the Senate. While the prefect's accusers raised a number of issues, the letter was their damning exhibit. Arvandus wrecked whatever defense he had by overconfidence. When found guilty of treason he was amazed. A sentence of death was commuted to banishment with a heavy fine. His message had failed to reach its addressee, but the damage was done, the treason accomplished. The proposal had been made public and Euric took the hint, realizing the hollowness of the Empire in Gaul.

After the Britons had crossed the Loire and got into their exposed forward position, Euric thrust ahead. It was now, probably, early in the year 470. Jordanes again: "Euric, king of the Visigoths, came against them with an innumerable army, and after a long fight he routed Riotimus, king of the Britons, before the Romans could join him." The royal phrase is there, spelled out. The Romans who never came would have been troops promised by Syagrius. Gregory of Tours, sixth-century author of a classic *History of the Franks*, adds details. He is a little hazy as to when, but he knows where. "The Britons were expelled from Bourges by the Goths after the killing of many of them at Bourg-de-Déols." Déols is just over the River Indre from Châteauroux, and thereabouts the tragic battle was fought. Riothamus had gone forward boldly and tried bravely, but the horde of barbarians overwhelmed him. Jordanes once more: "When he had lost a great part of his army, he fled with all the men he could gather together, and came to the Burgundians, a neighbouring tribe then allied to the Romans." Gregory's words show the course of his retreat. A line from Déols back through Bourges, prolonged on the map, passes into a neighboring part of Burgundy. There Riothamus vanishes from history. As for the surviving Britons whom he could *not* "gather together," there are signs that Euric may have taken them prisoner and resettled them in part of his own domains, Aquitaine by the Bay of Biscay.

This King of the Britons poses a fascinating historical "if." He and Ambrosius in Britain and Aegidius and Syagrius in their portion of Gaul did not stand for the shattered Empire exactly, but they did stand for *Romanitas.* Furthermore, the British settlement in Armorica was forging a link. If there had been no treachery, if a concerted effort had repulsed Euric, the Empire might have revived in northwestern Europe; not through a return to provincial status, but through the rise of a new center with its own emperors. But with the British defeat, all was over, or virtually so. Anthemius, the enterprising but ill-served Greek, was deposed and murdered in 472. Four years and four Emperors later, the line in the West came to an end.

Yet the vast crumbling was also creative. The Franks turned against Syagrius, and in 486 their next king, Clovis, captured his capital, Soissons. Clovis rose to supremacy in northern Gaul and drove the Visigoths back toward Spain. Gaul became the land of the Franks—eventually France.

In Armorica the settlers were drifting off on a course of their own. Their colonized part of Gaul shrank into Brittany, and, in due course, accepted Frankish suzerainty. Yet Brittany did gain some distinctiveness. Not only did rich emigrants found local dynasties, but those years also brought a migration of churchmen, the "saints" of Brittany—missionaries, teachers, founders of religious communities, many from Wales. Few at first but numerous later, they played a crucial role in shaping a new society. Over the next eighty years fresh waves of colonists were to confirm the nature of the country. The native Armoricans were absorbed into a Breton nation.

In Britain itself Ambrosius may still have been active after 470. However, there were no more high kings, apart, possibly, from aspirants who failed to make the claim good. There could no longer be a "King of the Britons" in any effectual sense. A breakup was in progress. The regions were finally becoming separate kingdoms with dynasties of their own. The nation was on the road to radical changes in the sixth century and after, with its language evolving into separate forms spoken by separate branches—Welsh, Cornish, and, over the Channel, Breton.

The Saxons could no longer be contained. They did not raid at will anymore, but further immigration was steadily building up their strength, and they had started to inch forward in a gradual land-taking. To judge from the *Anglo-Saxon Chronicle,* the Kentish host took the offensive in 473. Also, deprived of most of their holdings in the Loire Valley, the Continental Saxons were casting their eyes on Britain again. Saxons began entering the island at new points, first, it seems, in what is now Sussex, in the year 477 (according to the *Chronicle*). Landings near the Isle of Wight followed, the first (again according to the *Chronicle*) being effected by a leader called Cerdic in 495. Saxon kingdoms were taking shape as well as British ones. In some areas the new encroachments were unresisted. In others the counterattacks begun by Ambrosius caused intermittent conflict.

Yet this was not a second collapse, for the Picts were nullified and the Saxons were moving cautiously. Their *Chronicle* still records no defeats, but again something can be inferred from the rarity and petering-out of victory claims. Bishop Germanus's biographer, writing about 480, is the only external witness for the state of Britain, and he can still call it prosperous.

Prosperous, but altered forever. Changes which had begun decades earlier were taking hold. The island no longer had a coinage. Most of the towns, though not deserted, were beyond reclamation. Even where there was still urban building, as at Wroxeter in Shropshire, the builders remodeled the town in timber. Generally the Britons were finding a new-old life-style by going back to the land and tribal ways. Some reoccupied ancient Celtic hill forts, setting up homesteads within the earthwork defenses.

Ever since the beginning of the resurgence they had been finding new leaders besides the two we know, Ambrosius and Riothamus. That is certain, because they won victories and continued to win them, and without leadership victories are not won. The nature of leadership would have had to change with changing conditions. We might see a sort of parallel in the United States during the half century after independence, with its long-planted civilization in the former colonies, and its hinterland of wild country and Indians. A frontiersman such as Davy Crockett knew how to fight Indians in the wilderness, and could also sit in Congress at Washington. As Britain altered, the "Washington" element shrank and the "wilderness" element increased. Nevertheless, its Crocketts carried on.

The recovery had gone through a phase of hope, then turned out to be indecisive. But it had a long way to go yet, and a second

The Emperor Constantius Chlorus, father of Constantine the Great. The reverse of the medallion shows Constantius entering London following his defeat of the British rebellion launched by Carausius. The inscription reads REDDITOR LUCIS AETERNAE, "Restorer of the Eternal Light." *Credit: The British Museum*

Arthur was born into the age of late antiquity, the art of which evokes an interest in the world of the soul. *Credit: Sotheby Parke Bernet*

Barletta Colossus. The best representation of a late Roman Emperor in the pose of *Restitutor Orbis* is of Marcian. He ruled in Constantinople in the early part of the reign indicated for Riothamus.   *Credit: Hirmer Verlag Munich*

Above: In the absence of any surviving representations of British high kings, we can at least glimpse how a visiting Constantinople artist or follower of a British High King in the North would have styled them. The "hourglass" look affected in Riothamus's time can be seen in this "Brussels" head. *Credit: A.C.L.-Brussel*

Left: The imperial general Stilicho answered an appeal for help from Britain about 398. His Romans drove the barbarians back, but official Rome never fully returned. *Credit: Mansell Collection*

Above: This helmet is from the Sutton Hoo Saxon prince's ship burial. A comparable archaeological find of Arthurian British royalty has eluded discovery.
Credit: The British Museum

Right: The reconstruction of a Saxon chief's parade armor of Roman type is helped by the Sutton Hoo discoveries. Shield and boots reflect the custom of fighting on foot.

Above: The Belgrade Cameo. A brilliant fragment preserves the Roman tradition of cavalier and heroic leader while dramatizing the late Roman resort to cavalry as an answer to raiding barbarians. *Credit: Narodni Muzej Beograd*

Left: The reconstruction of the dress of an Arthurian "knight" is based on archaeological evidence and references in early Welsh poetry. Clothes, sword, shield, and spear are suited to fighting on horseback. *Credit: Original drawing by D. Lloyd Owen*

Corbridge lanx. A masterpiece buried away in Northumberland by the British, typical of the princely silver available in the successive generation to Arthur's court. It serves as a reminder of how close in memory were the aristocratic British to pagan belief and Hellenic culture. *Credit: The Duke of Northumberland Collection*

Achilles lanx. That the future hero Arthur grew up inspired by poetry about the exploits of Homeric heroes is suggested by the occurrence of Achilles themes in much art imported into Britain, such as this Carthage example. *Credit: Private Collection*

Cadbury-Camelot excavations: conjectural reconstruction of a cruciform church of uncertain date. *Credit: Drawn by Bryan Whitton*

Reconstruction of the Arthurian gatehouse with rampart and breastwork at Cadbury. *Credit: Thames and Hudson (Publishers) Ltd.*

The Arthurian Grail myth seems to combine a crusader society's fascination with holy relics and preceding Celtic lore about pagan sacred vessels. Two cups, one pagan and the other Christian, date within a century of Arthur's time.

The Antioch Chalice, first believed to date from the century after Christ's Last Supper, is now regarded as contemporary with Arthurian Britain. *Credit: The Metropolitan Museum of Art, Cloisters Collection*

This gold "cage" was probably designed to enclose a glass bowl and was used to celebrate Dionysus at the pagan grape harvest festival. It dates from a century or so earlier. *Credit: Sotheby Parke Bernet*

peak of success to rise to, an even higher one. The legend destined to come out of it would be unique; the course of events in Britain was unique itself. Alone among Rome's provincials, the Britons had achieved self-rule before the barbarians moved in. Alone they had fought back, surmounted disaster, and laid the foundations of a heroic tradition.

This then is the context of Arthur's "history." As presented by Geoffrey of Monmouth the "history" is fantastic and unhistorical. Yet quite clearly it cannot be dismissed as based on nothing at all. The fiction has factual moorings. Britain did become independent; Vortigern did reign; the Saxons did come, in something like the way Geoffrey describes. There was catastrophe; there was resurgence. Since the resurgence came to be summed up and symbolized in the figure of Arthur, historians have sometimes called it the Arthurian Fact. That implies nothing, one way or the other, as to whether he existed. But he is more than a symbol of the resurgence alone. The story makes him a hero proper to that age, embodying one of its cherished dreams. Within his own sphere of action he is a *Restitutor.* Sidonius shows how persistent that notion was, and how easily poetry and rhetoric could attach it to real people, even on flimsy grounds.

Geoffrey's characters are seldom much like their living originals. No amount of searching could be expected to turn up anyone substantiating Arthur in detail. Yet, all things considered, we can fairly hope to identify an Arthur figure of status, a worthy original: someone with enough of the qualities Geoffrey needed for his fiction and enough substance to give that fiction its medieval impact, as an official history which nobody could subvert.

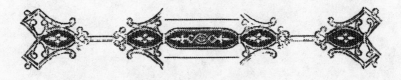

Part II

ARTHUR

4

The Old Welsh Trail

A Mysterious Preface

Confronting the tale of Arthur, the first question we have to ask is
what Geoffrey read or heard. Does he drop any hints himself as to
where he got it? If so, does he lead us to older matter showing
who Arthur was and where he fits in?

Geoffrey does a great deal more than drop hints. He tells us
exactly where he got it: not only the tale of Arthur but the whole
of his *History of the Kings of Britain.* The trouble is that his
explanation is hardly less puzzling than the *History.* After com-
pleting the book he prefaced it with a dedication to Robert, Earl
of Gloucester, a bastard son of King Henry I whose illegitimacy
did not debar him from importance. The preface begins:

> Whenever I have chanced to think about the history of
> the kings of Britain, on those occasions when I have
> been turning over a great many such matters in my
> mind, it has seemed a remarkable thing to me that,
> apart from such mention of them as Gildas and Bede
> [Gildas and Bede are authors whom we shall need to
> consider later] had each made in a brilliant book on the
> subject . . . I have not been able to discover anything
> at all on the kings who lived here before the Incarna-
> tion of Christ, or indeed about Arthur and all the others
> who followed on after the Incarnation. Yet the deeds of

these men were such that they deserve to be praised for all time. What is more, these deeds were handed joyfully down in oral tradition, just as if they had been committed to writing, by many peoples who had only their memory to rely on.

It looks as if Geoffrey is going to justify his *History* by appealing to oral tradition, which, of course, can't be checked. But no. He goes on to make a startling claim.

At a time when I was giving a good deal of attention to such matters, Walter, Archdeacon of Oxford, a man skilled in the art of public speaking and well-informed about the history of foreign countries, presented me with a certain very ancient book written in the British language. This book, attractively composed to form a consecutive and orderly narrative, set out all the deeds of these men. . . . At Walter's request I have taken the trouble to translate the book into Latin.

So Geoffrey wants us to think that the *History* is simply a Latin version of a much older book. The "British language" might mean either Welsh or Breton. Both were descended from the language of the Britons, and in Geoffrey's day they had not diverged as far as they have since. At the end of the *History* he says Walter the archdeacon brought the book *ex Britannia*, which is more likely to mean "from Brittany" than "from Wales." In another place he speaks of Walter as supplementing the ancient book with word-of-mouth information.

An archdeacon handled administrative and supervisory work in a bishop's diocese. Walter was a real person, and Geoffrey was in Oxford at the same time as he was. Their names appear together on deeds relating to various church properties. As to Geoffrey's assertions in his preface, no comment by Walter is on record, but seemingly he acquiesced. After all, readers would have asked him about the ancient book. This does not prove its existence. He could perfectly well have spun a yarn for their benefit. Archdeacons were not noted for having the highest ethical standards among the clergy. A theme of debate in the Middle

Ages, tongue in cheek to some extent but not totally, was "whether an archdeacon could be saved."

There is no known trace of the book today, and no one believes Geoffrey's claim in the form in which he makes it. The *History* has far too many fanciful details belonging to a twelfth-century milieu. For instance, he includes Normans in Arthur's army. They are as glaring an anachronism as Texans would be in a story of Joan of Arc, and he could not have found them in an ancient book. If he did simply invent it, with Walter's connivance, he would only have been following a well-known medieval practice. The Middle Ages valued authority more than originality, and many authors claimed falsely to have got their material from earlier sources; it made their work more respectable. The most that can reasonably be said is that Geoffrey may have drawn on a Breton work, now lost, for some part of his story. He gets Breton names right, and his kings who rescue Britain, including Arthur's father, are of royal stock repatriated from Brittany—just the kind of prestigious fancy that might have been current across the Channel.

The ancient book, then, is not a solution, but a problem which has to be regretfully shelved, with a hope of working back to it later. Meanwhile, there are the two authors whom Geoffrey names, Gildas and Bede. He implies truly that they were not much help with his British kings. Yet if we look at what they say, we can see where he got some of the Arthurian scaffolding.

Gildas was a British monk who lived in the sixth century. He counts rather uncertainly as a saint, but his writing reveals a bitter, uncharitable outlook which seems less than saintly. In the 540s he produced a book on *The Ruin and Conquest of Britain,* denouncing several contemporary rulers, and blaming his fellow countrymen in the past for their sins and stupidities, which, in his view, brought the Saxon invasion as a divine judgment. He is primarily a preacher, and his book is not so much "brilliant"—Geoffrey's word—as infuriating, because he has so much sermonizing in it instead of the history we would value. Even the part where he does give history has dreadful mistakes and misunderstandings. Still, historians treat his survey with a degree of respect, and turn to it in places for want of anything better.

We have already traversed most of the relevant ground he covers. He mentions the Britons' appeal to the Roman General

Aëtius, whom he miscalls "Agitius," for help against the barbarians. He tells of their national council, in agreement with the *superbus tyrannus* (this is where we find the Latin form of the High King title), inviting Saxons into the country. Then he has the horrible story of revolt and raiding, right across to the western sea. After the Saxons' withdrawal to their home bases—an important event which he attests—comes the launching of counteraction by Ambrosius Aurelianus, "last of the Romans."

Gildas goes on to say that the fortunes of war swayed back and forth for a long while. Finally the Britons won a decisive success at the "siege of Mount Badon," which was "almost the last slaughter of the villains." He seems to put it forty-three or forty-four years back from his time of writing, that is, somewhere about the year 500. A relative lull ensued. As the battle was within living memory, he is surely telling the truth about this victory and the respite it brought. On the whole, archaeology bears him out; the Saxon advance halted in most areas. He accuses his contemporaries of throwing away the gains of recovery, but his witness to the recovery itself cannot be shaken. Badon was somewhere in southern Britain. An ancient hill fort in Wiltshire, Liddington Castle, has a village of Badbury close by and is a good candidate. Excavation has shown that its earthwork ramparts were refurbished at more or less the right time. A British force could have dug in there, endured a Saxon siege, and then routed the discouraged enemy in a sortie. The same could have happened on a hill near Bath which has also been proposed.

As for Bede, the other author named in the preface, he lived in northern England in the eighth century. He was a much greater scholar than Gildas and wrote a much better history. Unfortunately, it only becomes so in a later period. Where he overlaps Gildas he largely copies from him, so that he does not add much. But he does add something. He mentions the pretender Constantine and his son Constans, and gives a full account of the visit to Britain by the bishops Germanus and Lupus. Also he partly supplies one of the strangest lacks in Gildas, an extreme scarcity of names. Vortigern, Hengist, Horsa, all become specific in Bede. He adds a further important detail, the Anglo-Pictish alliance in the revolt.

However wildly Geoffrey contorts and inflates, he plainly owes a debt to these authors. Besides the obvious things, he has the Saxon-crushing battle at Bath, which is his location for Badon. When he cites Gildas and Bede in his preface he is not misleading us, and he takes further, post-Arthurian matter from both of them.

But he doesn't take Arthur from either, because Arthur is not there. Gildas names only one Briton throughout the fifth century and the early sixth, Ambrosius. The trouble with this cleric is that he is exhorting, not writing history for its own sake. He regards most Britons as unworthy to be commemorated. Bede, another cleric, though usually a less narrow one, follows him here. Their silence about Arthur is not an argument against his reality, though some modern writers have tried to make it so. It tells against the existence of Geoffrey's colossus, whom no one could have ignored, but not against the existence of a Briton whom Geoffrey could have based him on. Gildas's own testimony to decades of fighting, with victories, shows that there were other leaders in Britain besides the one he names. With an original Arthur, he might have been silent because of his prejudices, or because of a gap in his information. When he is dealing with events beyond living memory that information is certainly sparse; he leaves out important people who can be proved to have lived. All the same, Geoffrey's two authors seem to get us into a dead end.

Twelve Plus One Battles

Geoffrey mentions Gildas again, several times, and continues to be frustrating. He quotes him as writing things which there is no trace of his having written, such as a Latin translation of early British laws. Whatever Geoffrey means, he may be giving a clue. When he speaks of Gildas the name may cover other writings than the *Ruin and Conquest* tract. Now, a book does exist called the *Historia Brittonum,* History of the Britons, which is much earlier than Geoffrey's and was once widely thought to be by Gildas. Perhaps Geoffrey thought so himself, so that when he speaks of Gildas he includes this book. Whether he does or not, he certainly knows it. Passages of his own *History* draw on it, interweaving bits with items from the genuine Gildas, and from Bede. And here Geoffrey did find his famous King. Not only here, but with details which he could, and did, use.

Several copies of the *Historia Brittonum* survive. The chief one is in a manuscript volume in the British Museum, catalogued as Harley 3859, that is, number 3859 in a collection so called. It includes various texts from various sources. The one which matters for Arthur, though in Latin, comes from Wales. In that country descendants of the Britons maintained their independence, and handed down traditions of the pre-Saxon age when their ancestors held all Britain. The longest portion of this text is the *Historia Brittonum* itself. After it come a chronicle usually called the *Annales Cambriae*, Welsh Annals, and some genealogies of Welsh princely families.

The *Historia Brittonum* takes us much closer than Geoffrey to any realities there may be. It was compiled between 800 and 820. With Gildas out of the picture, it has generally been ascribed to Nennius, a monk of Bangor in northern Wales. Right or wrong, Nennius is a convenient name for the compiler. He put together a jumble of materials, "making one heap," in his own disarming words, "of all he found." The result is chaotic. Yet the chaos inspires a kind of trust. He is so plainly not a literary artist that we can believe he is quoting real traditions and early records. He hardly seems capable of making them up.

Geoffrey undoubtedly made use of this book, and not only for post-Roman times. For instance, Nennius has a version of the legend of Brutus the Trojan. In the fifth century several of Geoffrey's themes make an embryonic appearance: the story of Vortigern again, with his heathen marriage; the campaign and death of his son Vortimer; the massacre of nobles; the fortress that collapsed; and the boy prophet, though Nennius calls him Ambrosius and confuses him with the general—it is Geoffrey who makes him Merlin. Most of these episodes are sketched briefly and crudely. Geoffrey not only enlarges them but changes the order, proof of his readiness to rehandle things to suit himself.

Nennius has very little about the real Ambrosius, and nothing about Uther. Instead he tells of another resistance leader.

In that time the Saxons strengthened in multitude and grew in Britain. On the death of Hengist, however, Octha his son passed from the northern part of Britain to the region of the Kentishmen and from him arise the kings of the Kentishmen.

Then Arthur fought against them in those days with the kings of the Britons, but he himself was leader of battles [in the Latin, *dux bellorum*]. The first battle was at the mouth of the river which is called Glein. The second and third and fourth and fifth upon another river which is called Dubglas and is in the district Linnuis. The sixth battle upon the river which is called Bassas. The seventh battle was in the Caledonian wood, that is, Cat Coit Celidon. The eighth battle was in Fort Guinnion in which Arthur carried the image of St Mary, ever virgin, on his shoulders and the pagans were turned to flight that day and a great slaughter was upon them through the virtue of Our Lord Jesus Christ and through the virtue of St Mary the Virgin, his mother. The ninth battle was waged in the City of the Legion. The tenth battle he waged on the shore of the river which is called Tribruit. The eleventh battle took place on the mountain which is called Agned. The twelfth battle was on Mount Badon, in which nine hundred and sixty men fell in one day from one charge by Arthur, and no one overthrew them except himself alone. And in all the battles he stood forth as victor.

Since Nennius has so much that is fabulous in other parts of his book, there is no guarantee that he is factual here. He may be, but the question is open to debate. The list is thought to be adapted from a lost poem in Arthur's praise. Early Welsh poems have survived which extol men of martial note by reeling off place names with a few words about their triumphs at each. A mere list might seem a poor and bald panegyric. However, though the poem theory was not known to Tennyson, he judged this list to be apt for metrical treatment in praise of Arthur, eked out with a few phrases of his own. In effect he reversed the process and reconstituted the poem, after his fashion, in English. It comes in his idyll "Lancelot and Elaine." Someone has asked Lancelot about the King's wars. (The white horse is a symbol of the Saxons.)

Lancelot spoke
And answer'd him at full, as having been

With Arthur in the fight which all day long
Rang by the white mouth of the violent Glem;
And in the four wild battles by the shore
Of Duglas; that on Bassa; then the war
That thunder'd in and out the gloomy skirts
Of Celidon the forest; and again
By Castle Gurnion, where the glorious King
Had on his cuirass worn our Lady's Head,
Carv'd of one emerald center'd in a sun
Of silver rays, that lighten'd as he breathed;
And at Caerleon had he help'd his lord,
When the strong neighings of the wild white Horse
Set every gilded parapet shuddering;
And up in Agned-Cathregonion too,
And down the waste sand-shores of Trath Treroit,
Where many a heathen fell; "and on the mount
Of Badon I myself beheld the King
Charge at the head of all his Table Round,
And all his legions crying Christ and him,
And break them; and I saw him, after, stand
High on a heap of slain, from spur to plume
Red as the rising sun with heathen blood,
And seeing me, with a great voice he cried,
'They are broken, they are broken!' "

In whatever copy Tennyson used, most of the names were
spelled differently. They are obscure, and this counts in Nennius's favor. A writer of fiction would have located Arthur's battles
at well-known places. But these names are archaic, dating from a
time before the map of Britain was changed by conquerors who
spoke English. Nearly all are now blotted out. Nennius is at least
giving fairly old tradition, not something concocted in his own
day.

The mention of Hengist and his son is confusing, because it
makes it look as if all Arthur's battles were fought against the
Kentishmen. But the "kings of the Britons" would never have
concentrated against this one group, in one corner of the island.
The Hengist sentence has to be a parenthesis. Arthur's opponents
are the Saxons in general. Two of the names point somewhat
waveringly to Lincolnshire, and to areas where the settlers were
dug in early. The "river which is called Glein" may be the Glen,
in the South of the present county, and the "district Linnuis" may
be Lindsey, the part of the county extending north from Lincoln.

Two of the other sites are much more certain. The "Caledonian wood" is a formerly forested area in southern Scotland. "The City of the Legion" for Geoffrey means Caerleon, and Tennyson follows him, but in Nennius's list it means Chester, a former Roman army base near the northern end of the Welsh border. Finally, the "battle . . . on Mount Badon" is the major victory which Gildas records. Gildas, in the sixth century, leaves the Britons' commander nameless. Now, in the ninth, he is said to have been Arthur.

Once again we can catch Geoffrey picking up items for his *History*, though here he picks up surprisingly few. Three battles fought by his young King Arthur come from this list—the one fought by the River Douglas, which is Nennius's "Dubglas"; the one near Lincoln, "in the district Linnuis"; and the one in the Caledon Wood. Also, once again, his battle at Bath is Badon, made a victory of Arthur on the strength—very likely—of the list. Yet all these battles together, even built up as he builds them up, account for only a fraction of his Arthur story. And if we try to work backward and outward from the list into history, it is not much use. Some of it, possibly most of it, *may* be historical. None of it positively is.

How much does Nennius really say? Even Arthur's status is left in doubt. He is the Britons' war leader, and in a Britain which has regional kings he holds some sort of paramountcy. As what? As a High King in fact, or name, or glorified retrospect, or only as a commander in chief, coordinating regional efforts? Who can tell? Nennius simply takes it for granted that the reader knows who Arthur was, and gives not a word of explanation.

Then again, it is hard to make out when all this is supposed to have happened. Hengist's death, being an aside, is no help. Nennius's chronology everywhere is fearfully muddled. In the preceding chapters he has been talking about the death of Vortigern, who may have died about 455, and the career of St. Patrick, who did die about 460. Arthur's exploits might seem to belong to whatever opposition the Britons were putting up during the last phase of Saxon ravaging, in the late 450s or early 460s. That view is supported by the only battle sites which look firm. Fighting in Scotland implies Picts, who were allies of the main enemy in the Saxon revolt, but not later. Fighting in Chester makes sense only in terms of combating raids right across the country, which happened in the revolt, but not later. As we shall see, one of the most brilliant findings of recent scholarship is that there was a tradition, known to historians in the Middle Ages, which put Arthur in just this period.

However, the only battle which can be proved real is Badon, and Gildas fixes it around 500, rather late for someone who was a national leader forty years earlier. To which it might be retorted that in this battle Nennius's Arthur has become plainly legendary, a larger-than-life hero slaying 960 men single-handed; so that his connection with Badon can be set aside as a fantasy, tacked long afterward on to a list of his deeds which placed them in the 450s or 460s.

It is all interesting, but meager. When we turn to the *Annales Cambriae*, which follow Nennius in the manuscript, they are more discomposing still. This chronicle belongs to the tenth century. In essence it is a table of years beginning with a year 1 which is A.D. 447. Many of the years have events written in. Some of these were posted from older chronicles and may even have been recorded at the time. In view of the title, the early portion looks very odd. It mentions nothing Welsh and nothing even in Britain till the year 72. Several entries in previous years are concerned with Ireland. The reason is that an annalist, copying Welsh records that started in the sixth century, also copied items from Irish ones that started in the fifth, giving a composite result.

Year 72 is 518, and the entry is: "The battle of Badon in which Arthur carried the cross of Our Lord Jesus Christ on his shoulders for three days and three nights and the Britons were victors." In Year 93, that is, 539, comes the following: "The strife of Camlann in which Arthur and Medraut fell. And there was plague in Britain and in Ireland."

The first of these entries connects Arthur with Badon again, and is open to the same sort of objection as the sentence in Nennius. It need not be as outlandish as it seems. "Shoulders" (as perhaps also in Nennius's sentence about the eighth battle) may be a mistranslation of a Welsh word meaning "shield." The cross could be an emblem, or maybe a holy relic, a piece of the True Cross found by Helena. But "three days and three nights" still has a legendary air. To make matters worse—much worse—the date 518 is inconsistent with Gildas, who wrote when the battle was within living memory.

As for the second entry, Arthur's fall in a tragic battle at Camlann or Camlan is a recurrent theme of Welsh tradition. Geoffrey knew it, and the *Annales* entry may have supplied him with the hint for the final battle with Modred on the banks of the Camel. But it supplied no more. The entry doesn't say that "Medraut" was Arthur's traitorous deputy, in league with the barbarians. It doesn't even say that they fought on opposite sides. The real location is not clear. Camlann probably means "crooked bank," and more than one river has the "crooked" element in its name. The only place actually called Camlan today is a valley in Merioneth in northwestern Wales with a small river flowing down it.

Since the item before the Badon one records the death of a bishop at the age of 350, this chronicle's early statements hardly inspire confidence. There is something amiss in its dating of Arthur, which stretches out his career far into the sixth century. On the other hand, apart from him, every person the chronicle mentions seems to have been real, so the chances are that he was real too.

Welsh poems and tales, or summaries of them, prove Arthur's renown before Geoffrey as a warrior and a leader of warriors. A poem speaks of his grave as a mystery, pointing perhaps to an early form of the folk belief in his immortality. One or two verses about him take us further back in time than Nennius does, perhaps as much as two centuries earlier. But they are not informative, and this further material leaves the same curious query over his status. In one poem he is called an *ameraudur*, which is the Latin *imperator*. That word might have its original meaning as "commander in chief," but it could also mean "emperor." Irish writers apply it to their high kings. One who is called so is the King who reigned in St. Patrick's time. Another is the great Brian Boru, unifier of a divided Ireland more than five hundred years later. Arthur the *ameraudur* might therefore be Arthur the High King.

In Pursuit

Until recently, modern attempts to get at the "historical Arthur" all depended on this Welsh matter. Serious scholars who tried it (they were never numerous, though there were plenty of ama-

teurs of varying sanity) had no doubt what to think of Geoffrey of
Monmouth. He could never be relied on for history. Moreover,
he had hoaxed the Middle Ages so thoroughly that nothing after
him counted as evidence. Some later poems and literary items
might be independent of him, but all references to Arthur that
professed to be historical were simply echoes of his own supremely mendacious work. In that work itself a few of the
passages about Arthur might have a faraway historical basis. But
Arthur could not have been a great ruler, not in the Britain
portrayed by Gildas. Most of his deeds were palpable moonshine.
That was true especially of his campaigning in Gaul. To look
outside Britain would be a waste of time.

Those were the assumptions, open or tacit, which narrowed
the field. They excluded Geoffrey from any consideration whatever. They excluded all evidence later than Geoffrey. They excluded all evidence outside Britain. In practice, furthermore,
they confined evidence *in* Britain to the Welsh matter and not
much else. Only the Welsh, as descendants of the fifth-century
Britons, recorded anything concrete with a bearing on Arthur.
The Cornish had the same background, and might be given a
little attention, but their testimony was scanty. Study of Nennius
and the rest in that spirit could lead to only one verdict. Before
Geoffrey, Arthur was on serious record solely as a mighty warrior
and leader of warriors, with a mystery over his fate. The only
items in Geoffrey's story with a traditional basis were some of the
battles in Britain and Arthur's cryptic departure. On the one
hand, therefore, everything else in Geoffrey (that is, four fifths of
the story) was confirmed as being merely his own invention;
while on the other, the "historical Arthur" meant whoever could
be reconstructed from the Welsh matter.

The first major impulse for the attempt came from E. K.
Chambers, better known for his work on Elizabethan drama. In
1927 he published *Arthur of Britain,* a sweeping survey of Arthurian literature. It took in not only Geoffrey and the medieval
romancers but the older documents, even local folklore. Chambers remained noncommittal as to Arthur's reality, but described
him in words which suggested where to look for him. Arthur, he
said, was ". . . the legend-hung champion of a dying order,
through whom we reach back, beyond the advent of the chill
barbarians from the north, to the slow spread of Mediterranean

civilization by the shores of the Atlantic, and to that *pax Romana*, of which this island was the ultimate outpost." Such language was an invitation. In due course the reconstruction of the "historical Arthur" began in earnest.

There were obvious cruxes. For instance, how far could Nennius be trusted? Did Arthur fight all those battles, or were some of them credited to him later, when he was a popular hero in bardic verse? If the former, he was highly mobile, a national leader with a command covering Roman Britain. If the latter, he was probably a local chief inflated by legend. A question then arises: Why was that local chief so hugely inflated, rather than any other? Supporters of a local Arthur argued that one leader could not have fought in such widely scattered places. However, well-attested wars in the next few centuries prove that he could have done it. Such a wide-ranging Arthur would be a credible leader for the second half of the fifth century and perhaps the first decade or so of the sixth, before the breakup had gone so far as to rule out a unifying command.

In 1936 R. G. Collingwood, coauthor of a standard work on *Roman Britain and the English Settlements*, presented a theory which held the field for some years. Accepting all the victories—and hence the mobility—as authentic, he explained Arthur by a guess at the position he really held. How could a Briton have turned the tide so completely against the Saxons? An easy answer would be that the Britons outnumbered them. But their larger numbers were never brought to bear, never organized. Collingwood offered a more ingenious answer: that Arthur was not a King, but a general who revived the cavalry of the later Empire, an arm developed for mobile defense in depth.

In the last phase of Roman Britain, one of its supreme officers was the *Comes Britanniarum*, "Count of the Britains" (plural because Britain had been split up into five provinces). He commanded cavalry units and had a roving commission to go anywhere. Warriors on horseback were not so dominant then as in the Middle Ages, because the stirrup had not reached western Europe. However, the Saxons were not horsemen at all. Mounted Britons would have had clear advantages through speed, surprise, psychological impact. They could have fought, in Robert Graves's phrase, as mounted commandos. Some of the oldest Welsh poetry, written around the year 600, speaks of nobles rid-ing to battle. Their forebears may have done the same with Arthur as leader. Collingwood, at any rate, suggested that Arthur was a *Comes Britanniarum,* appointed or self-appointed. He won his battles by the use of mobile horsemen against the pedestrian Saxons, and could move such men rapidly about the country. To call them "the original knights" would be to blur distinctions, but Collingwood remarked, fairly, that they would furnish just a trifle more substance behind chivalric romance. His theory as a whole yielded to criticism, but the cavalry idea survived, and has stayed popular and plausible.

As a hero of romance, the knight belongs to the more civilized part of the Middle Ages, running roughly from the twelfth century to the fifteenth. During most of that period the armored warrior on horseback was an immensely formidable battlefield figure, a sort of equivalent to the modern tank. Distinctiveness in war helped to give him status in peace, and various arts and attitudes went with it, making up what was known as chivalry. There were knightly pastimes, such as hunting and hawking; knightly interests, such as heraldry; knightly sports, such as jousting. Knights were sometimes formed into orders sponsored by kings and nobles (whence the notion of the Round Table), or on a religious basis. In the romances knights are glorified as bold adventurers who live by a chivalrous code, and conduct their love life by special aristocratic rules.

Ancient Rome had a social class of "knights"—*equites,* "horsemen"—but no men like the medieval knights could have existed in Arthur's time. Mailed cavalry, however, had played a major role in warfare for more than a century. A question that arises is whether the accounts of the knights of Arthur, in Geoffrey and later writers, could echo some tradition of British cavalry on the late-imperial model.

The next major development was that Professor Kenneth Jackson applied philological expertise to the battle list, identifying the River Glen, Lindsey, the Caledonian wood, Chester. His essay on "The Arthur of History" in a 1959 volume, *Arthurian Literature in the Middle Ages,* dismissed most of Collingwood but recognized an Arthur who "might well have existed" as organizer of the war effort in southern Britain, loosely around the year 500. Dissentient scholars preferred to put Arthur in the North and reduce his status. A topic for debate which had arisen was Arthur's home territory and whether or not his real career was confined to it. The northern school had a long spell of influence, but it finally waned. Its partisans stressed that some of the earliest poems with Arthur's name in them were composed in what is now northern England, at a time when its language was still a form of Welsh. But the poetry was a poor argument, because it mentioned people who were certainly not Northerners. All it proved was an early poetic fame in that part of the country, which was not surprising, because the North happened to be the home of the first important poets in the Welsh language. Another claim by this party was that the Camlann where Arthur fell was a fort on Hadrian's Wall northeast of Carlisle, called Camboglanna. This idea failed, in the end, to stand up convincingly.

Against the northern school it was pointed out that the only traditions giving Arthur a birthplace and a home put them in the West Country, between Land's End and Bath. Tintagel may be Geoffrey's idea, but no legend of any weight offers another birthplace to rival it. The early Welsh give Arthur a home in Cornwall at "Kelliwic," perhaps an ancient fort called Castle Killibury, a few miles south of Tintagel itself. Welshmen, surely, would have produced a home in Wales if they could! These and other beliefs linking Arthur with Cornwall, and with Somerset, seem to have been too deep-rooted to challenge. They may not be literal truth, they may reflect a geographical drift of storytelling, but the drift is in the West Country. And if Arthur was a major figure, he is more likely to have arisen, like Ambrosius, in the Romanized country near the Channel than in the remote, turbulent, thinly peopled North.

One by-product of these debates was a realization that the simplest argument for Arthur's reality was the plainest thing of all: his name. Arthur is actually a Roman name, Artorius, remolded by generations of change in speech, as Ambrosius became Emrys. An Artorius can be proved in Roman Britain, Lucius Artorius Castus, who held an army command in 184. Britons were still giving their children Roman names in the fifth century and a little later, but, as a rule, not much later. A Briton called Artorius could be a real person born in the fifth century, and spoken of afterward by the Welsh and others in their own pronunciation. He could hardly be a hero of Celtic mythology, or a fairy-tale character invented long afterward. Moreover, with this

particular Roman name, something unusual happened. It en-
joyed a brief revival. In the decades after 550, despite the general
vanishing of Roman names, at least four Arthurs are on record in
the princely houses of Wales and Scotland. Such an out-of-line
choice by at least four sets of parents, a long way apart, points to a
common inspiration at work—the widespread fame of a proto-
type living somewhat before: a man after whom it was natural,
patriotic perhaps, to name boys.

The debates also revealed the other side of the coin. Scholars
who tried to refute Arthur's existence, as distinct from merely
fence-sitting, were unsuccessful. Some claimed that the legendary Arthur was pure myth, a Celtic god reduced to human stature
by Christian legend. None ever produced a Celtic god called
Artorius, or anything else which could plausibly have evolved
into Arthur. The mythic school is still not quite dead, but the
claims of its advocates have always collapsed when put to a practical test. They have never given a convincing account in detail.
They have never explained where the notion of Arthur came
from—how it planted itself in the place and period it did, how it
developed—so as to cover all the data with no human original.
Incantatory repetition of the word "myth" is no answer.

The Inconclusive Quest

While these issues were being tossed slowly back and forth, the
work of archaeologists was affecting the picture, also slowly. It
was showing that the legends had tantalizing touches of rightness. Those who told them, Geoffrey and others, were not wholly
ignorant of the Britain where they placed their stories. It had
long been obvious that Geoffrey knew something of the preceding Roman Britain. Here and there in his *History* the imperial
map is seen lingering in the fifth century, as it did. Roman
Silchester is a place for crowning kings; Roman Caerleon is a
place for holding court. What began to emerge, from the 1930s
on, was that Geoffrey and other legend-weavers before and after
him knew something also of the restructured Britain which
emerged as the Roman pattern faded away.

There was, for instance, the matter of Tintagel and Geoffrey's choice of it for Arthur's begetting and (presumably) birth.
The scene is approached today from Tintagel village. A visitor

passes down a ravine to a cove, with a beach below and massive headlands on either side. To the left, a path goes up to the promontory Geoffrey is thinking of. On it are the remains of a twelfth-century castle and smaller buildings. Skeptics have claimed that when Geoffrey picked this place he was merely flattering the Norman founder of the castle. That motive may have been present. But excavation by C. A. Ralegh Radford disclosed features of the headland which nobody had suspected.

Radford discovered what came to be called Tintagel pottery. He dug up fragments of high-quality vessels, of a type used for luxury goods such as wine. They had been imported from the eastern Mediterranean region, and could be dated to the later part of the fifth century or the sixth. This imported ware gave the first major break into the "Arthurian" period in Britain. Somewhere hereabouts a wealthy household had flourished at a date corresponding to the pottery and perhaps a little before—that is, in more or less "Arthurian" times. Similar finds, in various parts of the British Isles, in due course helped to show further where the better-off lived.

At Tintagel itself Radford decided that the early dwellers on the headland were monks, whose community was rich enough to buy imports from far away. Subsequent study, in the light of findings on other sites, made it more likely that Tintagel was a princely stronghold. That proved nothing about Gorlois, Ygerna, or Arthur. It did suggest that the right sort of people were in possession of Tintagel at about the right time. Even if the monastic theory should be correct after all, an early occupation was real. When Geoffrey wrote, no traces of it would have been visible. In composing his story he was drawing on older information which told him this was a plausible locale, certainly as to date, probably as to character. Cornish folklore? Oral tradition?

Then there was the case of Vortigern's fortress over the pool, and the boy prophet. The site is Dinas Emrys, at the southern fringe of the Snowdonian mountain mass. Sitting on a craggy height, this Iron Age hill fort has triple earthwork ramparts enclosing a plateau. Excavation here by H. N. Savory showed traces of a small-scale occupation in Roman times, including an actual pool—an artificial one—if, admittedly, no dragons. In the fifth century someone new moved in, someone of wealth, who left objects implying Christianity and a degree of comfort. The name

Emrys points to Ambrosius, as in Nennius's confused account of the prophet. Nennius asserts that he took over the place after Vortigern abandoned it. Geoffrey, who makes out that the prophet was Merlin, tries to hold everything together by explaining that Merlin was "also called Ambrosius." The real fifth-century occupant was probably none of these, yet the occupation was real, and by a person of note. Nennius and Geoffrey did know something about that hill.

Radford carried on from his work at Tintagel. In 1935–36 he unearthed foundations of early buildings at Castle Dore, also in Cornwall, in a district associated in various ways with the Arthur-related romance of Tristan, the theme of Wagner's opera. In 1962–63 he went to Glastonbury in Somerset, a place with several Arthurian connections. The monks of its abbey once announced the discovery of an early grave which they claimed was Arthur's (a story to be told later). Excavation proved that this too was not undiluted fiction. They did discover an early grave and Radford rediscovered it, though the monks had removed its occupant, whoever he was. In 1964–66 Philip Rahtz also went to Glastonbury and excavated the top of the hill above, called the Tor. He found remains of buildings belonging to the fifth or sixth century, perhaps parts of a small fort or signal station, perhaps the cells of monks.

It was a further archaeological project which, for a while, drew this phase of the quest together. At South Cadbury in Somerset, within sight of Glastonbury Tor, is a hill fort known as Cadbury Castle. Its summit is about five hundred feet above sea level. There was never a castle here in the medieval sense. The hill itself is the castle, fortified by four lines of earthwork ramparts which defend a summit enclosure of eighteen acres, rising to a central plateau. As an inhabited place, Cadbury dates from pre-Roman centuries. A village once covered the plateau and trusted for its safety to the earthwork defenses. This particular hill fort, one among many, has been special for a long time because of a belief that it was Camelot, Arthur's capital in romance as it took shape after Geoffrey.

A writer in 1542, John Leland, says: "At the very south end of the church of South-Cadbyri standeth Camallate, sometime a famous town or castle. . . . The people can tell nothing there but that they have heard say Arthur much resorted to Camalat."

Critics have argued that there was no real local tradition, except perhaps for some hazy story of Arthur, and Leland merely made a guess inspired by two villages a few miles off, Queen Camel and West Camel. However, he speaks of the hill's identity as a recognized fact, and his spelling with an *a* in the last syllable may echo a local pronunciation which can be heard still. The *a* is pronounced as in "father."

In more recent times there has been no doubt concerning the hill's folklore. It has a legend of Arthur lying asleep in a cave, which can be traced back further than Welsh legends of the same type. The cave has iron or golden gates, which occasionally open, allowing a glimpse inside. Victorian archaeologists were once asked by an old man if they planned to look for the King. The highest part of the hill is Arthur's Palace, a name on record as early as 1586. On Midsummer Eve, or Midsummer Night, or Christmas Eve—nobody is sure which, and it may be only every seventh year—the ghosts of Arthur and his horsemen ride over the hilltop and down through the ancient gateway. Beneath the hill are remnants of a track leading toward Glastonbury, twelve miles off. This is Arthur's Lane or Hunting Causeway, and on winter nights, they say, the galloping of spectral riders can be heard along it.

The Camelot of romance is a medieval dream city which never existed anywhere. But Cadbury could be Camelot in a mundane sense as the far-off reality behind it, the personal citadel of the original Arthur. In the mid-1950s that idea began to be aired seriously. Part of the summit area was ploughed. A local archaeologist, Mary Harfield, wandered over it while walking her dog. She collected flints and pottery scraps in the ploughed-up soil. Radford examined them and picked out imported ware such as he had found at Tintagel. Those fragments showed that the hill had been occupied in the post-Roman period as well as the pre-Roman, and that the occupants were people of standing, who imported luxury goods from distant countries. Perhaps, then, the Arthurian notion had something in it. As a result the Camelot Research Committee was eventually formed, which excavated parts of the hilltop (it was too big to excavate fully) in 1966–70, under the direction of Leslie Alcock.

Eloquent facts emerged about the earthworks. One grim discovery, at a bend in the top rampart, was the skeleton of a young man rammed head downward into a pit, his knees and chin drawn together. A pre-Roman reconstruction had been carried out on top of him. Seemingly he was a human sacrifice for divine strengthening of the wall. That practice is echoed in the tale of Vortigern's fortress and the young victim demanded by his soothsayers.

For the post-Roman "Arthur" period the archaeology was richer than anyone had expected or dared to predict. On the high ground called Arthur's Palace the foundations of a fair-sized hall came to light. It had been timber-built, with skilled workmanship. At the break in the ramparts where the ghosts ride through were the remains of a gatehouse. A cobbled road had climbed into the enclosure through double doors in a nearly square tower.

More impressive still were the results of several cuts through the top rampart. In the same period, more or less, it had been reconstructed again. An unmortared stone wall sixteen feet thick, with blocks of Roman masonry built into it, girdled the hilltop. The total perimeter was close to three quarters of a mile. Gaps in the courses of stone showed where massive timber posts, now rotted away, sustained a breastwork on the outside. Beams had run across, binding the structure together and supporting a platform where soldiers would have stood behind the breastwork's protection.

The implication was clear. In the second half of the fifth century, or somewhat later, someone with great resources of manpower reoccupied the vacant hill and renewed its defenses on a grandiose scale. The impression made by the system as a whole was one of overlapping eras. The gatehouse seemed to have touches of Roman architecture, and the rampart used Roman materials. But these were incorporated in a structure of Celtic type, which, like many post-Roman things in Britain, spoke of a rebirth of pre-Roman ways. *Romanitas* lingered in the mind of the master planner, but he worked with men whose practicality took a different, more national form.

To this extent, then, tradition was borne out. It happened that the musical *Camelot* was being filmed during the excavations. A map which is displayed briefly in one scene shows Camelot in Somerset. The location was chosen as a direct result of an inquiry to the committee.

In 1971 Leslie Alcock published a book, *Arthur's Britain.*
Mainly on archaeology, it included a discussion of Arthur himself
to justify the use of his name. He followed it up with *Cadbury-
Camelot,* an account of the excavations which included more
discussion. Alcock reviewed the Welsh matter and judged that
Nennius's battles were credible. However, he did not insist on
them. What he did insist on was the reliability of the items in the
Annales Cambriae about the battles of Badon and Camlann.
More precisely, he suggested that the Badon one might be chal-
lenged, but not the Camlann one. If everything else had to go,
that would still stand up, at least as the record of a fact. The date
might be wrong and he thought it probably was. Like most who
followed the Welsh trail, Alcock put Arthur's main activities in
the last decade or two of the fifth century—a view which was
arrived at by starting from Gildas's date for Badon, accepting
Arthur's role in the battle, and then fitting everything else to
that. Arthur as presented by Alcock conformed to the thinking
that had developed over the years. He was a soldier and commander in chief, making use of cavalry and organizing the war
effort as the general of an unknown High King. Alcock believed
that a vague High Kingship might have survived till Badon, despite the lack of evidence. Coming down firmly against the northern theory, he interpreted Cadbury as a military base, the unique
headquarters of his war leader. (That was not to be his last word,
however.)

Soon afterward John Morris, a professional historian, published *The Age of Arthur.* He used the same evidence, but with a
less controlled imagination, and built up the war leader into a
kind of Emperor. Though pouring scorn on Geoffrey of Monmouth, he broke with his predecessors on Arthur's status, main-
taining that he could have been—and, in fact, was—a major ruler.
Morris's readers could be excused for feeling that this titan lacked
substance.

> Arthur the ruler is as elusive as Arthur the conqueror.
> . . . A few notices describe events and incidents that
> happened while he ruled. None describe the man him-
> self, his character or his policy, his aims or his personal
> achievement. He remains a mighty shadow, a figure

looming large behind every record of his time, yet
never clearly seen.

Anyone so mighty ought surely to be recorded somewhere, and
"clearly seen" at some point.

Such a paragraph was an invitation, as Chambers's had been
before. In 1977 the tide turned. Alcock and Morris were both
savaged by David Dumville, who argued that the Welsh matter
was worthless as history, and that the whole historical-Arthur
case had never amounted to more than saying "no smoke without
fire." In 1982 Alcock acknowledged the force of some of the
criticism, and declared himself now "agnostic" regarding Arthur
personally.

What had happened? Certain truths had sunk in.

To begin with, an Arthur who is credible as far as he goes is
not the same as an Arthur who can be proved. None of the Welsh
matter comes anywhere near to being contemporary. This need
not be fatal, because writers copy from previous writers, and
even a late text can faithfully reproduce a much earlier one.
Alcock tried at first to maintain that the Camlann item, though in
a tenth-century chronicle, was posted from another written
down at the time. After reflection, however, few agreed. In the
end it has to be recognized that a book like Nennius's, put together so long after the event, *may* give facts but cannot alone be
proved to do so.

There are other difficulties. No method of fixing the dates
will work. Arthur's career spreads out so far that the evidence
cannot all be valid. How to decide which parts of it are? Nennius
has his two locatable battles, which both fit the state of affairs in
the mid-fifth century and no relevant later time. He also has
Badon, pegged by Gildas to 500 or thereabouts. His talk of "kings
of the Britons" might seem to swing the balance toward the last
part of the century, when Britain had fissured into separate kingdoms. But no; in another place he speaks of regional kings earlier
with a High King over them, so there is no pointer here. Then, of
course, the *Annales Cambriae* have an incompatible Badon in
518 and extend Arthur's active career to 539.

All might be resolved by a single phrase lining up Arthur
with known history outside Britain. The Welsh matter has no
such phrase. It never says, for example, that he fought Saxons

when so-and-so was Emperor. It never supplies a chronological fix. This is not too much to ask for, since we do get one for Vortigern, which links the year of his rise with Roman records, putting it in 425. Dating is by no means a minor issue. It affects everything else. An early Arthur would be a Roman type of person like Ambrosius, and probably active over a wide, fairly cohesive territory, whereas a late Arthur would be far more Celtic and probably a regional leader only.

A further difficulty cuts deeper. Anyone in pursuit of an elusive figure like this will try to prune away legend, and isolate clear-cut, trustworthy statements. The drawback with Arthur in his early Welsh setting is that this cannot be done. We never get a clear-cut, trustworthy statement. Nennius's list builds up to the Badon sentence, which promptly undermines the whole thing with its flight of bardic hyperbole about the 960 men. The Badon entry in the *Annales,* with its three days and nights, is also dubious. As for the poems and tales, that, precisely, is what they are. Some historians have singled out the Camlann item as the one firm Arthurian statement. However, it hangs in a void, with nothing to show where it came from, no means of checking it against history, and an almost incredible date. To treat Camlann as the sole verity leads to the absurd notion that the entire Arthurian legend grew around a petty chief, one among dozens, squabbling with another petty chief, one among dozens, in an obscurity so deep that hardly anybody noticed.

The net result of the fifty-year discussion was to persuade most inquirers that there had been a real Arthur of some sort. Despite all obstacles, it was easier to believe that he did exist than that he didn't. But he had no convincing outline. The proof was that scholars had reconstructed him in half a dozen different ways, disagreeing about his dates, his location, his status, his importance. Speculative writers had added a flood of further theories, all likewise contradicting each other. By 1980 the proper attitude to the Welsh items was fairly clear. They could be seen as pointing vaguely to a real British leader, probably an outstanding one. Cadbury-Camelot could be seen as supporting them. As history, however, they fell short. The right course was not to drop them in despair, but to look beyond for facts which would bring them into focus, and fit them into an adequate explanation.

5

New Discoveries

Lateral Thinking

My own involvement with the problem of Arthur began as a by-
product of other interests, mythological and historical. For some
years I trod, more or less, in the footsteps of the professional
scholars. Then I drew somewhat closer as secretary of the Camelot Research Committee, which excavated Cadbury. One result
was my editing a book, *The Quest for Arthur's Britain,* to which
Ralegh Radford, Leslie Alcock, and Philip Rahtz generously con-
tributed.

Early in 1980, BBC Television ran a series of programs on the
archaeology of Britain during the early Christian era. The pre-
senter was Michael Wood. His style was ebullient, with special
effects such as swords flying through the air. A newspaper critic
spoke of "the *Star Wars* school of archaeology." Each program
was related to a person, and the fifth and sixth centuries could
only be related to Arthur. Wood's archaeological sequences were
interesting; his attempt to settle the Arthur question itself was ill-
conceived. It amounted to a few words about Nennius and the
Annales Cambriae with a nearly negative conclusion. This
seemed to me to fly in the face of common sense. If Arthur was
fictitious or at best insignificant, why the legend? How did he
supplant the leaders who did exist? Nevertheless, I saw that Wood
had a case. I am indebted to him for prompting a reappraisal of

the whole topic, leading me to a fresh conception which I believe, in principle, is the answer.

One thing which struck me was that the exclusion of Geoffrey had diverted attention from an issue which loomed enormous the moment I turned back to him. I saw that the Welsh matter, even taken at its maximum, came nowhere near to accounting for his Arthur story. The parts which he owes to it—some of the warfare in Britain, and perhaps the cryptic departure with no known grave—add up, in Thorpe's translation, to ten pages or so out of fifty. Furthermore, most of the things that make Arthur unique and climactic have no pre-Geoffrey Welsh basis: his strange birth, his quality as a *Restitutor* figure, his splendid array of followers, his international fame, his campaigning in Gaul which brings him into the Roman sphere as a Briton whom emperors have to reckon with.

To be fair, a late Welsh tale, "Culhwch and Olwen," makes Arthur a prince with a kind of court, and hints at adventures overseas. But the court is bizarre, including grotesque fairy-tale characters, and the foreign contacts are mentioned only in passing, not explained or made functional. The atmosphere is quite unlike, and the warrior-prince developed thus is a very different hero from Geoffrey's. "Culhwch and Olwen" is a tale which, most likely, has sprung from the realm of Celtic imagination.

In Geoffrey's *History* the Roman embroilment takes up more than half the story, raising Arthur to his apogee. Concerning this elaborate business no Welsh tale or poem gives the slightest hint. The point is not that Geoffrey spins a long pseudohistory out of a little real history, or what may be such. The point is that he produces something "other." Arthur the warrior is an established hero of the Welsh, as Vortigern is an established villain. When Geoffrey composes his tale about the villain he simply embroiders the tradition. When he composes his tale about the hero he might be expected to do the same. That, however, is not what he does. He restricts Arthur in his Welsh-affirmed military guise to a fraction of the story, part of a towering structure which could not be evolved from it.

As I reconsidered the Welsh items, my feeling was that they gave early layers of legend rather than facts, though sometimes they were close to facts. Insofar as they were close, they were limited, and, to judge from Geoffrey, gave only an aspect of a grander original that he worked upon. Welsh bards could understand martial prowess and make up verses about it, so the martial prowess of Arthur, whoever he might be, was what they commemorated. However, it could well be only one feature of a man with a more distinctive importance. Arthur was perhaps a parallel case to another figure of roughly the same period. A Gothic King, Theodoric, conquered Italy after the Western Empire ended, and controlled it from 493 to 526. He was one of the greatest rulers of late antiquity, bringing peace, prosperity, and religious freedom after the torments Italy had endured so long. Medieval German poets made him a hero of their minstrelsy, putting him in their chief epic, the *Nibelungenlied*. But they reduced him to a knight called Dietrich of Bern (that is, the Italian city of Verona), and turned him into a liegeman of Attila the Hun, shifting him several decades for the purpose—Attila died in 453. Working back to Arthur via the Welsh matter alone might be rather like working back to Theodoric via the *Nibelungenlied*. Anyone who tried that would end up with a picture of a warlike noble contemporary with Attila, and miss most of the reality.

One question, although crucial, had not been seriously asked, because of the assumptions the scholars had worked with. When Geoffrey wrote of Arthur had he anything in mind which he got from outside the Welsh tradition?

This brought me back to his claim to have translated the *History* from a "very ancient book in the British language." As it stood, it was too much to swallow. Yet he might be exaggerating a truth. He could have had a book, now lost, which gave him ideas for at least some of the *History*. Since the "British language" might well be Breton, and he showed a pro-Breton bias and an interest in Brittany, the possibility did open a door into the world beyond Wales. Without the book it seemed that I could get no further. Yet perhaps I could. If I could pinpoint any specific thing which Geoffrey supposedly took from it, the part of the *History* where that thing occurred would be the part to explore. Thus, maybe, I could detect traces of an unrecognized source.

The search for the "specific thing" proved surprisingly easy. Geoffrey did the pinpointing himself, and, encouragingly, the passage was one that concerned Arthur. According to him the book gave him the facts, or some of them, for Arthur's last battle.

Having mentioned Modred's treason and the Queen's infidelity, he goes on, addressing himself to the same Robert of Gloucester whom he addresses in the preface:

> About this particular matter, most noble Duke, Geoffrey of Monmouth prefers to say nothing. He will, however, in his own poor style and without wasting words, describe the battle which our most famous King fought against his nephew, once he had returned to Britain after his victory; for that he found in the British treatise already referred to. He heard it, too, from Walter of Oxford, a man most learned in all branches of history.

More is implied here than meets the eye. Geoffrey could have got the bare name of the fatal battle, Camlann, from the Welsh matter. Probably he did, by way of Walter or otherwise. So, what was the special contribution of the "British treatise"? Presumably some or all of what he added, before and after the parenthesis quoted—the circumstances from which he created the drama of the downfall: Modred's position as deputy ruler, his betrayal of Arthur, his league with the barbarians, and the interweaving of all this with the Gallic war which made his stab in the back possible. Certainly it is quite at variance with the sketchy Welsh legends of Arthur and "Medraut," which tell only of a sort of barbaric feud.

I guessed, therefore, that if the ancient book existed, it had material for the end of Arthur's career as Geoffrey described it. This would be non-Welsh material about the making of the disaster, with treachery in it and an episode overseas, because his reference included Arthur's returning to Britain. Taking a closer look at that part of the story, I realized that he told it twice. In the "prophecies of Merlin" which he inserted near the end of Vortigern's reign, he made Merlin foretell (among much else) the career of Arthur, the "Boar of Cornwall." In all this passage of the "prophecies" he was sketching a portion of the story which he had not yet come to, as he then expected to tell it. But I now noticed something which had never been given due weight, that several of the "prophecies" were not exactly fulfilled in the sequel. After writing them Geoffrey had changed his plans as he went along. Among other divergences, there was a clear hint that in his early thinking, Arthur was going to depart differently.

This is what Merlin is made to say to Vortigern.

> The race that is oppressed shall prevail in the end, for it will resist the savagery of the invaders.
>
> The Boar of Cornwall shall bring relief from these invaders, for it will trample their necks beneath its feet.
>
> The Islands of the Ocean shall be given into the power of the Boar and it shall lord it over the forests of Gaul.
>
> The House of Romulus shall dread the Boar's savagery and the end of the Boar will be shrouded in mystery.

Nothing in this to suggest Camlann. It looks as if Geoffrey's first conception placed Arthur's exit in Gaul and introduced Romans, the House of Romulus. But when he reached that point in his actual writing he had learned the Camlann tradition or given further thought to it, and instead brought Arthur home for the cryptic passing. His imagination, however, had first fastened on something else. He retained it, and combined it with the Welsh Camlann tale in a new literary creation. Something from the ancient book? War in Gaul and a high-level betrayal as the makings of Arthur's downfall, the tragic pathway to Avalon?

By getting as far as this, I had established two facts. For Geoffrey the denouement was always involved with the Gallic warfare. And the denouement was the only episode in the whole *History* where he pointed, specifically, to the ancient book as a source. Previous searchers had failed to notice because of a mental block. Their assumption that the Gallic parts of the story were pure fiction meant that there was no point in considering them. Only Arthur's career in Britain counted, and only some of that. Yet an impartial look at the *History* shows that this is utterly out of keeping with Geoffrey's own attitude. The Gallic business, in two installments, is patently important to him. It is present in his mind from the outset, as Merlin's prophecy shows. It raises Arthur to the peak of his glory. With the prior diplomacy and debates counted in, it takes up more than half the account of his reign. Assessed by space, he is more a Gallic conqueror than anything else. At one point in the campaign Geoffrey slips in the unusual phrase "so the story goes." He wants to persuade his readers that he has got the Gallic business from somewhere, not made it up.

As I reflected further, it struck me that authors who come after Geoffrey take a similar view. They put Arthur on the Continent as well as in Britain. The first of the great romancers, Chrétien de Troyes, makes him hold court in Brittany. The chief German poet of the Grail, Wolfram von Eschenbach, locates him at the Breton city of Nantes through most of the story, sending him back to Britain only at the close. Romancers who deal with Arthur's wars show what they think important. Most of them pay little attention to the Saxon-quelling battles in Britain. The warfare in Gaul, now called France, remains. It takes up less space than it does in Geoffrey, because the romancers are less interested in war. But it remains. In the classic English version by Malory it even divides into two wars, one against Rome, and the other, long after, against a rebellious Lancelot.

I knew that scholars who had discussed this issue had attempted to explain it away. They said Geoffrey invented exploits for Arthur modeled on those of emperors who were proclaimed in Britain and crossed the Channel: Maximus, for instance, in 383. Or they said he tried to please the Normans who ruled in England by making Arthur's realm include lands they claimed on the Continent. Certainly he could have done either. Yet thoughts like these presupposed a basic decision to portray an Arthur for whom the Welsh gave no warrant. That was a weighty decision; it implied solid reasons, and preexisting sources.

Dissatisfied with the assumption that only events in Britain counted, I resolved to challenge it. I would try taking the Gallic part seriously. Not literally, as if it were or could be history, but seriously, as perhaps pointing back to something which Geoffrey drew upon. The Continental events might even turn out to have a firmer substratum than the ones in Britain. If the ancient book came from Brittany, it would make sense. I would be looking for Arthur by asking a new question, in a new way: *On what real happenings (if any) did Geoffrey base the Gallic warfare; and what real person (if any) was here the original for his King?*

This was an exercise in what has been called lateral thinking. It held out a hope of progress even if the clue that suggested it,

Geoffrey's statement about the downfall of Arthur being in the book, was a lie after all. There was no need for it to be true. Nevertheless, I thought it would be pleasant if I could find documentation which fitted in with it, and tied the threads together.

Closing In

I wondered, for a start, whether I could get any bearings with the dates. When was Arthur's warfare in Gaul alleged to have happened?

Geoffrey's chronology seldom hangs together, and in the early fifth century, before Arthur, the muddle is bad. But Arthur's family works out fairly well. His grandfather Constantine reigns after Maximus but not very long after. Constantine's reign ends prematurely and Vortigern soon takes over. When the bishops visit Britain in 429 Vortigern has been King for some time. Meanwhile, Constantine's sons, Aurelius Ambrosius and Uther, are growing up. The former ousts Vortigern. His own reign is brief and is probably meant to lie within the 430s. His brother Uther succeeds him and Arthur is born shortly after, coming to the throne at the age of fifteen. The periods of time mentioned in Arthur's own reign are hard to reconcile completely, but it lasts about twenty-five years. He cannot be much past forty when he departs for Avalon.

None of this can be taken for a moment as genuine dating, but it shows, within broad limits, where Arthur is put in Geoffrey's scheme. He is the grandson of a man who is dead well before 429, and no juggling of the generation between will make him anything but a fifth-century ruler. Geoffrey has done some juggling himself to insure this, cutting off both Vortigern and Ambrosius when their originals still had many years to live. His Arthur flourishes, probably, in the third quarter of the century.

Turning to Gaul and considering his concerns there, I saw that there were clues in the way Geoffrey pictured the Roman Empire. The *History* has it surviving in the West, with Gaul still officially Roman, though too shakily to prevent a conqueror from moving in. Lucius, Arthur's chief opponent, is a strange person. In the first campaign he is not mentioned; in the second his status is unclear. His title, "procurator," was given to deputies of the Emperor in minor provinces. That makes him sound less than absolute, and, in fact, the Senate in Rome has power to give him orders. Later Geoffrey calls him an Emperor a few times. But he also mentions another Emperor, who is in power throughout both campaigns, and seems not to be in Rome, yet is the one whose emperorship is unquestionable, who really counts.

Geoffrey is writing with a background awareness of a situation which we already know—the situation as it was after the death of Valentinian III in 455. Roman Gaul was breaking up but not quite defunct, and the Western emperors were short-lived and ineffectual but not quite extinct. This phase lasted till 476, after which there were no Western emperors at all. Constantinople, however, remained steady throughout, with a powerful ruler.

Taking stock of these facts, I judged that any basis for the Gallic campaigning must lie between 455 and 476. To my astonishment, I hit on a far more specific point which confirmed the dating and tightened it up. Not merely once but three times, and during both Arthur's marches into Gaul, Geoffrey names the "real" Emperor, the one at Constantinople—and we can recognize him. First: "The province of Gaul was at that time under the jurisdiction of the Tribune Frollo, who ruled it in the name of the Emperor Leo." Second: "Lucius Hiberius . . . could not make up his mind whether to engage in a full-scale battle with Arthur or to withdraw inside Autun and there await reinforcements from the Emperor Leo." And third, at the report of Modred's treason: "Arthur immediately cancelled the attack which he had planned to make on Leo, the Emperor of the Romans." This can only mean Leo I, who reigned at Constantinople from 457 to 474. Leo II was a child who succeeded him and died almost at once, and no further Leo reigned till centuries later.

The significance of Leo needs underlining. Geoffrey is giving a chronological fix, a tie-in of Arthur with known history outside Britain. For no visible reason he rubs it in, giving it three times. It is the only explicit and certain fix in Arthur's whole reign. What is more, it is the only one anybody gives him at all, up to Geoffrey's time. Nothing comparable competes with it. Geoffrey, rejected as a weaver of fantasy, supplies what the purportedly historical Welsh matter never does.

While Leo is the key name, two others deserve attention. Geoffrey speaks of a Pope called Sulpicius. No such Pope ever existed. But Sulpicius is usually thought to be a garbling of Simplicius, the name of a Pope who reigned from 468 to 483. In other words, he was Pope during six full years when Leo was Emperor, 468 to 474. They overlap. A history or chronicle for those years, which supplied Geoffrey with Leo, could have supplied him with Simplicius too.

A possibility of the same sort may arise with Lucius himself. No such Emperor ever existed. But one of the last of the dwindling Western series was Glycerius. In a chronicle which Geoffrey may well have known, by Sigebert of Gembloux, this ephemeral person is called Lucerius and assigned, incorrectly, to the years 469–70, again during Leo's reign in the East. An arresting conclusion follows. If some book that gave Geoffrey material focused his interest on just those years, 469–70, he could have made out not only that the Eastern Emperor was Leo but that the Western Emperor was Lucerius and the Pope was Simplicius—from which, by changes he was quite capable of, he could have got his Lucius and Sulpicius. There is nothing historical here, only the names and the offices held. But the way all three coincide, within a small span of time, is striking.

Geoffrey's sequel to Arthur confirms the time scheme. His next chronological fix comes in 597, when he mentions another fact attested outside Britain, the dispatch of a Christian mission from Rome to Kent. He has a great deal happen in the interval, and clearly pictures it as long, even doing some more jugglery to lengthen it. But, of course, he also has that one detail which glaringly doesn't fit, the date given for Arthur's passing-away to Avalon, 542. There is no accepted explanation for it. Early writings are full of blunders when it comes to precise, numerical dates, and when all the rest tells an incompatible tale, it is fair to shelve this one for the moment. If the rest continues to make sense, it will be fair also to reconsider it and ask where it may have come from.

With points such as these in mind I reviewed what Arthur is represented as doing. The account of his first Gallic campaign is short, and mostly taken up with his romantic single combat with Frollo. The second campaign is the one that matters. He ships his army across the Channel, advances to the fringes of Burgundy, and is then betrayed by the deputy ruler Modred, who makes a pact with the barbarian enemy. His last explicit Gallic location is among the pro-Roman Burgundians. After the fatal battle brought on by the treachery he departs in the direction of Avalon, with no recorded death.

Once again, Merlin's prophecy suggests that at first Geoffrey did not intend a return to Britain. He picked up Camlann later and combined it with his Gallic story, whatever it was, saddling Modred with a treason which the Welsh never ascribe to him. One telltale detail confirms this view. The mythic island where Arthur goes is a paradisal "Place of Apples," or "Apple Orchard," or so the name is generally taken to mean—certainly by Geoffrey. In Welsh it is Ynys Avallach. Geoffrey's Latin equivalent is *Insula Avallonis*. But this is not really equivalent, since it doesn't correspond to the Welsh. It has been influenced by the spelling of a real place called Avallon. Avallon is a Gaulish name with the same meaning, and the real Avallon is in Burgundy—where Arthur's Gallic career ends. Again we glimpse an earlier and different passing of Arthur, on the Continent and not in Britain.

So then, did Geoffrey get any ideas from historical events in Gaul? Step by step, the range of time for them can be narrowed. If there were any, we can say the following:

1. They happened during the last phase of the Empire in the West, between 455 and 476.
2. They happened when Leo was Emperor in the East. This cuts the range to 457–74.
3. They happened, most probably, when Simplicius was Pope. He does overlap Leo, but the overlap is confined to the six years 468–74.
4. There are grounds for thinking that they happened when "Lucerius" is said by a chronicle to have been Emperor in the West. The years in question lie within the Leo-Simplicius overlap. They are 469–70.

In those years and only those years, Geoffrey could have found all the names together. The first and second steps are surer than the third and fourth. But any train of events within that last couple of years would be practically self-proved.

Face to Face

To state the question like that was to answer it. Strangely, I had
come within inches of the answer in my early book *From Caesar
to Arthur,* published in 1960, but had backed away. After the
reexamination, there could be no serious doubt whose career
inspired this portion of Arthur's, especially the last phase, where
Geoffrey does indicate that he drew on an unknown source. I
now realized that the search for Arthur via the Welsh items had
been, to some extent, misconceived. It was an attempt to find an
additional British leader besides the ones on historical record,
and it ended by demanding an act of faith. Such an act might still
be justified to complete the picture. But at least half of Geoffrey's
story could be explained without it. Identifying the man at the
point of origin was not a matter of finding anyone. It was a matter
of recognition. He was already there, and documented. He was
the King known on the Continent as Riothamus, to whom
Sidonius wrote a letter. We traced his career (pages 53–56).

Riothamus too led an army of Britons into Gaul, and was the
only British King who did. He too advanced to the neighborhood
of Burgundy. He too was betrayed by a deputy ruler who treated
with barbarian enemies. He too is last located in Gaul among the
pro-Roman Burgundians. He too disappears after a fatal battle,
without any recorded death. The line of his retreat, prolonged on
a map, shows that he was going in the direction of the real
Avallon. As for the date, he was on the Continent not only in
Leo's reign but in those precise years, 469–70, from which Geoffrey, browsing among chronicles, could have got his names for all
three dignitaries: his Eastern Emperor, his Western Emperor,
and his Pope.

There could even be a bonus. A fourth name which his
browsing might have turned up, within the same couple of years,
is Childeric. Childeric was the Frankish King whose pact with the
Saxons preserved their remnants in the Loire Valley. In this case
Geoffrey would have got a name only; but he could have got that,
plus a vague association with Saxons and double-dealing; and
Childeric, in the form Cheldric, is the name he gives to the Saxon
overlord with whom Modred makes his treacherous treaty.

Once again, we are not dealing with history but with fiction.

Yet so many themes and details in Arthur's Gallic enterprise echo Riothamus's that the source of inspiration is in no doubt. Geoffrey manipulates the data, inflating and twisting and rearranging, very much as he manipulates data in other places. The relation between his fiction and the facts is the usual one.

If the King's name was Riothamus, why should he appear in the *History* as Arthur? This, I could see at once, was not too grave an obstacle. Geoffrey might be doing very much what he did with Nennius's boy prophet, whom he read about as Ambrosius but to whom he gave the more exciting name Merlin. In smoothing this over by saying Merlin was "also called Ambrosius," Geoffrey took advantage of a known fact: that some Britons in the fifth century had two names, one British and one Roman. St. Patrick, for instance, was called Maun or Magonus as well as Patricius. It could have been so with the King, either in Geoffrey's imagination or in truth. Riothamus is a Latin rendering of a British name, and Arthur, as we have seen, is the Roman name Artorius. He could have had both.

But a little delving suggested a better idea. In its original British form, Riothamus would have been Rigotamos. The first part of this would mean "king" if taken as a noun, "kingly" or "royal" if taken as an adjective. The second part is a superlative ending like "-est" in English, as in words like "kindest." So Rigotamos might mean the "king-most" or "supreme king." A modern word formed in the same way is "generalissimo." Or perhaps it should be read as "most kingly" or "supremely royal." Either way, my impression was that it could be a title or honorific for the High King, and not, strictly speaking, his name. In that case he would have had a name as well. Artorius?

Powerful persons have sometimes been referred to formally in just such a way. The Mongol conqueror who is always known as Genghis Khan was actually named Temujin; Genghis Khan means "very mighty ruler." The name of the first Roman Emperor was Octavian, but he is always called Augustus, meaning roughly "His Majesty." The word "augustus" meant "majestic" before it was applied to him, and afterward it became a title of all the emperors. In more recent times the German Kaiser was "the all-highest."

So when continentals wrote of this King as Riothamus, were they using a title or honorific in the same way? Did it simply mean the High King? The notion was all the more alluring because Vortigern expresses the same idea, and so indeed does Vortimer, the name given to the man who (according to Geoffrey) replaced Vortigern for a while, and (according to Nennius as well) was his son. The High Kingship of the Britons never stabilized and might have been expressed in different ways. Rival high kings might have employed different designations. At any rate, the form Riothamus or Rigotamos seemed to line this one up with his predecessors, and it was too far-fetched to suppose that it was a baptismal name which just happened to fit so neatly.

I took advice on the question, and was delighted to learn that Professor Léon Fleuriot, the distinguished historian of Brittany, had also discussed Rigotamos and judged it to be a title. He took it as a noun, the "king-most" or "supreme king." Later Professor Kenneth Jackson, the same who expounded Nennius's battle list, disputed Fleuriot's reading. He preferred the interpretation "supremely royal" and claimed that it was a personal name. It is true that in Wales it eventually became one, as indeed Vortigern did. But the parallels with the other British kings, and with Roman and German emperors, would surely make it honorific rather than personal at its first appearance.

In evoking this figure of the High King at the root of Geoffrey's story, I was aware of two difficulties.

The first was that the main enemy was wrong. For Geoffrey's Arthur the Romans were opponents. For Riothamus they were allies, however unreliable and, in the end, absent. To this it could be answered that changes of enemy are not unknown in heroic literature when the story demands them. The French epic of the death of Charlemagne's paladin Roland turns the enemy from Basques, as they actually were, into Saracens. Geoffrey makes at least one similar change earlier in his *History.* When he got to Arthur he could hardly make his King a mere Roman auxiliary. For his literary purpose no enemy but the Empire was great enough. However, there is more. He left one eloquent detail stuck in his text. At the council held before the major Gallic campaign, one of Arthur's subkings speaks of going overseas to fight Romans *and Germans.* These "Germans" could be Saxons or Goths or both. Geoffrey forgets them. Not being needed for his story, they can only be related to whatever he read—what else but an account of Riothamus, who fought Goths and probably Saxons?

The other stumbling block was Geoffrey's mysterious date for the King's passing, 542. Hitherto nobody had explained it. But on studying the ways in which early authors did confuse dates, I found that Riothamus could give the answer here too. The reason was that before A.D. dating became standard, there was an older Christian method which began from another starting point, and differed by twenty-eight years. As a result, historical writings sometimes have a twenty-eight-year error due to a mix-up between the systems. Nennius himself has it, twice. Riothamus's probable exit in 470, recorded by the old method, would have been dated 442. Set down mistakenly as an A.D. date, somewhere along the line of copyists, this would have been plainly too early for the King's passing. Geoffrey would have seen that even he could not make it work.

We can guess what happened. For some reason he was determined to use the document where he found it, at whatever cost in inconsistency with his other materials. Perhaps not knowing the type of error involved, he opted for a more obvious and familiar mistake of a hundred years. He "corrected" 442 to 542, giving the date as we now so awkwardly have it. Such an alteration was all too easy, and this very date was to undergo it at the hands of Geoffrey's adapter Wace, ending up as 642! The "correction" only upset things in the other direction, making the end too late instead of too early. But it fudged the story, spreading it out into a vague tract of time where it was easier to fit in Camlann (plus a few anachronistic Welsh saints to make Arthur's court more interesting), and where, for most readers, the absurdity was less palpable. To sum up: whatever the exact process, Riothamus's passing in 470 gives a date from which 542 could have been arrived at by recognized errors. And thus, at last, the mystery of the discrepant year is resolved.

With all these facts coming together, even odd and obscure ones, could I accept that Arthur *was* Riothamus in plain terms? Not quite yet. After publishing my first presentation of the idea, I learned that someone had hit on it long before, and pointed out a choice it entailed. His name was Sharon Turner, and he wrote a *History of the Anglo-Saxons* which was a pioneer work of scholarship. The first volume came out in 1799. In his discussion of the first Saxon settlements in Britain, Turner argues against a notion, current in his day, that Hengist completely smashed the Britons during the 450s and 460s. He is closer to the modern view than some more recent historians. With no archaeology to help him, he lays his finger on a "simple and authentic fact": that "at this very period the Britons were so warlike that twelve thousand went to Gaul, on the solicitations of the emperor, to assist the natives against the Visigoths." In a footnote he explains that he means "the expedition of Riothamus," and continues: "Either this Riothamus was Arthur, or it was from his expedition that Geoffrey, or the Breton bards, took the idea of Arthur's battles in Gaul." Having had his moment of vision, Turner veered away and put Arthur later. But there it is.

His either-or is very much to the point. Maybe Riothamus was Arthur, just like that, but maybe the connection is due merely to literary fancy. To show that the two were one, something more is needed—evidence that other people, before Geoffrey or independently of him, also spoke of Riothamus and called him Arthur. The terms of the inquiry, of course, are now altered. It is no longer a question of trying to prove that a historical Arthur existed. Riothamus, the High King, did exist. Sidonius's letter would be proof enough by itself. The question now is whether the traditions and legends of Arthur are, at however many removes, about this man.

The evidence is there. Some of it I found myself, some came to light through the work of a friend and colleague.

Arthur the Immortal

Geoffrey glances at the doubt over Arthur's end, but he is non-committal. Folk belief went much further. It affirmed that he never died, and would return as a kind of messiah. In early versions he was to be a Celtic messiah, triumphing over English and Normans and all other non-Celtic overlords. That belief can be traced before Geoffrey, and it has features which suggest that the undying King whom people called Arthur was none other than Riothamus.

All the indications are that it started in Brittany as part of a cycle of popular tradition. It may have reached Cornwall early. The Welsh said Arthur's grave was a mystery, but there is no proof that they adopted his deathlessness or return till the middle of the twelfth century. Since this legend arose on the Continent, it is logical to look there for whatever inspired it.

The belief that a famous person is not truly dead is a recurring one. As a rule, the person is an impressive figure who raises hopes, then passes from the world amid disaster and unfulfilled promise. Modern instances are the Irish patriot Parnell, the Mexican peasant leader Zapata, even President Kennedy. The belief can also take shape in a spirit of dread or horror, as it did with Nero and Hitler. Usually, of course, it fades out. Sometimes, however, a vanished hero is an Arthur who goes on indefinitely. The German Emperor Frederick is in his ninth century of sleep inside a mountain. But the survival legend closest to Arthur's—at least in its original form—is one that concerns Sebastian, King of Portugal.

In 1578, at the age of twenty-four, he led an inadequate army against the Moors. The ill-conceived crusade quickly collapsed. Sebastian was routed at Alcazarquivir in Morocco and presumed dead. Soon after, the Spanish took possession of Portugal. Promptly a popular rumor began circulating. Sebastian was alive; he would return and liberate his country. Four impostors pretended to be the King, including a potter's son and a cook. Portugal recovered its independence, yet Sebastian was not forgotten. He became immortal. In 1807, during the Napoleonic Wars, his reappearance was looked for again. The belief spread to the Portuguese colony of Brazil, where some of the aboriginal people still hope for a demigod called Sebastian as a savior from poverty and oppression.

Riothamus passed away very much as Sebastian did, overwhelmed in battle by superior numbers, a long way from home. History is silent about his fate, and for his fellow countrymen it probably remained uncertain. The settlers in Armorica, closer to the event, would have had more cause for remembrance than the insular Britons. Their legend of the undying Arthur makes complete sense if Arthur is identical with the High King, and there is no other documented King of Britons or Bretons who qualifies in the same way. It is likely that the identity was an accepted thing for them, or rather, simply, that they always knew him by a name, not a title.

A by-product of the parallel with Sebastian is the proof that even if the High King acted irresponsibly in taking troops out of Britain, it would have been no bar to his enshrinement in folklore. Sebastian was irresponsible, crazily so. Yet no one cared afterward.

Arthur in Brittany

Another clue points the same way. From an early stage of my Arthurian searching, I was haunted by a suspicion of evidence among the Bretons which had been missed—ancient book or no ancient book. There was one actual document which E. K. Chambers had quoted, which I took note of in my own discussions, yet which everybody else seemed to ignore or dismiss. This was the dauntingly titled *Legend of St. Goeznovius.* Goeznovius Latinizes Goueznou, the name of a saint of Brittany. The author gives his own name as William and the date of composition as 1019. Before getting to his main story he has a preface about the Britons' migration across the Channel and various sequels to it. His opening paragraphs are a mixture of truth and legend. He shows some genuine knowledge, and diverges sharply from other accounts of the same happenings, in Geoffrey and Welsh writers —which means he has information of his own. After a while he becomes more factual, with an elaborate explanation of the wave of saints going to Brittany during the late fifth century and the sixth. It brings in Arthur, and has implications as to when he flourished and who he was.

The treatment of *Goeznovius* by experts is a sad little cautionary tale. Chambers, in 1927, published a transcript from it. In 1939 another eminent scholar, J. S. P. Tatlock, tried to blow it to pieces. He claimed in an article that its date was bogus, it was not written before Geoffrey's *History* but after, and its author took everything from there, so nothing he said had any value. Tatlock gave almost no hard evidence to support his view, and much that has come to light on other Arthurian matters has sapped his credibility. But a few years later he produced a major work on Geoffrey which gave him a massive air of authority, and the scholars' assumption that "nothing outside Britain counted" disposed them to agree with him on *Goeznovius,* or rather to accept what he said without examining it. If it had not been for his article, the Arthur question might have been resolved long ago.

As it was, effective rethinking had to wait forty years. At last Professor Fleuriot, the Breton historian already mentioned, defended the date 1019 as authentic. About the same time I was able to prove in print that the preface could not have been derived from Geoffrey whatever its date.

Goeznovius is in Latin, so it is not Geoffrey's ancient book. Its author, William (as we may as well call him), cites an "Ystoria Britanica" as his source. Neither of them copied the other, but a shared body of data seems to be hovering in the background of both. Here is William's account of the Britons during the fifth century.

In course of time the usurping king Vortigern, to buttress the defence of the kingdom of Great Britain which he unrighteously held, summoned warlike men from the land of Saxony and made them his allies in the kingdom. Since they were pagans and of devilish character, lusting by their nature to shed human blood, they drew many evils upon the Britons.

Presently their pride was checked for a while through the great Arthur, king of the Britons. They were largely cleared from the island and reduced to subjection. But when this same Arthur, after many victories which he won gloriously in Britain and in Gaul, was summoned at last from human activity, the way was open for the Saxons to go again into the island, and there was great oppression of the Britons, destruction of churches, and persecution of saints. This persecution went on through the times of many kings, Saxons and Britons, striving back and forth. . . .

In those days, many holy men gave themselves up to martyrdom; others, in conformity to the Gospel, left the greater Britain which is now the Saxon's homeland, and sailed across to the lesser Britain [i.e., Brittany].

The first thing to notice is that this passage supplies what nothing Welsh ever does: plain, nonlegendary statements about Arthur, in a context where they can be tested. "Summoned . . . from human activity" may acknowledge a mystery over the

King's end; it doesn't assert that he was immortal. The second thing to notice is that historical checking works out well.

William puts Arthur's victories in Britain after the Saxon revolt, but not long after. The word translated "presently" is *postmodum,* which implies sooner rather than later. Furthermore, he has nothing about Ambrosius or Uther, or indeed any gap between Vortigern's reign and Arthur's. On the face of it he is putting Arthur not much past the middle of the fifth century. That is confirmed by his connecting Arthur with the retirement of the raiding Saxons to their enclaves, presented in pro-British terms as their being "largely cleared from the island," and with the subsequent phase when the Britons probably thought them to be scared off and contained. He is talking about the Britons' recovery in the 460s. Their phase of ascendancy after the battle of Badon came far too long afterward to be relevant here, and in any case it brought only a lull, not a major Saxon withdrawal.

Arthur's victories in Gaul confirm this dating further. He seems here to be fighting Saxons abroad as well as at home. No mention is made of other adversaries, Geoffrey's Romans for example. There was only one period when a King could have gone on from fighting Saxons in Britain to fighting them in Gaul. The British-Saxon confrontation north of the Loire began after the migration to Armorica toward 460. It ended with the Saxons' collapse near Angers toward 470. *Goeznovius,* therefore, puts Arthur's Gallic warfare in the 460s, probably the late 460s when the Loire Saxons were tackled and defeated.

So to William's final touches. With Arthur's departure, "the way was open for the Saxons to go again into the island." Whether or not his departure was the reason, that is what did happen. It was during the 470s, after their defeat in Gaul, that they began a fresh series of entries into Britain at new points. The *Anglo-Saxon Chronicle* gives 477 for the first landing in Sussex, and the process went on for twenty or thirty years. This was also the time when the Britons' territory was falling apart. The fluctuating warfare which Gildas records drifted on till Badon. William has both these particulars. He speaks now of many British kings, not one, and of "striving back and forth"—almost echoing Gildas, who says that "sometimes our citizens and sometimes the enemy had the best of it." Lastly, the saints' migration seems to have started during those later decades of the fifth century. Again William is correct.

What it all amounts to is that his version of these events is surprisingly good. Arthur is built plausibly into a story which has eight features apart from him.

1. Vortigern settles Saxons in Britain as auxiliary troops.
2. They turn against their British employers and harry them.
3. They withdraw, or are compelled to withdraw, into a confined zone.
4. Britons fight in Gaul, apparently against Saxons there too.
5. After defeat on the Continent, the Saxons make new incursions into the island.
6. The Britons become divided, passing into a phase with many kings.
7. There is a period of to-and-fro warfare.
8. The saints emigrate.

The *Goeznovius* preface gets all these things right, and in the right order. It is much better than any other known account of them that was available in William's time. Indeed, it is much better than any other for hundreds of years after him. He could have read, say, Nennius. He could never have got such a summary from Nennius, or anything like it. Even if Tatlock were to be right and he did read Geoffrey, he could not have turned Geoffrey's long, fanciful narrative into such a compactly good one, unless he had some older and sounder document which enabled him to select and emend.

William, then, embeds Arthur in history as no one else convincingly does. He dates Arthur's Gallic presence in the late 460s, as Geoffrey dates it, but he does so in a different way, not by names but by circumstances. The conclusion with both of them is the same. Both have the Gallic connection, and when William talks about an Arthur who goes to Gaul, he is talking about the man called Riothamus whose career is sketched in Jordanes's *Gothic History*. His Arthur is "king of the Britons," and that is the phrase Jordanes uses. His Arthur leads British forces into Gaul and apparently fights Saxons there, in the late 460s. Riothamus led British forces into Gaul in the late 460s and very probably fought Saxons there. Arthur is "summoned . . . from human activity" between the Saxons' collapse in or around 469 and the new Saxon landings in Britain about 477. Riothamus departed, with no recorded death, in (probably) 470. *Goeznovius* credits Arthur with Gallic victories; Jordanes mentions none, but Jordanes is concerned with the Goths, not the Saxons, and at least the Saxons on the Loire were defeated and Britons were involved.

William, of course, is writing too long after the events to be reliable in himself. His word cannot be trusted unsupported for facts of history. But the man he calls Arthur coincides with the High King, and his rightness where he can be checked proves that Brittany had good records to draw upon. One thing more. This author, who is so much better informed than most, makes Arthur live when he could have fought most of Nennius's battles in Britain. But he doesn't make him live long enough to fight at Badon and Camlann. That is an issue which will have to wait.

Arthur in Chronicles

As my explorations progressed, I wondered whether a problem which seemed obvious to me had been obvious to others. On the basis of the Welsh matter, I thought no method of dating Arthur would work, because he was spread out too far. The same would apply to Geoffrey's *History* for any reader who took the "wild" date 542 at face value. But was I being too difficult? Or had readers in the Middle Ages noticed the same perplexities? This line of questioning led, again, to traces of a tradition in which Arthur and Riothamus were one.

I soon found medieval authors whose thoughts had moved as mine had. One was a monk of Glastonbury, the writer of a long marginal note in a history of his abbey. This note sums up Geoffrey's story of the passing of Arthur, complete with the date 542, but at the end it adds that the King was "almost a centenarian." Geoffrey has no hint of this. The monk had read the rest of the Arthur narrative and could see no other way to hold it together. I came across a similar notion in a thirteenth-century French romance, where the King lives into his nineties and is still an active warrior.

The issue could be expected to grow more serious in the

Merlin's Tree is the subject of an ancient tradition:
   "When Myrddin's Tree shall tumble down,
   Then shall fall Carmarthen Town."

The South Wales town bedded the oak in concrete. It has since been removed; a fragment is kept in the museum. (Myrddin is the old Welsh form of the magician's name.) *Credit: Reece Winstone*

Tintagel in Cornwall is traditionally thought of as the place of Arthur s concep-
tion and is the site of archaeologists' initiation into the mysteries of Arthurian
Britain. Here Merlin's enchantment aided Uther Pendragon's seduction of
Ygerna. *Credit: Edwin Smith*

Above: Tintagel's headland and adjacent coast. The ruins near the isthmus belong to the medieval castle. Many of the others are from the Arthurian era. *Credit: Aerofilms*

Left: The pillar of a cross commemorating the Welsh King Eliseg and tracing his ancestry back to the Roman Emperor Maximus and Arthur's predecessor, Vortigern. *Credit: Royal Commission on Ancient and Historical Monuments*

THE ARTHURIAN NORTH

Above: Arthur's Seat is an old volcano's remains to the east of Edinburgh and its famous castle. The Arthurian era poet Aneirin laments how later British knights rode out to their deaths from a "Din Eydin" in this locality. *Credit: British Tourist Authority*

Opposite page: Bamburgh Castle is on the site of a British fort which was called "Din Guayrdi" before the Northumberland English made it Bamburgh. Malory took the name Joyous Gard as his home for Sir Lancelot. Here he gave hospitality to Tristan and Iseult. *Credit: Edwin Smith*

Above: The Isles of Scilly off Cornwall may give some reality to the old Arthurian tale of the land called Lyonesse, over which Tristan reigned and which the sea was later to claim. *Credit: Aerofilms*

Below: Portchester Castle with its Roman walls built to repel the Saxons and its later Norman keep is believed by some to have been the scene of Geraint's exploits in battle as recorded in an Old Welsh poem. *Credit: British Tourist Authority*

Left: Quimper in Brittany is one of the centers associated with British settlement in the mid-fifth century. The medieval cathedral has a statue of Budic, possibly a successor of Riothamus. *Credit: French Government Tourist Office*

Below: The French town of Avallon lay on the line of march for Riothamus after his betrayal in battle to the Goths and his escape into Burgundy. *Credit: French Government Tourist Office*

Glastonbury Tor. It is the West Country which has the most Arthurian lore, and nowhere more than mysterious Glastonbury in Somerset, the ancient "Summer Country." Glastonbury is associated with Arthur's Isle of Avalon. Indeed, the man-carved Tor there is believed to have then been almost surrounded by marsh and water. *Credit: Aerofilms*

medieval chroniclers, who would hardly have rested content with such brute-force solutions. There were many of them, writing at various times through the Middle Ages, using materials which were often much earlier. At my suggestion, Professor Barbara Moorman most generously made a search, which had a remarkable outcome.

Most of the chroniclers, she reported, avoid Arthur. They either prefer not to commit themselves or find the difficulties too much for them. The ones who tackle him fall, essentially, into two groups. Those in the larger group treat Geoffrey's work as history, and try to pin Arthur down by the wild date for his passing, without attempting a careful study. Two eccentrics who put him absurdly early may have taken the date in a previous form, 442, from a lost first edition. Many more simply grab at 542 and try to manage with a sixth-century Arthur. They seldom give any impression of critical thinking or independent research.

Those in the other, smaller group do give that impression, and are much more interesting. Even when they know Geoffrey's work, they seem to know other material as well. Sometimes they conserve Arthur by modifying the story, or relating him to facts which are not so much as hinted at in the *History*. And they put him in a part of the time scale that excludes the wild date altogether. If they are aware of it, they are aware of it as an error.

Between 1227 and 1251 a Cistercian monk, Alberic, compiled a year-by-year chronicle based chiefly on French information. He tried to fit some of Geoffrey's kings into the time sequence. This is the first attempt:

> 434. In the history of the Britons [is an account] of King Vortigern and the tower he built, and of those things which were under the tower's foundation, and of the manner in which they were interpreted through Merlin the prophet.

A few years later comes the monarch whom Geoffrey works in as Vortigern's successor, with the length of his reign:

> 440. Aurelius Ambrosius, king of the Britons, 2 years.

And the successor of Aurelius Ambrosius:

> 442. Uther Pendragon, king of the Britons, 17 years.

And Uther's son:

> 459. Arthur, the very famous king of the Britons, reigns 16 years.

With a separate demise:

> 475. King Arthur mortally wounded went away to the Isle of Avalon.

Nothing here about the sixth century. Alberic has decided where Arthur belongs. He, or someone he has followed, even shortens Arthur's reign in defiance of Geoffrey, pulling back his departure. It would be worth knowing why, because the result is most intriguing. Alberic has misplaced the starting point of the three-reign series through an oversight in reading Geoffrey. Aurelius Ambrosius should supplant Vortigern much sooner after the Merlin episode. If we make a correction, shifting back his accession to 435, the three reigns take us to 454 for Arthur's accession and 470 for his passing. On that reading he could, most precisely, be Riothamus.

Whether or not there is anything in that, Alberic's conclusion is clear. He has Arthur reigning in the 460s plus a few years before and after. Nor does he stand alone. In another chronicle, the *Salzburg Annals,* someone a little later than Alberic has inserted an Arthurian reference. The main entry for the year 461 notes the death of Pope Leo the Great (the one who used moral suasion against the Huns and Vandals) and the accession of Pope Hilarius. After it is an addition: "At this time Arthur, of whom many stories are told, reigned in Britain." Geoffrey does not mention these popes. The chronicler, therefore, has information from somewhere else.

Jean des Preis, who lived from 1338 to 1400, is one of those who do have a sixth-century Arthur. Yet he knows a rival opinion which he feels he has to rebut. Writing of the year 467 (468 as reckoned now) and the death of Pope Hilarius, he quotes another chronicler called Martinus Polonus as saying that Arthur reigned in the time of that Pope. Jean's reason for disagreeing is none too clear, and seems to involve the doubtful authority of Merlin. In any case he provides further evidence, backhandedly, of a dating in the 460s.

Toward the end of the fourteenth century Jacques de Guise,

a learned Franciscan, wrote a history of Hainaut (now part of Belgium). In one chapter he speaks of Hainaut as being oppressed in the time of "Arthur and the Goths, Huns and Vandals." The Huns began to fade out as troublers of western Europe a year or so after Attila's death in 453, so an Arthur flourishing in their time cannot be much later than that. Further on, Jacques mentions "histories of the Britons," putting Arthur in the mid-fifth century, and his Gallic warfare in the reign of the Emperor Leo. This is from Geoffrey. But further on again, Jacques speaks of Arthur as having been King during the rule of General Aegidius in northern Gaul, that is, in the years 461–64. Which is not from Geoffrey, who never mentions him.

The naming of Aegidius is arresting here, since, as we saw, the settlement in Armorica may have involved him in contacts with important Britons. The theme reappears in a chronicle by Philippe de Vigneulles, compiled in 1525 from a miscellany of older matter. Philippe is writing about the Franks in northern Gaul.

> Childerich, son of Meroveus, held the kingdom and began to reign in the year 470. But according to Gauguin, he had not been reigning long when, by his libidinous conduct, he aroused the indignation and hatred of most of his princes and nobles; and he fled to Bassine, a friend of his, the wife of the king of Thuringia. In his place was chosen Gillon the Roman, who was then established at Soissons. And this Gillon, they say, had many dealings with King Arthur of England. But after a while the aforesaid Childerich, by the advice and aid of his friend Guinemault, who was one of the chief men of his realm, returned home and was restored to his realm and lordship.

Most of this can be found in Gregory of Tours, the sixth-century historian who records the Britons' defeat in Berry. The debauched King is Childeric, who, it will be remembered, was flourishing at that time. His reign actually began in 456. Philippe's 470 is due to a scribal error. He uses Roman numerals, IIIICLXX, and the final XX is a mistake for VI which has crept in somewhere—an easier blunder, for anyone working with medieval manuscripts, than might be supposed. Childeric's lady friend is Basina. He eventually married her, and their son was Clovis, the effective founder of France. And "Gillon the Roman," who took over the government in his absence, is Aegidius himself. This is proved by Gregory's account of the same events, by the mention of Soissons, and by a reference to Syagrius as Gillon's son. Thus a sentence about Aegidius having dealings with Arthur is embedded in largely factual matter, on record as far back as the sixth century. It is perfectly credible as a scrap of history preserved nowhere else.

Taken together, these items suggest a well-marked tradition of an early Arthur, which was independent of Geoffrey, or nearly so. That is true whether or not we leave Alberic untampered with. But if he did use an older note of the three reigns, and made a slip with the starting point, the five-year correction gives a framework which contains everything and is never in conflict with known facts.

1. Arthur begins to reign in 454 (Alberic, corrected).
2. This is close enough to Attila to justify saying the time of "Arthur and the Goths, Huns and Vandals" (Jacques de Guise).
3. He is King during Aegidius's rule in Gaul, 461–64 (Jacques de Guise), and has dealings with him (Philippe de Vigneulles).
4. He is King at the death of Pope Leo in 461, and during the papacy of Hilarius, 461–68 (the Salzburg item and Martinus Polonus).
5. He campaigns in Gaul when Leo I is Emperor, as per Geoffrey, 469–70 (Jacques de Guise).
6. He departs in 470 (Alberic, corrected).

As with *Goeznovius,* and more so, items as late as these are not direct evidence for history. But, taken with the rest, they are evidence for a solid tradition. The chroniclers could all be transmitting facts from further back, even from a single source. And when they speak of Arthur they could all be referring to our High King, with a reign running from about 454 to 470. The *Anglo-Saxon Chronicle* has Vortigern still living in 455, but this is his last appearance, the margin of error is wide, and the rise of a successor about that time, Arthur-Riothamus as we may call him, would present no difficulties. When I was once asked to draft a synopsis for a television serial featuring an Arthur understood in this way, a careful assessment of many factors led me to choose 454 for his accession. I arrived at it with no knowledge of Barbara Moorman's findings.

In the High King called Riothamus we have, at last, a documented person as the starting point of the legend. He is the only such person on record who does anything Arthurian. Or to put it more precisely, he is the only one to whom any large part of the story can be related. The bedrock proofs of his existence, Sidonius's letter and Jordanes's history, refer to him by the title or honorific. But we now have evidence in four quite different settings—not only Geoffrey's fiction, but the folklore of the Celtic fringe, Breton hagiography, and Franco-German chronicle-writing—for the name Arthur denoting this King. Each manifestation has features of its own. Even apart from questions of date, no one of the four could have produced the other three. This looks like the solution.

One medieval historian poked fun at Geoffrey because he professed to know all the British kings, yet missed Riothamus. But Geoffrey didn't miss him. Unlike his critic, he had a very good idea who Riothamus was.

6

The Wellsprings
of Romance

On Home Ground

Where the High King appears in the records, they apply to Gaul and to that part of the Arthur story. Continental authors in the fifth and sixth centuries shed no light on his background or career before he came over "by the way of Ocean." They fail to link their Riothamus with Arthur in Britain. Nevertheless, one point that arises does take us back with him to the island. Indirectly the linking does happen, putting Arthur together and drawing in the Welsh matter.

This point is a seeming paradox. Here in Gaul is the most important British King of the time, the only one who is firmly attested, the only one whom an Emperor sought out as an ally. Yet on the face of it, nobody back in Britain knows anything about him. On the face of it, he is never mentioned in Gildas, or Bede, or Nennius, or the *Annales Cambriae*, or the Welsh poems and tales. Which, if true, would be bewildering. The obvious answer is that he must be mentioned; or rather, that someone who *is* mentioned must be the same person, differently labeled. Everything so far suggests that we know the someone and he is Arthur. Still, it would be wrong to jump to conclusions. Riothamus could have been the title of another royal or prominent Briton. We have to try an elimination. The others who are mentioned are Vortigern, Vortimer, Ceredig, Uther, and (to keep the chief claimant to the last) Ambrosius Aurelianus. We must ask whether the King known as Riothamus could be identical with any of these instead of Arthur.

Vortigern is out of the question. He is too early, and while we may discount the blackening of his character, his historic role was quite different. Vortimer is a shade more interesting. However, all we are really told of him is that he fought Saxons in Britain and died in Britain, and that it all happened well before Vortigern's death. This does not square with Riothamus and his Gallic disappearance much later. Ceredig or Coroticus of the Clyde was certainly real, but he is ruled out by his remoteness and unimportance. Uther is neither remote nor unimportant, but he is not real. Before Geoffrey he only figures, as "Uthr Pendragon," in uninformative Welsh verse. Even his fatherhood of Arthur has been put down to a false reading. The Welsh *uthr* means "terrible," and the phrase "Arthur the terrible" could have been misconstrued as "Arthur son of Uthr." There is simply nothing to take hold of. Geoffrey's account, if founded on fact, would rule Uther out as Riothamus because he is on the Continent only as a boy, and never goes there again as King.

Ambrosius remains. The idea that Riothamus was Ambrosius, and that the distinction between the King and the general is wrong, must be taken more seriously. Professor Fleuriot maintains it. He accepts that the Britons had a great leader in the third quarter of the fifth century, whose title was Riothamus, and whose exploits went into the making of the Arthur of legend. He believes, however, that the ruler was Ambrosius, and his deeds were credited later to somebody else named Arthur. He cites a version of Nennius's book, written in 1072, which says Ambrosius was in Brittany. He also points to two Breton places called Macoer Aurilian, "Aurelian's Wall," which could suggest Ambrosius Aurelianus as Amesbury does in Britain.

Fleuriot's study is valuable. However, the actual equation Riothamus = Ambrosius has not carried conviction. A major obstacle is that Ambrosius is the only fifth-century Briton whom Gildas names or gives any particulars of, and Gildas does not call him a King. He speaks of him purely as a war leader, organizing the Britons for their counteroffensive. Nennius, in a passing phrase, does make him a King, with some sort of paramountcy among the "kings of the British nation"; but this is legend. Elsewhere Nennius preserves his rank in its Welsh form, calling him

Emrys *gwledig,* and those who had this "landholder" office were regional rulers only. Finally, even legend says nothing about Ambrosius's campaigning in Gaul.

Probably Alcock's view is correct. Ambrosius was a general responsible to a High King, Vortigern's successor; in other words, to Riothamus—whoever he was. As a pro-Roman leader he may have had something to do with the Armorican settlements, in concert with the pro-Roman Aegidius. That would account for any "Aurelian" place names in Brittany. Afterward he may have acted as regent in Britain during the absence of Riothamus—whoever he was.

Surely, however, we need no longer say "whoever he was." Elimination has forced an answer. A person as important as this High King has to be a remembered Briton, and although there are five others to match him with besides Arthur, they all fail. Arthur is the only one left for him to be. Which, by the way, disposes of the argument that because Gildas doesn't mention Arthur, Arthur never existed. Gildas doesn't mention Riothamus, yet he undoubtedly did exist. The explanation is simply that for Gildas he was beyond living memory. If he was the same as Arthur, Arthur was too.

Belatedly and surprisingly Cadbury-Camelot turned out to favor the identification. Alcock's project had a series of sequels after the end of work on the site in 1970. During the next few years archaeologists dug into other hill forts, and showed that many more of them had been reoccupied in the same period. Hence, they urged (echoed by Michael Wood on television), Cadbury was not unique, and there were no grounds for singling it out as the citadel of a special person. Alcock meanwhile, as professor of archaeology at Glasgow, was working on sites in Scotland. In October 1982 he gave a lecture at the British Academy, with a fresh assessment of Cadbury in the light of all that had happened in the interval. While steering clear of Arthur, he put forward the thesis that "Arthurian" Cadbury, Cadbury II as he called it, still stood up as special, and more strikingly so, but with different implications.

Despite all the work on other hill forts, no one, he pointed out, had found the same military architecture anywhere else in England or Wales. Other post-Roman ramparts were simpler, without the combined use of stones and timber. The only parallels were in Scotland. The most relevant of these was at Alclud, the rock of Dumbarton, which was the capital of the Clyde kingdom founded by Ceredig. However, the northern forts were much smaller. Cadbury's size and the timber-stone architecture made it all the more plainly unique in Britain.

Unique as what? Alcock recalled that when Nennius tells of Vortigern's would-be fortress in Wales, he says the builders assembled "timber and stones." The words hint that these were thought to be the proper materials for a High King's stronghold in the fifth century. Alcock suggested that Cadbury was special, not as the headquarters of a commander in chief, but as the capital or residence of a King. Alclud, the nearest thing to a parallel, certainly was.

Cadbury now makes better sense in political terms. It looks like the citadel of a King with resources of manpower which, in the Britain of his time, were unrivaled. It is worth reverting for a moment to Leland, who, in 1542, called this place Camelot. He has been accused of making a mere guess, or retailing local gossip not much better than that. But the hill which he indicated has turned out to be the only known place in Britain with the right features. A mere guess would have had to be incredibly lucky to hit on it. Even a modern archaeologist could not have made such a guess simply by looking at the hill, without digging. Leland heard a tradition of some sort.

With the High King called Riothamus, the conclusion is forceful. He could have been the refortifier. Alcock's first discussion put the earliest date for the work at about 470—a little tight, but even with that there was a margin of doubt, and the High King could at least have begun it. At the British Academy he acknowledged that the margin had widened. Nothing would exclude the 460s or even the 450s. As for the resources of manpower, the High King had those, as Jordanes's account of his army proves. We could go further. We could say that he is not merely a candidate, he is the only one with any substance; the only documented person who could have been the royal refortifier of Cadbury. And of the various names which British antiquity supplies, the only one associated with Cadbury is Arthur. Here the two coincide again. An awesome convergence.

Once More the War Leader

Should we conclude that the High King's name, his baptismal name, was Arthur—that is, in its Roman form, Artorius?

That is the simplest theory, and it may be right. However, there are others. It could be that he was not named Arthur, but came to be confused at an early stage with someone who was, so that traditions of both were drawn together under that name. If so, the legendary King would be a composite. Several Arthurian figures are. Merlin combines two characters, arguably three. Mark of Cornwall, in the romance of Tristan and Iseult, probably combines two. King Arthur himself might be a similar case. But with no hard evidence for a separate Arthur early enough, this is speculative.

It could also be that Arthur was not the High King's name but a nickname or sobriquet, perhaps bestowed in his lifetime, perhaps later. Two Roman emperors have gone down in history under nicknames, Caligula and Caracalla. This could be the case for Arthur. As observed before, there was at least one Artorius in Roman Britain, the general Lucius Artorius Castus. He led a British force to Armorica in 184 to suppress a rising. Such an event might have been remembered (there is some very oblique evidence that it was), and the High King might have been nicknamed Artorius as the leader of another British force going to the same country. A poet, for example, might have hailed him in panegyrical verse as a "second Artorius," which could easily have become Artorius pure and simple.

This is a fancy, but an intriguing one, because of the contact with Sidonius, whose panegyrics of emperors were well known. Did the Briton's court in Gaul include a poet fluent in Latin, who read Sidonius's effusions and composed one in honor of his own leader? There were still Britons capable of it. Such a poem could account for a great deal of the Arthurian legend. Sidonius extolled emperors by recalling battles they had won; the British poet might have recalled fights against the Saxons in Britain, and thereby supplied the basic text, if at several removes, for some of Nennius's battle list. Sidonius extolled emperors by making them *Restitutor* figures; the British poet might have saluted the "second Artorius" as a *Restitutor* in Britain presiding over the recovery, and thereby defined the shape of the royal legend as it was one day to emerge in Geoffrey. To pursue the fancy further, a Breton epic or chronicle including a summary of the poem, with an added sketch of the betrayal and downfall, might have been Geoffrey's ancient book.

Whatever the source of the list in Nennius, does Arthur-Riothamus qualify as the war leader of Welsh tradition? Could he have fought those battles in Britain before going overseas?

With seven of them, in four different localities, he qualifies well. These far-flung clashes fit into the middle of the fifth century better than any relevant later period. Roman Britain had not been left so far behind. The roads were in better repair. Cities, however damaged and depressed, had more residual value as bases. The battles fought north and south of Lincoln, if they were, make sense in terms of combating early penetrations via the Humber and The Wash. They are less plausible afterward, when the settlers hereabouts were more numerous and more deeply entrenched. As for the two battle sites which are reasonably certain, Celidon and Chester, we have seen that they belong in the mid-fifth century and the anarchy of the federates' rebellion.

We might picture Arthur-Riothamus leading British units in a medley of minor actions during the late 450s and perhaps the early 460s. The wide scattering accords with the image of a High King struggling to win control of his territory in disordered times. Next would come the Saxon withdrawal which Gildas attests. The Britons would doubtless have regarded this as due to their own efforts under their King, and been emboldened to regroup for action against the settlements under his general, Ambrosius.

Four of the battle sites—"the river which is called Bassas," "Fort Guinnion," "the river which is called Tribruit," and "the mountain which is called Agned"—have defied identification. If any of them were on the Continent, that would be very interesting indeed. Ronald Millar wrote an amusing book called *Will the Real King Arthur Please Stand Up?* in which he located not only these four battles, but all twelve, in Brittany. That is going too far. Yet Agned could be worth studying. It comes last, apart from Badon, and could find a place in Arthur-Riothamus's Gallic enterprise. Moreover, it has something odd about it. Several copies of Nennius have "Breguoin" instead. This is a much-modified version of Bremenium, the name of a Roman outpost north of Hadrian's Wall. A battle was indeed fought among its abandoned buildings, but by a northern British King in the late sixth century. It looks as if someone thought Agned didn't count, struck it out, and made up the twelve by crediting this other battle to Arthur. Was the name Agned suspect as being no longer known in Britain?

Though called a mountain, *mons* in Latin, the site need not have been more than a hill. A startling possibility is that Agned is Angers, where the Loire Saxons were beaten, probably when Arthur-Riothamus was in the neighborhood. It has rising ground where some of the fighting may have taken place. Gregory of Tours in the sixth century gives Angers the Latin names Andegavi and Andegavum. When writing of the Saxons and their collapse he uses both spellings. Given either, in Gregory or elsewhere, scribal contraction and corruption would have been quite equal to producing Agned. This explanation could not compete with a known and confirmed Agned in Britain, but none exists, and even the possibility is exciting, in a place where a major Saxon defeat is on record and the King of the Britons may have played a part. To judge from *Goeznovius*, he was believed to have done so.

After Arthur-Riothamus's passing there was no King of the Britons, or none recognized widely enough to count. Dissolution was under way. Whether or not this was cause and effect, we can glimpse the makings of the Arthurian tragedy, the legend of a national leader sadly lost. To that extent the sequel after 470 is in keeping. But as we go on we come to the second phase of British recovery, and to the difficulty over Badon, with Camlann coming after it. We confront the time spread which prevents any dating of Arthur from covering everything. If Arthur-Riothamus's career ended when it seems to have done, in 470, he could not have fought those two later battles.

Alcock virtually abandoned his defense of the *Annales* entries about them in his British Academy lecture. These are now discounted as historical evidence, and the chief question is where they came from. There is no problem as to why the *Annales* should mention those two battles and not the more credibly Arthurian ones in the fifth century. Whatever the British records were that went into the chronicle, they started only in the sixth century; they did not extend back to Arthur-Riothamus at all.

What then should be done about Badon and Camlann? Of course there are questions which cannot now be answered. We don't know what happened to Arthur-Riothamus after his escape into Burgundy. Certainly he vanishes without trace. Certainly the mystery over the passing, and the prophecy of a second coming, suggest that he never got back to Britain. Yet he may have done so after an interval, and played a military role. An unlooked-for return after a report of his death could even have promoted belief in another return, after he did die. But all this is fancy. In any case, a further life of several decades, with nothing on record in it but a couple of battles, is hardly likely.

No linkage of Arthur's name with Badon can be proved before Nennius in the ninth century, and no linkage of it with Camlann—indeed, no Camlann—can be proved before the *Annales* in the tenth. The long misty interval gives ample scope for misunderstanding and legend-weaving. One possible answer has surfaced already: that the Arthur of legend and romance combines two originals. The first would be Arthur-Riothamus, the second a warrior who led the Britons at Badon and fell at Camlann. In course of time the two were confused, forming a synthetic hero. Perhaps. But if a single Arthur can explain everything, it is wiser not to bring in a second without evidence for him. The well-informed author of *Goeznovius* knows only the one, who leaves the human scene long before Badon.

The prerequisite of a one-Arthur explanation is a proof that battles where he was not present, and could not have been, might still have become Arthurian battles. This in fact is not hypothetical. It has happened.

East of the Scottish town of Forfar is Nechtansmere, now called Dunnichen Moss. In 685 a battle was fought here between northern English and Picts. The date is wrong, the nationalities are wrong, yet in local legend the battle is a clash between Arthur and Modred, supposedly part of a feud leading up to Camlann. It was provoked by Modred's intrigue with Guinevere, who, in this version, goes to him willingly. Dumbarrow Hill to the east is called Arthur's Seat, like a more famous hill beside Edinburgh. Barry Hill, across the valley of Strathmore, is the stronghold to which Modred took the Queen. Several place names recall the tale, such as Arthurstone and Arthurbank. When the King recaptured his errant wife, it is said, he had her torn to pieces by stallions. A Pictish carved stone, formerly in a churchyard in the small town of Meigle, now in its museum, was once said to portray her execution. Actually it portrays Daniel in the Lions' Den.

Much the same sort of process underlies the equation of Camlann with the River Camel in Cornwall, started or popularized by Geoffrey. The battle is said to have taken place around the aptly named Slaughter Bridge, where Arthur and Modred fought hand to hand. A battle did take place. John Leland, the Tudor traveler who wrote on Cadbury, was told that "pieces of armour, rings, and brass furniture for horses are sometimes digged up here by countrymen." But the battle was fought by a Saxon King against the Cornish, in 823.

To judge from the version of Nennius which has the sixth-century non-Arthurian battle instead of Agned, such legend-making may have begun quite early. Hence, maybe, Arthur's role at Badon and the original Camlann, wherever it was. The battles were real, but legend and poetry put him in place of other leaders, or added his name to earlier versions. With Badon at any rate there were manifest reasons. A man whom bards and story-tellers had built up into a supreme hero had to be credited with the supreme victory, at the expense of lesser commanders, whom his authentic fame was great enough to eclipse. It was all the easier, since the Britons' second phase of success, toward 500, could readily be confused with the first, in which he did play a part. Thus Arthur acquired his extended life span. A story of the Welsh saint Cadoc, who flourished around the middle of the sixth century, proves independently (as we shall see) that legend did stretch Arthur's life impossibly far. Prolongations like this happened with other major figures. One was St. Patrick, who presents a problem quite like Arthur's. If everything is counted in, Patrick has to die at the age of one hundred and twenty, so some historians have proposed a "two Patricks" theory like the potential "two Arthurs" theory.

That may be enough, yet it is not satisfying. Arthur's connection with such weighty events should be more than a mere confusion or falsification. A remote but thought-provoking clue comes from another form of life-prolongation which is believed to account for the great ages of some of the biblical patriarchs. A man such as Abraham could blur and blend into the lore of his people, and come to be associated with all their doings. Tradition regarded the leader with his kinsfolk as, in effect, a unity. The acts of the group went on counting as his even after he was dead. One piece of evidence shows how a process rather like this could have supplied a matrix for stories extending Arthur's career.

A Welsh poem in a medieval collection, the *Black Book of Carmarthen,* extols a King called Geraint. His home country was Dumnonia, corresponding roughly to what is now the West Country, the long limb of England stretching down to Land's End. The scribe who gave the poem a heading thought it was about a Geraint who lived at the end of the sixth century, but this was an error. The Geraint of the poem flourished a hundred years before.

As it stands, the poem is centuries later, but it looks like a rehandling of one composed by a poet who was, or could have been, an eyewitness of the event he sings about. The theme is Geraint's prowess at the battle of Llongborth. Llongborth means "Warship Port," and the place is likely to be Portchester, by Portsmouth Harbour opposite the Isle of Wight. The *Anglo-Saxon Chronicle* mentions a clash hereabouts and assigns it to the year 501. Archaeology confirms that incoming Saxons occupied a Roman fort. So this may be a unique case, a Saxon-British battle in the relevant period which is put on record by both sides. It merits attention.

The poet praises Geraint in a series of three-line stanzas.

> Before Geraint, the enemy's scourge,
> I saw white horses, tensed, red.
> After the war-cry, bitter the grave. . . .
>
> In Llongborth I saw the clash of swords,
> Men in terror, bloody heads,
> Before Geraint the Great, his father's son.
>
> In Llongborth I saw spurs
> And men who did not flinch from spears,
> Who drank their wine from glass that glinted.

And so forth. But he interrupts the sequence with three lines about someone else.

> In Llongborth I saw Arthur's
> Brave men who cut with steel,
> The emperor, ruler in toil of battle.

After which he goes on with Geraint again.

The Arthur stanza is not a late insertion, which would have made the hero more prominent. Cool and concise, it hints at the poetic phrases which underlie Nennius's image of a war-leader fighting alongside regional kings. Arthur's "brave men" do fight alongside such a King, namely, Geraint. Arthur is called "the emperor," *ameraudur*, derived from the Latin *imperator*, which, as we saw, may correspond to "High King" (as sometimes in Ireland), though it may only mean "commander in chief." The main point, however, is that he is not present in person. A force described as "Arthur's men"—in the Welsh these words come together, with the adjective "brave" following—is fighting without him, somewhere about the date of Badon. The poem speaks of Geraint's men similarly, but with a marked contrast: the other stanzas leave no doubt that he was there and led them himself, whereas there is no further allusion to Arthur.

This reference to a body of soldiers bearing a leader's name, irrespective of his personal presence, recalls the late-Roman practice of naming military units after individuals. There were Honoriaci, Theodosiani, perhaps a British force named from Ambrosius. The phrase "Arthur's men" might even render a Latin word *Artoriani*. Jordanes says that when the Britons were betrayed in Berry, and Arthur-Riothamus escaped into Burgundy, he took with him "all the men he could gather together." Some might have returned to Britain and carried on as a unit, joining Ambrosius if he was still active. Recruitment of younger members could have kept such a force in being indefinitely, aiding regional kings against the Saxons. Hence the stanza with its passing recognition of "Arthur's men" at Llongborth.

This would, in a proxy sense, have extended Arthur's career. The stanza has an ambiguity which would have helped. One or two modern translators have preferred something like "Arthur [and] brave men." That seems far less probable, but if a doubt can arise with modern translators, it could have arisen before. The phrase "Arthur's men" on a bard's lips could have been wrongly heard or wrongly remembered as "Arthur and his men," making the late leader present in person. His association with Badon, when he was not actually there, could have been brought about by the presence of warriors fighting under his name. They would have supplied leadership, experience, encouragement. Possibly a bard made a poem about the Badon victory like the Llongborth poem, including praise for the deeds of "Arthur's men," and this became "Arthur and his men," turning an honorary presence or presence in spirit into a literal one, which there was ample willingness to believe in.

Camlann is the problem rather than Badon. Poets and storytellers would have wished to connect Arthur with a triumph, but why with a disaster, unless they had solid grounds? Here if anywhere is the case for a second, lesser Arthur, who came to be confused with the first. But the problem can be solved without him. Perhaps a quarrel broke out among the last remnant of "Arthur's men" which wiped them out as a force. A bard composed a lament telling how "Medraut stirred up the strife of Camlann and Arthur's men perished." In due course the phrase became "Arthur and his men." Perhaps they had been using Cadbury as a base, and fought to the death beside the River Cam, which flows nearby and is an acknowledged candidate for Camlann. Between the river and the hill a farmer once unearthed a multiple burial.

The King

To the question Was King Arthur real? we now have an answer. The Arthur of Geoffrey and the romancers is a legend. But he has a real original, the British High King who was in Gaul. This is the person Geoffrey and others are speaking of when they speak of Arthur, however distortedly some conceive him, however near some may be to losing sight of him. He was there all along; recognition has been delayed because the records are scanty and disjointed, and scholars have missed several of them through making unwarranted assumptions. Also, of course, because he is transmitted under a name in most contexts but under a title in those which prove his reality.

Anyone who followed the debates over the "historical Arthur" will ask a further question. Is the High King a radically new Arthur who consigns him to oblivion?

The first point to make is that Arthur-Riothamus is not actually new at all. He has priority. Sharon Turner hit on him long ago, but failed to pursue the insight, so that it dropped out of memory in a footnote. The second point is that the scholars' "historical Arthur" was never historical. He was a construct made of Welsh odds and ends, based on the impression that a real person lurked behind them. The impression was correct. However, history's real datum was not the construct but the Arthurian Fact, the Britons' resurgence. Arthur was the symbolic hero of this. On balance, those who studied the problem usually found it easier to believe that he had existed. But his cash value was only a medley of legends and demilegends about his martial exploits.

Arthur-Riothamus can accommodate most of these exploits. Extended by way of "Arthur's men," he can accommodate all of them, bringing the Welsh matter into focus at last. He is not a rival to a Welsh Arthur; he is an authentic figure in history with the Welsh Arthur as a bard-projected aspect. Insofar as the latter may seem different, the reason lies in the lapse of time and the change of circumstances. Welsh poetry took shape as the language did, in the sixth century. Its first notable school was in the wild North, more than a hundred years after Arthur-Riothamus. When bards took up the folk memories, they cast him in the mold of a society which, by then, was half barbarized itself. The fullness of the original was beyond their ken. They spread him out into a period they could grasp better, and confined their treatment of him to the heroic aspect they understood, altering him as those German minstrels altered the great Theodoric.

But the real Arthur-Riothamus grew up in a Britain where Roman culture survived, and many were still living who had been born into the Empire. Sidonius wrote to him in highly wrought Latin. We cannot at present add much about him, except this: his background and career make him more like the Arthur of legend, worthier and more intelligible as the inspiration for him, than any "historical Arthur" proposed hitherto. He was the High King in whose reign Britain was, for a while, retrieved from disaster. He was the Briton to whom an Emperor turned as Rome's last hope in the West. Under his leadership Britons reentered the imperial scheme and might, in their part of Europe, have set it up again. Hence he was the nearest thing to a *Restitutor* in that quarter which the last agonies produced. Some poem or chronicle, it would seem, commemorated him as such. It is certainly *as if* it did, and the substance found its way through unknown channels to Geoffrey of Monmouth.

In his *History of the Kings of Britain*, Geoffrey created not only a resurgent Arthurian Britain, but something like a resurgent Empire. He drew traditions together, reconstituting a King who embodied centuries of legend-making. He portrayed a young, charismatic Arthur quelling barbarians and reestablishing the realm. He gave the reign a new, pointed-up, dramatic shape, adopting not only the early campaign but Badon and Camlann, transformed in the interests of his artistry. Badon, as Bath, now came directly after the early battles, lifting the reign to a first climax in Britain. Geoffrey exploited Gildas's few words about a post-Badon lull, depicting a fresh start and a glorious peace, with the King presiding over his knighthood. Continental conquests followed. A second phase of peace evoked the magnificence of his court, and the stage was set for all the romances to come. After that, Geoffrey made the major Gallic campaign—correctly, in the time of Leo—raise the reign to a loftier climax, from which he brought it down in tragedy, through an embellished Camlann incorporating the hateful betrayal. Out of that last touch grew the story of the passing of Arthur which, in Malory's version or Tennyson's, haunts the memory even when the rest may have faded.

To find the basis and nature of his Arthurian achievement in no way reduces it. His creation of King Arthur is one of the most amazing things in literature.

Part III

THE UNFOLDING MYTH

7

Saints, Bards, Heroes

New Ways, New Lives

Arthur-Riothamus opens up vistas in "alternative" history, as it is sometimes called, the history of what might have been. His impact on real history is a different matter. To assess it we must turn back from the personalities to the peoples. By defining the context, we can begin to cross the gulf between the fifth and twelfth centuries, and trace legend-making on its way to the medieval explosion.

The Arthurian Fact is the Britons' rally and temporary success, primarily in their own island but also on the Continent. Their High King played a part in this and, under his real or poetic name Arthur, came to be credited with the major role and made symbolic. The reason may lie in his character, or his fame overseas, or his good fortune at the hands of poets. At present there is no way of telling. From the viewpoint of history it is chiefly the rally itself that matters—the historical fact which Arthur came to symbolize.

It rose to its final climax at the battle of Badon, with three or four decades of semiequilibrium following. Saxons were still encroaching in Hampshire, near Southampton Water, but the burials found by archaeologists show that they were few. Even the boasts of the *Anglo-Saxon Chronicle* never take them far inland, and to judge from Gildas's sketch of the period they went almost unnoticed. In some other areas the settlement process had even gone into reverse. Toward the middle of the sixth century we have a strange telescopic glimpse in the writings of Procopius, a court official at Constantinople. His knowledge of Britain is scanty, but besides travelers' tales of fogs and ghosts, he is able to report a little.

> Three very populous nations possess the island of Brittia, and there is a king over each of them. And the names of these nations are the Anglii, and the Frisians, and the Britons who have their name from the island. And so numerous are these nations that every year great numbers, with their wives and children, migrate thence to the Franks, and the Franks give them dwellings in that part of their land which seems most bare of men.

When Procopius says "Frisians," he means (as one or two other writers do) the original Saxons and their comrades the Jutes, named from their pre-British homeland in Holland. "A king over each" is an undue simplification, though he may have heard of shadowy claims to paramountcy by regional rulers. The triple migration out of Britain to the land of the Franks—that is, Gaul and a part of Germany—is his most striking fact, and a fact it is. The migration of Britons is of course the settlement in Armorica, which was forging ahead strongly in the sixth century with fresh waves of colonists. Most of them came from the West Country. As a result, Brittany and Cornwall were linked for centuries, politically, culturally and economically. Procopius's other migrations are the remarkable ones, yet separate records, plus archaeology, bear him out. Descendants of Vortigern's federates actually were drifting back to the Continent. In 531 a Frankish King received a party of Angles who had crossed over from Britain looking for a home. He enlisted them as soldiers and settled the party in a German district to which they gave a name, Engilin. Clearly, back in the island, British firmness had deterred some of the new people from pressing forward.

This breathing space was a legacy of the "Arthur" phase, and it helped a whole network of British kingdoms to stabilize and survive. They included Dumnonia, or Dyfneint, in the Southwest; Gwent, Dyfed, Powys, and Gwynedd in Wales; Elmet in the

Pennines; Rheged in Cumbria; Clyde, or Strathclyde, an enlargement of Ceredig's domain, in the far North; and beside it, Manau
Guotodin around Edinburgh. Some of the rulers claimed power
on the grounds of their descent, real or alleged, from officehold-
ers in the imperial twilight.

We can put names to several in and around the 540s. Gildas
attacks Britain's kings in general for squabbling among themselves, and picks out five to denounce their sins in detail. One is
Constantine, King of Dumnonia, whom Geoffrey exaggerates to
make him Arthur's successor. Three others, in Geoffrey's hands,
are also inflated into kings of all Britain and strung out after
Constantine, helping to bridge a gap of time which he is not sure
what to do with. The most important of them in real history is
Maelgwn, King of Gwynedd in northern Wales. Memorial inscriptions which tell something about his subjects show that his
kingdom preserved more *Romanitas* than most. He was a tall,
brave, generous man, fiercely energetic, but erratic and unprincipled. He held court in the island of Anglesey—Gildas calls him
"the dragon of the isle"—and tried to assert a hegemony over
other kings, but without much success. The High Kingship, void
by then for most of a lifetime, was past resuscitation.

The kingdoms' security encouraged a fresh development.
The Church sprang to life, especially in Wales. Its stirring was due
largely to a single apostle, St. Illtud, who had grown up while the
fighting against the Saxons was still going on. Allegedly he was
born to emigrant parents in Armorica, and retraced their steps
back to Britain. There he is said to have become a soldier of
Arthur, being his cousin. This part of the story may be a distant
echo of a post-470 assembling of "Arthur's men." Leaving the
army, he founded the monastery of Llantwit Major in southern
Wales.

It was not the first monastery in Britain. No one knows
where or how the monastic way of life had planted itself. The
earliest Briton known to have been a monk is Constans, the son of
the pretender who was proclaimed in 407. Much later, as we saw,
communities were formed in Armorica by fifth-century migrants
who were surely exporting a system they had learned already.
The first monasteries were simple, with groups of hermits living
in cells around a small building used for communal purposes,
chiefly worship. Priority has been claimed by Glastonbury in

Somerset, where Christian hermits settled at a pre-Christian holy place. Even if this was not the first community, it was the first that endured, the first institution in which the Christianity of the Britons got on its feet and stayed upright.

Illtud, however, passed it by and went his own way. The basis of his foundation at Llantwit was work on the land, but he possessed learning as well as practical talents. Gildas calls him "the polished teacher of almost all Britain," and by about 500 his community was becoming a school of leadership, its destined graduates including Gildas himself, Maelgwn, and another monastic founder, St. Samson. Thanks to Illtud's disciples the British Church evolved a new style, adapted to a society where urban centers had ceased to matter much. As the Roman towns had declined, or been wrecked by Saxons, the importance of the bishops had declined with them. Bishops yielded slowly to abbots as the Church's dominant figures, and for many years its key structures were communities like Illtud's.

Their members had a good deal of freedom and many traveled widely, from the Pictish borderlands to Brittany. Behind them was the missionary impulse given to British Christianity by Ninian and Patrick. They went as teachers, doctors, advisers; they improved agriculture, launched public works such as the repair of seawalls, and even planned defense against pirates. Their schools were open to students from Ireland, and their Irish pupils eventually outdid them, making Ireland, for a while, the most civilized country of western Europe. One consequence of the high status of the monk was a high status for the nun. There were communities of women as well as men, sometimes of both, and in them women could recapture their long-ago Druidic importance.

The broader Celtic Church that branched out from western Britain was to flourish for centuries over a large part of the British Isles, fresh and vigorous, and not too heavily encumbered with wealth and officialdom. Celtic Christianity was Catholic, but with a difference that revealed itself in various ways, and conspicuously in its attitude to the old gods and mythologies. This attitude was to be of prime importance in the making of legends, including Arthur's.

On Europe's outer fringes the Celts had retained more of their ancient character. Also, they had not been subjected to the same pressures as Christians on the Continent. Throughout the Mediterranean lands the Church had a long record of martyrdom at the hands of pagan persecutors, egged on by pagan priesthoods. Christians, therefore, saw paganism as diabolic, with gods who were demons, deceivers of the human race. In Britain it was otherwise, since persecution there had been slight. Beyond the Roman frontier it had never happened at all, and the few Christians among the Irish and Picts, so far as we know, were left in peace. So however loudly Celtic clerics might inveigh against paganism, they never found the same feeling of enmity to work upon. In such a milieu, Celtic Christianity could not fail to be subtly different in spirit. Pagan mythology could no longer be literally believed, but it could be adapted. Ancient deities (suitably demoted) could be viewed with friendliness, and survive as kings and queens and enchanters and fairy folk, in the story-telling and poetry of a Christian culture.

Such were some of the results of the Britons' stubborn holding-out. It affected the Saxons also. While they did conquer in the end, the conquest was sporadic and piecemeal. The tide began to flow in their favor in the 540s when an epidemic known as the Yellow Plague spread from the Continent with imported goods. It reached the British part of the island, but not the Saxon part; the Saxons did not import the same goods, and the Britons did not infect them, because resentment and bitterness were inhibiting contact. King Maelgwn of Gwynedd was the plague's principal victim. Many more died, and the Celtic population became relatively weaker.

Yet even when the advance resumed, it did not take the form of a single onslaught. In Anglo-Saxondom itself small kingdoms had solidified during the years of peace. By now they were sharply distinct from one another, with dynasties of their own. A nominal supremacy passed from King to King. Ceawlin of Wessex, Aethelbert of Kent, Raedwald of East Anglia, successively held the title "Bretwalda," "Britain-ruler," but at this stage it was mainly honorary. No Bretwalda could coordinate the regional sovereigns, and they pursued their own policies with varying fortunes. During the second half of the sixth century, triumphant West Saxons broke through to the River Severn not far from Welsh territory. On the other hand, the northern Angles were held back for decades by the kings of Rheged in Cumbria, and forces from Strathclyde that fought as their allies.

In the seventh century general success came at last, and the occupation covered most of what is now England. By then, however, the occupiers themselves had altered, and had far less of their former heathen destructiveness. Roman missions in the South and Celtic missions in the North had Christianized Anglo-Saxondom, so that the England which emerged was not a barbaric blank. It was soon producing distinguished figures: Bede, the great scholar whom we know; Caedmon, counted as the first English poet; Boniface, a missionary himself, who organized the German Church; Alcuin, the foremost political thinker of his day.

Nor was this England a place of intolerant racial "purity." Barriers were crumbling, and a Celtic strain survived in the population. The first clear partnership of Saxons and Britons, the first clear step toward the United Kingdom, occurred at Glastonbury. When the West Saxons arrived, in about 658, their King Cenwalh was a convert to the new faith. Finding a British monastery, he treated it with respect, left its abbot in charge, and made a grant of land. The advent of Saxon monks and abbots did not disrupt its continuity. Glastonbury became a temple of reconciliation, with Irishmen joining it as well. Because of its origins in "Arthurian" Britain, it was one of the places where stories of Arthur were to take shape.

To sum up, the phase after Badon saw several historic processes at work in the island, all tending to avert total ruin, to nurture fresh possibilities, to raise the level of culture. These trends took the course they did because of the long delay in the barbarian conquest, a delay due to the revival associated with Arthur. We cannot know what would have happened otherwise, but we know what did happen, and much of it was good. It would be absurd to credit this to any one Briton. It is not so absurd to see these facts as following on from the Arthurian Fact.

Saga-making

From the Clyde to the Loire the seeds of Arthur's legend were sown. Over all those hundreds of miles descendants of his Britons maintained their identity. It ceased, however, to be a single identity. The language which all had spoken in the fifth century

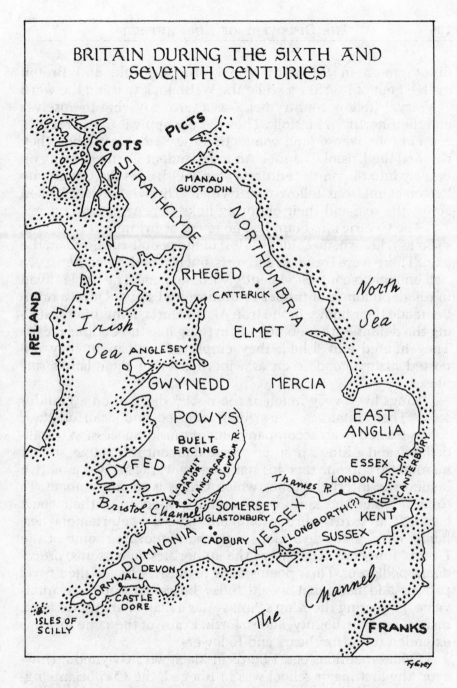

BRITAIN DURING THE SIXTH AND SEVENTH CENTURIES

Showing positions of the chief regional kingdoms. Two of the Anglo-Saxon ones, Northumbria and Mercia, grew greatly during the period. Also shown are places where Arthurian traditions developed.

disintegrated in the sixth, and Welsh, Cornish, and Breton evolved out of it. After a while the Welsh took to using the word "Cymry," "fellow countrymen," as a term covering themselves and their northern kinsfolk. They did not apply it to their southern kinsfolk, whose land connection the Saxons cut when they reached the Bristol Channel. An independent Cornwall hung on bravely into the ninth century, yet in Welsh eyes the Cornish no longer counted as fellow countrymen. Disowned, they looked across the sea, and their enduring links were with Brittany.

The Cymric kingdoms had no towns of any importance, and, so far as is known, no coinage. Most of the people subsisted on the land. There were freemen and serfs, but few of the freemen were rich enough to contrast violently with the poor. The nobles lived in rough buildings of timber or unmortared stone. Quite a number made their homes in the Iron Age hill forts, sometimes restoring the defenses, though not on anything like the Cadbury scale. They hunted and fished; they employed craftsmen; they imported luxury goods such as wine, bartering their land's surpluses.

Kings lived very much as the nobles did, but on a grander scale. Their retainers were finely dressed and colorful; their courts feasted to an accompaniment of music. Succession was ill-defined, and a King's position was seldom entirely stable, so that he might try to enhance his standing by war. This was a motive behind the internal clashes which Gildas is so angry about. In time of peace the kings drew moral support from their court bards. The bards were prominent figures—entertainers certainly, but a great deal more than that, inheriting some of the Druids' functions. They were the authorities on customs, precedents, pedigrees. Their poems, sung to music, extolled their royal patrons and had what would today be called public relations value, projecting the King's "image" as a man of august descent, martial renown, bounty, and so forth. Praise of the same sort was extended to his forebears and followers.

Gildas mentions court bards in Maelgwn's Gwynedd. However, the first major school was in Rheged, the Cumbrian kingdom. It included two poets of lasting fame, Taliesin and Aneirin, some of whose work survives. This has been claimed as the oldest poetry in any living language of Europe, though their Welsh is not modern Welsh.

Through the bards' poetry, their oral storytelling and popularization, the Arthur of the Welsh took shape. His nucleus was a tradition of battles, so the bards made him primarily a warrior. His status apart from that was uncertain, with words applied to him which could mean "emperor" or "commander in chief" or "king." Some copies of Nennius say that "there were many more noble than he," hinting at lowly origins. The same could have been said of some of the greatest Roman emperors, including the soldiers who pulled the Empire together after the crisis of the third century, and gave life to the *Restitutor* idea. The saga of Arthur's leadership drew in other heroes, whom the bards also sang about and made into companions of his, as some perhaps actually were. Bardic genealogical lore preserved names and relationships which Geoffrey was to use most inventively.

The earliest long poetic work has the earliest mention of Arthur by that name: it is brief, but significant. About 598 a prince of Manau Guotodin in Scotland assembled a force from various parts of Britain. After a period of preparation the army journeyed south to attack the Angles at Catraeth, which was the former Roman fort of Cataractonium, now Catterick in Yorkshire. The Britons, outnumbered, fought bravely and nearly all were killed: nearly all the nobles, at any rate. The bard Aneirin was present and composed a series of laments for the fallen which were gathered together under the title *Gododdin*. More verses were added by later poets, so it cannot be proved that the line which names Arthur was in the original, but there is no compelling reason to query it.

What Aneirin says is that a warrior called Gwawrddur "glutted black ravens on the wall of the fort, though he was not Arthur." "Glutting the ravens" was a stock phrase for "killing enemies." The words may mean that although Gwawrddur was not Arthur, he was an equally good raven-glutter, or that he was a valiant fighter though admittedly no Arthur. On either reading they show that Arthur had become proverbial for prowess in battle. That, by the way, is all they show. While the poem is northern, its mention of Arthur does not imply that he was a Northerner, since it mentions warriors who were not, including one from the West Country.

Gododdin gives glimpses of the nobles feasting round open fires, in halls lit by rush candles and pinewood torches. They drink wine and mead from cups of gold, silver, glass, and horn. They attend church and they take baths. Their brightly colored clothing is held by brooches and decorated with beads of amber. In war they wear leather cuirasses and probably simple chain mail; they have swords, white shields, and spears; they ride to the battlefield and apparently fight on horseback.

> Men went to Catraeth, they were renowned,
> Wine and mead in gold cups was their drink,
> A year in noble ceremonial. . . .

> Men went to Catraeth with a war-cry,
> Speedy steeds and dark armour and shields,
> Spear-shafts held high and spear-points sharp-edged,
> And glittering coats-of-mail and swords.
> He led the way, he thrust through armies,
> Five companies fell before his blades.
> Rhufawn Hir gave gold to the altar,
> And a rich reward to the minstrel. . . .

> Warriors rose together, formed ranks,
> With a single mind they assaulted.
> Short their lives, long their kinsmen long for them.
> Seven times their sum of English they slew:
> Their fighting turned wives into widows;
> Many a mother with tear-filled eyelids. . . .

> Wretched am I, my strength worn away,
> Bearing the pain of death in anguish,
> And more, the heavy grief of seeing
> Our warriors falling head over heels.
> And long the moaning and the mourning
> For the countryside's stalwart soldiers. . . .

> May their souls be, after the battle,
> Welcomed to heaven's land of plenty.

Tragedy is closing over the remnant of Arthur's heroic world. A tragedy of Arthur himself, a *Morte d'Arthur,* is the natural literary outcome.

After Aneirin the poems with Arthur in them are mostly anonymous, or ascribed wrongly to Taliesin. One is the Llongborth poem where he is "emperor," and "Arthur's men" make their appearance. Another, of a weirder kind, is best considered in a different context. Stray allusions to Arthur's horse, his kinsfolk (including a son, Llacheu), and his general greatness confirm a growing reputation.

Two poems call for special notice. The first is in dialogue form, and shows how he was pictured as a leader heading a band of paladins. He arrives at the gateway of a fortress and seeks admission.

"Who is the porter?"

"Glewlwyd Mighty-grasp.
  Who asks it?"

"Arthur and Cai the Fair."

"What following hast thou?"

"The best of men are mine."

"Into my house thou shalt not come,
  Unless thou plead for them."

"I will plead for them,
  And thou shalt see them."

Arthur, it seems, has no authority over Glewlwyd. The lines may reflect tales about his early career. His position then could have been comparable to Cromwell's in the English Civil War, when he was leading his famous troop of Ironsides, but was still far from political power. In response to Glewlwyd's demand, Arthur names ten followers. He describes one of them as "Uthr Pendragon's man," though with no hint that the Pendragon is his own father. He speaks highly of Bedwyr, who is the original Bedevere, and his warlike deeds "on the shores of Tryvrwyd." This is the unknown river which Nennius calls Tribruit in the battle list. The fullest praise is for Cai, the original Kay, who is noted for drinking as much as four men, and for slaying witches and monsters. Among the latter is Palug's Cat, which lived in Anglesey and ate 180 warriors. The cat is mentioned in other places. As a kitten it swam ashore from the strait between Anglesey and the mainland, and Palug's sons looked after it, realizing too late that this was unwise. It is spoken of as "speckled." If not a creature of pure fancy, it may have been a leopard which escaped from a ship bringing exotic cargo for a King of Gwynedd. Folk memory would soon have enlarged it.

One further poem is noteworthy for a single line, the earliest Welsh hint at a riddle over Arthur's end. *The Song of the Graves* is a list of warriors with their real or supposed places of burial. A few casual words pick out one of them as unique: *"Anoeth bid bet y Arthur."* The precise meaning of *anoeth* has been debated, but the undoubted sense is "a mystery the grave of Arthur."

Besides Welsh poetry there was Welsh storytelling. Much of it was nostalgic, looking back to a heroic age in the "Island of Britain," the "Island of the Mighty." This age was really a fusion of two periods, the first vaguely before the Roman conquest, the second running from the late fourth century to the seventh. Bardic imagination could blend them, or at least fudge the distinction, because it glossed over the Roman phase between. The second came to be dominated by Arthur. Characters from a wide spread of time were drawn into his saga and added to his company.

Few stories have come down entire, and of those which have, several are too late to show what was being said before Geoffrey. However, the collection known as the *Mabinogion* includes several early ones. Also we have a tantalizing body of "triads"—plot summaries grouped in threes. The motive for the grouping is practical. Each triad has a heading, which applies to all three of the stories summarized, so that any one of them is a reminder of the others. As an illustration, suppose a bard had recited stories from Shakespeare. He might have linked *Othello, Cymbeline,* and *The Winter's Tale* by making up a triad like this:

> Three Jealous Islanders.
> The first was Othello in Cyprus.
> The second was Posthumus in Britain.
> The third was Leontes in Sicily.

When the bard had told the tale of Othello his triad would have reminded him of *Cymbeline,* the play with Posthumus in it, giving him a ready-made encore.

Many triads are late, romantic concoctions, and many are forgeries, but as with the complete stories, some are early and genuine, and quite a number of the characters whom they name were real people. Those that mention Arthur have a curiously primitive air. Several refer to Camlann and his quarrel with

Medraut or Modred, making it sound more like a feud of equals than a subordinate's rebellion. Arthur is one of the Three Famous Prisoners and, unexpectedly, one of the Three Frivolous Bards. As to the latter description, we are told in another place that he annoyed Cai by extemporizing a verse about him, as someone today might make up a limerick. The triad which calls him a Famous Prisoner has been expanded to bring him in. It names three, then adds Arthur as a fourth "who was more famous"— proof of his being special. A cousin, it seems, helped him to escape, but the reason for his imprisonment is not given. Here again there may be a reminiscence of guerrilla adventures in his early career.

By careful study of these triads a fair amount can be pieced together, yet they remain frustrating, and they are far from being a substitute for the actual stories. With Arthur, only one such story has survived which is entirely pre-Geoffrey. This is so rich and thought-provoking that it belongs in a separate discussion. Meanwhile, a natural question is whether the poetry and stories have any Arthurian history in them. Probably none or very little, apart from the odd meaningful phrase like "Arthur's men." However, some of the characters they connect with Arthur may have been real. His comrades-in-arms Cai and Bedwyr stand a good chance; Cai's name is another Roman one, Caius. His enemy, Medraut, may well be authentic. A warrior called Gwalchmai has a shade more substance than most; he becomes Gawain. Women are more doubtful, but Arthur's wife is already Gwenhwyvaer, meaning "white phantom," which of course becomes Guinevere. At least it is likely that Arthur-Riothamus was married.

As early as the ninth century, Cornish matter was becoming intertwined with Welsh. The Cornish might not count as fellow countrymen, but they had traditions which the weavers of saga could not ignore, including the belief that Cornwall was Arthur's home territory. Claims about another hero had a solid basis in the shape of a memorial stone. It can still be seen near the little port of Fowey, and is the only known object from more or less Arthurian times with the name of one of the characters on it. The inscription reads DRUSTANUS HIC IACIT CUNOMORI FILIUS, "Drustanus lies here, the son of Cunomorus." Drustanus Latinizes a name which came to be spelled Tristan. The father is on record as having ruled in Cornwall, and Castle Dore, where

Radford discovered foundations of early buildings, is not far off. Storytellers asserted truly or falsely that Cunomorus was the same person as a King called Mark—that is, Marcus—who figured in the traditions of Wales. This was the genesis of the love-triangle legend of Tristan, Iseult, and her husband Mark, destined to have a long career in romance and opera. While Marcus Cunomorus would be a credible name, it seems likely that Marcus and Cunomorus were different, and King Mark in the legend is a composite character.

The love story of Tristan (whose name has several spellings including Tristram) is not Arthurian in its origin, and is composite rather than purely Cornish. However, it becomes a favorite part of the cycle, and is given a Cornish setting which corresponds loosely to whatever history there may be in it. Tristan is a prince from Lyonesse, supposedly a tract of land that extended Cornwall westward and is now submerged. He is both valiant and cultured, a musician and chess-player. When the Irish King demands tribute from Tristan's uncle, King Mark of Cornwall, Mark refuses and the dispute has to be settled by single combat. The Irish Queen's brother Marhaus comes over as champion, and Tristan, as Cornwall's champion, kills him.

Visiting Ireland, Tristan meets Iseult, the King's daughter. She is skillful in medicine and heals a wound which has troubled him. He has to leave when he is recognized as Marhaus's slayer. Mark sends him to Ireland again to seek Iseult as a bride for himself. Tristan restores friendly relations, but when he is on the way home with Iseult they unknowingly drink some wine with a love potion in it. She marries Mark as arranged, but is compulsively drawn to join Tristan at every opportunity. Their love survives a marriage of Tristan himself, contracted in Brittany. Lancelot befriends them and lets them live for a while in his own castle.

There are different versions of the end. Sometimes it is said that Mark slew Tristan with a spear while he was playing the harp, sometimes that Tristan died through the jealousy of his Breton wife.

If the original Tristan was the King's son, as the monument says, any original Iseult was a young stepmother. In the legend Tristan is the King's nephew. The storytellers may have changed the relationship to render the love affair less discreditable. Tristan was slow to make his way into the Welsh repertoire, but a triad shows that he did, if surprisingly. He is one of the Three Mighty Swineherds, so called because he looked after Mark's pigs while the regular swineherd took a message to Iseult for him. He protected them successfully against rustlers led, also surprisingly, by Arthur.

Beyond Cornwall, developments of the same sort were under way in Brittany. Tales and ballads of the Bretons were also to flow into Arthurian literature. That, however, was a later development. While the Welsh saga was being formed, very little was known or told outside Brittany itself, except for one or two legends about the way the Britons had colonized it.

Arthur and the Saints

Arthur was also taken up in a species of Welsh storytelling which was due not to bards but to clerics. This was hagiography, the writing of so-called lives of the saints. Welsh monasteries cherished traditions about their founders and other eminent members. Over the centuries the facts were usually swamped by legends, not only of a saint's career and achievements, but of his miracles. When official saints' lives came to be written they had far more fiction in them than history, and were largely made up of would-be glorification and edification.

One cliché in these works is a type of anecdote telling how a proud layman was taught a lesson by the saint, or by divine intervention on the saint's behalf. Arthur figures as the layman in several such, so that the lives, on the whole, put him in a poor light. Their authors raise the same queries over his status as the poets and storytellers, but in a spirit which is at best unsympathetic and sometimes hostile. They make him a domineering leader of soldiers; they make him a *tyrannus;* they make him a King, but with some doubt as to whether this is an uncontested and legitimate title. There are few signs of the fidelity to the Church which is implied in Nennius and the *Annales,* where he carries Christian emblems and wins battles by celestial aid.

All the Welsh lives which introduce him were written at the same place, the monastery of Llancarfan near the south Welsh coast. It was a center for the collection, recording, and (it must be said) improvement of ancient traditions. The Llancarfan texts with Arthur in them show the same kind of legend-making as the *Annales*. They spread out his career from the mid-fifth century far into the sixth in order to bring him into the lives of the main characters, for without stretching it, his life would not overlap theirs. However, in two cases the stretching is betrayed by his being given a rank which he could only have had much earlier, and which was long since obsolete when the saints lived.

Llancarfan's account of its own founder, St. Cadoc, starts by telling how Cadoc was born. His mother, Gwladys, eloped with Gwynnlyw, a local ruler in southern Wales. Cresting a hill in flight from her father, Brychan, another local ruler, the couple found Arthur playing dice with his knights Cai and Bedwyr. Arthur stopped them, and looked lustfully on Gwladys. The knights re- minded him of their duty to protect those in need (the earliest hint of an Arthurian chivalric code). When her father caught up, Arthur told him they were on Gwynnlyw's territory, so he could not take his daughter back. The couple married promptly and Cadoc was their firstborn.

Arthur reappears in the same life many years later. When Cadoc was abbot of Llancarfan, it says, he gave sanctuary to a man who had killed three of Arthur's soldiers. The fugitive stayed in the monastery for seven years. Arthur ran him to earth at last, and protested that sanctuary could not be extended so long. When a parley was held on the River Usk, with Arthur on one side and Cadoc on the other, adjudicators upheld Cadoc's right, but awarded Arthur a hundred cows as compensation. Arthur demanded that all the cows should be red in front and white behind. With supernatural aid, Cadoc and his monks produced a herd as requested, and drove them halfway across a ford. When Arthur's soldiers waded in to collect them the cows changed into bundles of fern. Abashed, he conceded Cadoc's right to give sanctuary for seven years, seven months, and seven days.

In the first of these Cadoc episodes Arthur is simply a mili- tary chief. In the second, after a lapse of time extending into the middle of the sixth century, he is called—impossibly—"king of Britain." Nothing reveals how he is supposed to have become so, and the story suggests a rather questionable authority. Another life, that of the great St. Illtud, makes him vaguely a King at a time when Illtud was young—well before 500. Two other lives qualify that view again. St. Carannog's tells how that early saint had a floating altar. He launched it from Wales into the Bristol Channel and vowed to preach wherever it landed. It ran aground on the farther shore near Dunster in Somerset. There Arthur presided as a regional prince, junior to a colleague named Cato. When Carannog arrived Arthur was in vain pursuit of a gigantic serpent which was harrying the neighborhood. He told Carannog he knew where the altar was, and would give it back if the holy man proved his worth by overcoming the serpent. Carannog found and banished it, whereupon Arthur produced the altar, which he had secreted himself. He had tried to use it as a table, but it threw off everything he put on it. A life of St. Padarn is also less than respectful. When Padarn was sitting in his cell, "a certain tyrant named Arthur," from foreign parts, burst in and coveted a fine tunic. Rebuffed, he tried to take it by force. Padarn said, "Let the earth swallow him," and it did. Arthur sank to his chin and had to beg forgiveness before he could get away.

The life of Gildas the historian was also written at Llancarfan by a monk named Caradoc, shortly before Geoffrey's *History;* Geoffrey mentions him. Here Arthur is "king of all Britain," though again with no history as such, and an uncertain-sounding authority—and as with Cadoc, this occurs well on in the sixth century when such a kingship was an impossibility. He impinges on Gildas because of the saint's elder brother Hueil, a piratical northern chief. Arthur captured him and put him to death, an act which made Gildas his enemy, but the two were finally reconciled. Years later Melwas, King of the Summer Land (Somerset), carried off Guinevere and kept her at Glastonbury. Arthur levied troops in Devon and Cornwall and marched to her rescue, but was hampered in his attempts to reach Glastonbury by the watery country round about. The abbot and Gildas, who was living there at the time, negotiated a treaty. The two kings made peace in the monastery church and the lady was restored. This is the first known version of a story that passes into romance, with Lancelot becoming the rescuer. It also gives the first certain connection of Arthur with Glastonbury. The early complex of buildings uncovered by Rahtz's excavation of the hill over the town, Glastonbury Tor, might—perhaps—have been Melwas's citadel.

The Bretons too had their hagiography. We have looked at the preface to the *Legend of St. Goeznovius,* a very important document indeed. Brittany has a life of St. Efflam rather like that of St. Carannog, in which Arthur fails to cope with a dragon, and the saint disposes of it. However, there is no sign that the Welsh knew these items.

The Welsh lives have no trustworthy Arthurian history in them, but they do have points of interest. Three (those of Cadoc, Carannog, and Padarn) portray Arthur as rapacious. This could be a reminiscence of warlords seizing monastic goods to maintain their troops. The lives resemble the lay tradition in the doubt they cast over his status. Yet their different pictures of him could all echo older storytelling about different phases of a real career, if that career was early enough. In the fifth century the same man could have begun as a local princeling with no very exalted background, formed a guerrilla band or private army, and risen to the far from absolute High Kingship through ability or marriage or some sort of coup—or all three combined. This would be quite plausible with Arthur-Riothamus, but not with anyone appreciably later, after the political breakup. The Arthur who confronts Cadoc and Gildas only makes even approximate sense as an anachronism—the holder of a fifth-century paramountcy which, in their time, had passed away.

Arthur on the Map

Meanwhile, Arthur's name had begun to generate local lore and become attached to the landscape. At the end of Nennius's book is an appendix on "The Marvels of Britain," compiled by Nennius or by someone soon after him, in the ninth century. Two consecutive items concern Arthur.

> There is another marvel in the region which is called Buelt. Here is a heap of stones, and on the top of the heap one stone bearing the footprint of a dog. When they hunted the boar Trwyth, Cabal which was the dog of Arthur the soldier, put his foot on that stone and marked it; and Arthur afterwards piled up a heap of stones and that stone on top, on which was the dog's footprint, and called it Carn Cabal. And men come and carry away the stone in their hands for a day and a

night, and the next morning there it is back again on its heap.

There is another marvel in the region which is called Ercing. Here is a burial mound near a spring which is known as Licat Amr, and the name of the man who is buried in the mound is Amr. He was the son of Arthur the soldier, and Arthur himself killed him there and buried him. And men come to measure the length of the mound, and find it sometimes six feet, sometimes nine, sometimes twelve, and sometimes fifteen. Whatever length you find it at one time, you will find it different at another, and I myself have proved this to be true.

Buelt was in south-central Wales, where Builth Wells preserves the name to this day. The hunting of the boar Twrch Trwyth is an early story found in the *Mabinogion.* The name of Arthur's dog, also found elsewhere, is from the Latin *caballus,* "horse." That looks peculiar, and there may have been a misunderstanding. Folklore locates the "marvel" at a hill called Corngafallt. Corngafallt means "Cabal's Cairn" and the hill does have cairns on top, but the identification has been disputed.

Ercing was mainly in what is now the English county of Herefordshire, on the Welsh border. Licat means an eye, or the source of a river, the place water flows from. Licat Amr is Gamber Head, a spring which is the source of the River Gamber. No one knows anything further of Arthur's grim deed. Nor does anyone know how the mound varied in size. The writer doesn't set this down as mere hearsay; he measured it himself. He may be thinking of a burial mound called Wormelow Tump, not far from Gamber Head, but unfortunately this has been leveled and can no longer be measured.

Later, but still before Geoffrey, two more Arthurian sites can be documented. A cleric, Hermann of Tournai, in a history of the shrine of Our Lady of Laon, describes a journey through England made by nine canons of that French city in 1113. Their cathedral had burned down and they were raising funds to rebuild it. With this in view they brought holy relics, and invited the sick to offer donations and pray for healing. On their way from Exeter in Devon to Bodmin in Cornwall, people told them they were entering the land of Arthur, and pointed out "Arthur's Chair" and "Arthur's Oven." These would have been rock formations or prehistoric stone huts. Arthur's Chair cannot now be identified, but Arthur's Oven may have been King's Oven, a stone structure on Dartmoor.

Since 1113 the process has gone enormously further. Arthur's name and fame are perpetuated at well over a hundred spots, stretching from the Isles of Scilly off Cornwall far into Scotland. There are four hills called Arthur's Seat, six stones called Arthur's Stone, eleven more called Arthur's Quoit. There are earthwork "Round Tables" and fancied battlefields.

Some are products of medieval or modern fancy, prompted by romance, yet many look like outgrowths from a senior body of tradition. Two facts tell in favor of this belief. In the first place, the sites and legends are not spread evenly over Britain. The vast majority are in those areas which kept a Celtic identity longest, or keep it still—the West Country, Wales, Cumbria, Northumberland, southern Scotland: regions where the real Arthur could have been active, or, at any rate, descendants of his Britons could have kept tales of him alive. Lore of this kind has seldom taken root anywhere else. Moreover, the topography has shape as well as extent. As remarked before, while there are stories of Arthur in so many counties, only the West Country gives him a birthplace or a home—or, it may be added, a grave.

The second reason for scenting a long past lies in the nature of the lore. Most of it simply does not suggest romance. The image of King Arthur and the knights of the Round Table has long been dominant and accepted, yet in this respect its impact has been slight. Countless imaginations have failed to impress it on the map. The Arthur of local legend is seldom the majestic head of a chivalrous court, and hardly figures at all in great cities and historic settings. He lurks in out-of-the-way places, and on sites so ancient that the centuries blur. Often he seems less like a monarch than a Titan or demigod of dateless antiquity. When he was walking through Carmarthen he felt a pebble in his shoe and threw it away; it flew seven miles and landed on the Gower Peninsula close to the Bristol Channel, where it remains as the capstone of a megalithic ruin. That pebble weighs twenty-five tons.

Arthur Among the Gods

Active in various ways is a process best described as mythification. The tolerance of Celtic Christians toward the old religion
enabled bits of its mythology to survive in their legends. Gods
and goddesses appear, semihumanized, in the *Mabinogion*. To
grasp how this affected Arthur, we need to look at some of them
and draw a distinction.

One is Beli. In his origins he is the god Belinus, worshiped
not only in Britain but in Gaul, even Italy. Welsh legend passes
him through weird transformations. He remains pagan in the
guise of a King conquered by the Emperor Maximus, yet he
becomes quasi-Christian at an earlier date as brother-in-law of
the Virgin Mary. His timelessness allows him to be grandfather to
another god, Bran, who can also be traced a long way back. In the
Mabinogion he is a giant, Bran the Blessed, ruling over Britain in
an age so remote that only a narrow channel divides Britain from
Ireland. Nevertheless, characters from historical times wander
blithely into the story.

A third god who changes roles is Nodons. In Wales he becomes both Nudd and Lludd, "of the silver hand." As Nudd he
has a son Gwyn who is lord of Annwn, the underworld, with a
palace inside Glastonbury Tor. As Lludd he has a daughter Creiddylad; the two have been seen as prototypes of Shakespeare's
Lear and Cordelia. However, he is also a British King Lud who, it
is said, improved Brutus's capital New Troy. It was renamed
Kaer-Lud, "Lud's City," and London is deviously derived from
this. Allegedly, one of the city's gates was called after him, Ludgate, and to this day the front approach to St. Paul's Cathedral is
Ludgate Hill. For good measure it may be added that the two
dragons which Merlin brought to light in Snowdonia were originally put there by Lludd, and that one of his brothers was the
chieftain Cassivellaunus, who led British resistance against Julius
Caesar.

Appraisal of Beli and the rest (there are more, of both sexes)
underlines the fragility of the notion that Arthur himself could
have started out as a god. Whereas inscriptions and other proofs
attest their divinity, nothing attests a British god with the name
Artorius. Gaul has traces of a god whose name began with "Art,"

but Britain has none, and anyhow no recorded form of the name would convert into Arthur. Some advocates of Arthur-as-god have tried to make out that he was a latecomer to the pantheon, worshiped in a pagan revival, and unknown earlier for that reason. The trouble is that there was no pagan revival late enough. Gildas abuses his fellow countrymen for virtually every sin except apostasy. If paganism had taken renewed hold, he would have denounced it. Finally, no god becomes a character of the sort Arthur is. Not one of them is given a proper history, or fitted even loosely into real history. They touch it here and there, glancingly and contradictorily, and that is all.*

A variant of the Arthur-as-god theory is the Arthur-as-purely-mythical-hero theory. One claim which is urged in its favor is that his name is a derivative or echo of a Celtic word for "bear." This would have been *art*, akin to the Greek *arktos* which comes through in the English "arctic," meaning the part of the world beneath the Bear constellations, Ursa Major and Ursa Minor. Many Asian and North American tribes hold bears in religious awe, and several myths tell of prodigious heroes born of unions between a bear and a human parent. Artgenos, "Son of the Bear," occurs as a Celtic name. One medieval writer does try to explain the name Arthur like this. But Arthur has nothing of the bear hero about him. At one point Geoffrey seems to be moving in this direction, when he tells of a dream the King had on his way to the Gallic war. In the dream a bear fights a dragon. When Arthur wakes and discusses it with his companions two interpretations are offered—but in both of them he is the dragon and not the bear!

The Arthur of the Welsh, then, cannot be deprived of his human and historical origin. But this does not prevent him from inhabiting a world where the ancient things press in. Like Maximus, a real Emperor, and Cassivellaunus, a real chieftain, he becomes involved with ex-deities, and themes from their myths are attached to him. A clear case is the tale of Bran's wonder-

---

* Exponents of this kind of theory show a rare talent for self-inflicted wounds. One, having noted a few feeble "parallels" in other mythologies, torpedoes his own credibility with one casual sentence. He says that a representation of Arthur in Otranto Cathedral is encircled by zodiacal signs, "just as Glastonbury was once encircled by a vast system of landscape gardening that represents the Zodiac." This is a "fringe" notion which no serious archaeologist accepts, and which the writer cannot even state correctly himself.

working head. This is one where the pagan antecedents are certain, because of archaeological proofs that the Celts had a cult venerating human heads.

Bran went to war in Ireland and was mortally wounded by a poisoned spear. He told his surviving comrades to cut off his head and take it back to Wales, going first to Harlech, then to Gwales in Penfro. After that they were to go to London, where they should bury the head with its face toward the Continent. They complied. At Harlech, never decaying, it kept them in a state of enchanted bliss for seven years. Then they took it to Gwales and were happy with it for eighty years more. At last one of them broke the spell. They carried the head to London and buried it on Tower Hill as Bran had told them, and it protected Britain against all foreign evils. Arthur, however, dug it up, saying Britain should not rely on talismans but on the military effort under his leadership. A triad condemns this act as one of the Three Wicked Uncoverings. The magic dissolved, and when British resolution waned the Saxons conquered. Even today the fancy of Bran's protection may linger on. The monarchy, it is said, will survive as long as the ravens do in the Tower of London, just by the place where the head was buried; and Bran means "Raven."

Bran may have a share in a far greater piece of mythification, Arthur's immortality and promised return. If this began with a doubt over Arthur-Riothamus, it was no more at first than normal wishful thinking about a lost leader. He had to be still alive, like Sebastian of Portugal. As with Sebastian, however, the belief became supernatural: the King could never die, even after centuries. That conviction, traceable first in Brittany, took hold strongly in Cornwall too. Hermann of Tournai, the same who reports Arthur's Chair and Arthur's Oven, tells of an incident in 1113 when the traveling French canons got to Bodmin. They displayed their relics. A Cornishman with a withered arm approached in hope of a cure. Something brought up the topic of Arthur, and he assured one of the party that the King was alive. The Frenchmen laughed, but the bystanders supported him and a fight broke out. The withered arm remained withered. Hermann, giving his account of this fracas, remarks that the French have the same problem with the Bretons, who insist that Arthur has never died, and seem to think he will come back to help them.

It is not certain when the Welsh began to talk in the same strain. *The Song of the Graves* does not go beyond saying that Arthur's grave is a mystery. The historian William of Malmesbury takes up the topic about 1125, and does add the "return" motif. "The grave of Arthur is nowhere beheld, whence ancient songs fable that he is still to come." However, he may mean Breton or Cornish songs. As to where Arthur is, there are two main notions: one, that he is in Avalon, pictured as an enchanted western island; the other, that he lies asleep in a cave. In the cave a company of his knights may be sleeping too. Neither idea is on record early, but both may well be old, because both seem to be derived from a single myth—one of the few myths of the British Celts to be put on record by a classical author. Though not a god, Arthur has acquired attributes of a god, and he has done it in two ways.

The classical author is Plutarch. In *The Silence of Oracles* he quotes a government agent named Demetrius who was in Britain in A.D. 82 and took down various things which the people told him. They included a myth about a god over the water. "There is, they said, an island where Cronus is imprisoned with Briareus keeping guard over him as he sleeps; for, as they put it, sleep is the bond forged for Cronus. They add that around him are many deities, his henchmen and attendants." Demetrius follows the ancients' annoying practice of giving foreign gods classical names, so we are not sure who is meant. In Greek mythology Cronus was leader of the Titans, the elder gods, and father of Zeus. He ruled the universe in a far-off golden age, but Zeus dethroned and banished him, and became world ruler himself. Briareus was a giant who survived from the older Cronian world. Demetrius has equated the British god with Cronus because of some likeness; perhaps merely that according to one account, Cronus's place of exile was across the Atlantic. Plutarch says more in another work, *The Face in the Moon*, seemingly giving a fuller version of what Demetrius reported. He speaks of some islands over the ocean from Britain, in the general direction of sunset.

The natives [of Britain] have a story that in one of these Cronus has been confined by Zeus, but that he, having a son for gaoler, is left sovereign lord of those islands and of the sea, which they call the Gulf of Cronus. . . .
The natural beauty of the isle is wonderful and the

mildness of the environing air. . . . Cronus himself
sleeps within a deep cave resting on rock which looks
like gold, this sleep being devised for him by Zeus in
place of chains. Birds fly in at the topmost part of the
rock, and bear him ambrosia, and the whole island is
pervaded by the fragrance shed from the rock.

The description adds that he has spirits around him who attended
him in the days of his power.

Here is a dethroned British god asleep in a cave, in a western
island with Avalonian qualities. He supplies both the versions of
Arthur's survival, including prototypes for the sleeping attendants. He may even be the source of one or two further touches.
Cronus sleeps on rock that looks like gold; in Geoffrey's *Life of
Merlin*, when Arthur is taken to the island, he is laid on a golden
bed. Cronus was overthrown by his son; in romance, Modred is
secretly Arthur's son. We might venture further, into more profound possibilities. Greeks dismissed Cronus's golden age as a
closed chapter, but Romans identified him with their god Saturn,
and in the poetry of Virgil his return is foretold. The golden age
will be renewed. Did the Britons say the same of their own lost
god? At any rate, it was prophesied of Arthur, and there could
even be a link with his historic role, because the Romans who had
once looked for a *Restitutor* sometimes quoted the very poem in
which Virgil speaks of a Saturnian reign being reestablished.
Annexing the myth of a golden-age deity who will come back and
"restore," Arthur, the man who actually was seen as a *Restitutor*,
might presumably come again in the same character and "restore" a golden age of his own. The parallel with the god might
even have been suggested first in a panegyrical poem of the kind
imagined in Chapter 6.

Some have claimed that the Celtic god equated with Cronus
was Bran—that is, the original divine Bran. He was more or less
humanized in Ireland as well as Wales, and an Irish tale takes him
across the western sea to a happy island, where he lives for many
years in a spellbound deathlessness. Intriguing from this point of
view is a third, folklore version of Arthur's survival, which is
much less familiar. Cervantes mentions it in *Don Quixote*, saying
that there are people in Britain who think Arthur was turned into
a raven. This seems to have been a Cornish idea. In spite of the

strength of Cornish convictions, that part of Britain has no version of the cave legend. In the eighteenth century, however, on Marazion Green near Penzance, a sportsman who shot at a raven was rebuked by an old man who protested that the bird might be Arthur. Since Bran is "Raven," his identification as the god in Demetrius's account would explain all three immortality motifs. On this showing, Arthur was assimilated to a being who was called the Raven, who slept in a cave with attendants round him, in a fortunate isle over western waters. There we would have the Cornish bird transformation, *and* the cave legend, *and* Avalon, all derived from one of the few ancient British myths for which there is hard evidence.

The cave legend has been recorded in fifteen or more locations, ranging from Cadbury Castle through Wales, to northern England and southern Scotland. A few real caves bear Arthur's name, but the typical tale is of a cave which can only be visited through magic or some rare chance, often with bad results for the visitor.

At Craig-y-Ddinas in the southern Welsh county of Glamorgan, a Welshman is said to have been shown the cave by an English wizard. A bell hung from the roof of the entrance passage. Arthur and his knights lay asleep in a circle, awaiting the day when they should wake up, and restore justice and peace throughout Britain. In the middle were a heap of gold and a heap of silver. The wizard told his companion that he could take whatever he could carry from one heap or the other, but not both, and must be careful not to touch the bell as he left. If he did, and it rang, one of the knights would wake and ask if it was day, and then the only thing to do was to reply, "No, sleep on." The Welshman took gold, so much that he walked clumsily and blundered against the bell. A knight woke and asked the question, and he gave the answer and escaped. The wizard warned him not to squander the gold. Needless to say, he did squander it. He returned to the cave for more, made the same mistake, and forgot the formula. More of the sleepers woke. They gave him a beating and took back the gold. For the rest of his life he was poverty-stricken and infirm from the beating, and could never find the cave again.

In other places the test is different. The story at Sewing-shields in Northumberland is that a farmer was knitting among

Above: The ideal of King Arthur affected by medieval artists was always as a monarch of their own era. This is a detail from the Christian Heroes tapestry, ca. 1385. *Credit: The Metropolitan Museum of Art, Cloisters Collection*

Left: The Third Crusade, led by Richard the Lion-Heart, spread Arthur's fame as far as the distant East and may explain this portrayal of him astride a camel from an early sixteenth-century Flemish stained glass roundel. *Credit: The Metropolitan Museum of Art, New York*

Opposite Page: On this Parisian tapestry (ca. 1385) King Arthur peers anxiously to his right at Guinevere, whose song appears directed to the knight on her right. *Credit: The Metropolitan Museum of Art, Cloisters Collection*

The art of courtly love: On the lid of a thirteenth-century French ivory casket knights joust for their ladies' favors and assault a "castle of love." Both sides use flowers for weapons. *Credit: The Metropolitan Museum of Art, Gift of J. Pierpont Morgan*

The knights are seated at the Round Table in this fourteenth-century French manuscript. Before them is the shrouded Grail. *Credit: Mansell Collection*

Opposite page:

Above: The celebrated "Round Table" in Winchester's Castle Hall dates to a reign in the range from Henry III to Edward III, when it was probably made as a centerpiece for a courtly entertainment. The rose at the center is the Tudor rose painted in later, reflecting the Tudor claim to an "Arthurian" lineage. *Credit: The Hampshire Chronicle*

Below: Edward III planned to revive the knighthood of the Round Table, but founded the Order of the Garter instead. His son, a true believer of the Arthurian ideal, was the Black Prince, whose effigy over his Canterbury tomb this is. *Credit: Edwin Smith*

Here at Leeds Castle the young widow of Henry V fell in love with Owen Tudor, a Welsh prince who claimed Arthurian descent. Their grandson was the future Henry VII. Leeds has been called "a vision of Camelot." *Credit: British Tourist Authority*

Henry VII is seen here smugly holding the Tudor rose, which symbolized the unity he brought to a country torn apart by the war between the White Rose of York and the Red Rose of Lancaster. He named his eldest son Arthur. *Credit: National Portrait Gallery, London*

Sir Galahad by G. F. Watts, R.A. Pre-Raphaelite painting's love for Arthurian themes reflected the popularity of Queen Victoria and her poet, Alfred Lord Tennyson, who together revived interest in the romances to such an extent that nobles in Scotland built fairy-tale castles. *Credit: Mansell Collection*

James Archer's Pre-Raphaelite *The Death of King Arthur* shows the once and future King about to be borne off across the water to the magic isle of Avalon by the mysterious women in his life.   *Credit: Mansell Collection*

the castle ruins (since demolished) when the wool fell down a crevice. He followed it to an underground chamber where Arthur was sleeping, together with Guinevere and their courtiers and a pack of hounds. Three objects lay on a table: a horn, a sheathed sword made of stone, and a garter. To restore Arthur to the world, the procedure was to draw the sword, cut the garter, and blow the horn. The farmer got as far as cutting the garter, and Arthur woke. Then, alas, he sheathed the sword. Arthur said:

> O woe betide that evil day
>   On which this witless wight was born,
> Who drew the sword, the garter cut,
>   But never blew the bugle-horn!

And went back to sleep. In a version told of the Eildon Hills, near Melrose in Scotland, the victim faces much the same test and makes the opposite mistake, blowing the horn without drawing the sword. As the sleepers stir he becomes panic-stricken, a violent wind blows him out of the cave, and he dies soon after. Alderley Edge in Cheshire and Richmond Castle in Yorkshire have similar stories of a visitor who comes to grief through failure of nerve.

Variants of the cave legend spread through Europe during the Middle Ages. Arthur was said to be inside the Sicilian volcano Etna, while other rulers, such as the German Emperor Frederick, were installed by legend in caves of their own. On both sides of the Channel, Arthur became involved with a related motif, the Wild Hunt, which figures in the folklore of several countries. Departed heroes emerge from whatever retreat they occupy, and rush through the clouds as sky-borne horsemen, with supernatural beings and ghosts. Sometimes they descend to earth. A French version with Arthur in it, the *Chasse Artu,* is primarily Breton. In Wales the chief hunter is Gwyn ap Nudd, the semihumanized son of the god Nodons. Gwyn's hounds, white-bodied and red-eared, round up the unquiet spirits of wrongdoers and, some say, unbaptized infants. Arthur's joining in the Hunt probably accounts for the phantom horsemen and "hunting causeway" at Cadbury. Farther north it may account also for the fearsome Arthur O'Bower. The children's writer Beatrix Potter quotes a riddle about him in *Squirrel Nutkin:*

> Arthur O'Bower has broken his band,
> He comes roaring up the land!
> The King of Scots with all his power
> Cannot turn Arthur of the Bower!

The answer is "the wind," which he personifies.

As lord of Annwn, the Welsh underworld or otherworld, Gwyn ap Nudd has strange subjects. A cryptic Welsh poem *The Spoils of Annwn* describes (if "describe" is the right word) how Arthur and his followers made a raid on his realm in quest of a magic caldron. The quest belongs to his mortal career, not its sequel, but the atmosphere is altogether unearthly. Composed in the tenth century, the poem is a forerunner of the Grail stories. Its imagery is pre-Christian. Annwn is a region of water-crossings and islands and eerie fortresses. The adventure is perilous, and as with the Grail quest, many never return from it. Arthur's ship *Prydwen* plies back and forth, taking three full loads of warriors, and only a handful of them escape.

One stanza has a special interest.

> The first word from the cauldron, when was it spoken?
> By the breath of nine damsels it is gently warmed.
> Is it not the cauldron of the chief of Annwn, in its fashion
> With a ridge around its edge of pearls?
> It will not boil the food of a coward or one forsworn. . . .
> Before the portals of the cold place the horns of light shall be
>   burning.
> And when we went with Arthur in his splendid labours,
> Except seven, none returned from Caer Vediwid.

The nine female custodians recall actual sisterhoods in the Celtic world. The Roman geographer Pomponius Mela, writing a little before Plutarch, tells of nine priestesses on the Île de Sein off the coast of Brittany. They cured the sick and were reputed to possess magical powers. Geoffrey presents Morgen, the lady of Avalon, as having similar talents—healing, flight, shape-shifting—and as heading a group of nine.

Fantasies

Stories like Plutarch's and Pomponius's have inspired theories of a more fundamental kind. Ancient, even non-Celtic myth has been detected in a whole medley of other ways, attaching itself to Arthur's name, surfacing in Welsh legend and medieval romance. Some have thought that the entire Arthurian cycle, or the bulk of it, is a mythology transplanted from a different time or place, and disguised. In other words, mythification is the key, not only to a few themes, but to virtually everything. It explains all that developed between the fifth century and the twelfth.

In 1891 Sir John Rhys argued that all the main Arthurian characters were Celtic deities and mythical figures. Even the themes of the romances were pre-Christian. He admitted a real Arthur, a fifth-century commander in chief, but merely as providing a pseudohistorical setting. The connection was suggested, perhaps, by his name happening to resemble a god's. This avoids the difficulties in making Arthur *only* a god. But Rhys's Celtic system depends on obsolete theories of myth, guesswork about the meanings of names, and "evidence" in romances as late as Malory's in the fifteenth century. It has few if any supporters today.

A kindred, more recent theory looks toward the Alps. In Savoy, and around Lake Geneva, there is a pocket of Arthurian place names and local legends. About 1260 a certain Étienne de Bourbon tells of a Savoyard woodcutter meeting a hunting party at night near the Mont du Chat. They said they were of Arthur's household, and he followed them into a palace full of dancers and banqueters. Offered a bed beside a beautiful lady, he took his pleasure and fell asleep, but woke lying in the open on a bundle of faggots. In another of the stories the Mont du Chat is the scene of a combat between Arthur and a cat of huge size, the "Chat" in question. According to one view the Lake Geneva area is the old Celtic heartland, and its Arthurian legends are the originals. They were transferred to Brittany and from there to Britain.

It really does not work. The saga of the terrible cat, for instance, began (as we saw) in Anglesey off the north coast of Wales. Its Welsh designation, Palug's Cat, is the original, and its French one, Chapalu, is a corruption of this. Nothing shows that the legends, in this setting, are very old. Still, it is interesting to find them here at all, not so immensely far from the last known location of Arthur-Riothamus.

John Darrah, author of *The Real Camelot,* is radical in terms of time rather than place. He accepts that the stories belong in

Britain, but shifts them back thousands of years. While Arthur was real, he annexed a mythology that took shape in the Bronze Age, the second millennium B.C. This was centered on a proto-Arthur who was more a divine symbol than a person. Darrah takes up a line of thought which depends largely on Frazer's celebrated *Golden Bough* anthropology. Darrah's main theme is sacred kingship, though there are several others. The germ of his work is Geoffrey's account of Merlin's bringing Stonehenge over the sea from the West. Geologists have maintained that some of the smaller uprights of that monument, the bluestones, were brought from the Prescelly Mountains in Wales by sea. If so, Geoffrey would seem to have known a valid tradition fully three thousand years old. Professor Stuart Piggott suggested that it was transmitted by a priesthood, who worked it up into "the only fragment left to us of a native Bronze Age literature." Darrah thinks more of the literature survived.

His real Camelot is Stonehenge, as the ritual center of early Britain. In support of his opinions he cites what is said by a Greek, Hecataeus of Abdera, about a "round temple" in the island. The Arthurian legend is a Bronze Age religious saga, variously adapted to Welsh storytelling and chivalric romance. Like Rhys, Darrah is willing to detect myths even in Malory. Two comments are called for, perhaps. One is that geologists now deny the necessity of the bluestones having come from Prescelly, though this may be true. The other is that Hecataeus's temple cannot be Stonehenge, because the Greek word translated as "round" never means "circular." It means "spherical," and since no British temple could have been spherical, it is probably a mistake for some other word.

A fourth theory, more exotic still, has had more support. This is the theory of the Sarmatian Connection, expounded by Helmut Nickel, C. Scott Littleton, and Ann C. Thomas. They draw attention to a tribe called the Ossetes, who live in a valley in the Caucasus and have a cycle of folktales about heroes known as the Narts. Several of these tales have Arthurian echoes. In one a dying warrior's sword has to be thrown into the water, as Excalibur is. In others much is made of a magic vessel recalling the Grail or the caldron of Annwn. The Ossetes are descended from the Sarmatians, a people who were once spread over eastern Europe. What is proposed is that the tales of the Narts are ancient

Sarmatian mythology. The same tales were brought to Britain by
Sarmatians imported as Roman auxiliary troops in the second
century A.D. Their commander was the already mentioned Lucius Artorius Castus. The name Artorius, it is urged, could have
gone the same way as Caesar and been adopted as a kind of title
by successive heads of a Sarmatian community in Britain. Such a
group could have kept its ethnic identity, and one of its leaders
could have been an Artorius who fought Saxons. The ancestral
mythology of the Narts, ready-made, would then have flowed
into his saga. (When the Sarmatian Connection was first publicly
aired, headline-writers found the phrase "Narts of the Round
Table" irresistible.)

These theories, and others, have drawn attention to facts
which are worth discussing. The cause for regret is that each
advocate claims to have the whole truth, the secret of the Arthurian legend. When asserted like that, every theory leaves gaps
and unanswered questions. If the whole legend belonged to the
Lake Geneva area, its transfer to Britain was a vast, complicated,
and mysterious fraud. Why did French romancers accept the
relocation without protest? If the whole legend was a religious
saga of the Bronze Age, it had, as Darrah says himself, "no bearing on the history of the fifth or sixth centuries A.D." Why was it
ever associated with someone who lived then, and was almost
certainly a Christian? If the whole legend was an import, confined to a colony of barbarians, it was utterly foreign to the peoples of Britain. How did it come to displace their own traditions,
and get transposed into British terms as a national mythos?

Further, of course, when views like these are maintained
unyieldingly they contradict each other and the case for each
wipes out the rest. Taken together, they reinforce a point urged
before: that those who make Arthur a myth, or predominantly a
myth, have never explained the "how" of it. We could now add
that this has not been for want of trying. Several have tried, and
they have all come up with different "hows," none satisfactory
and all mutually destructive.

Yet it is shortsighted to write such notions off entirely. The
effect of pondering several together is a feeling that the legend is
richer, more complex, than any one theorist has allowed. A reading of the romances amply confirms that view. But even before
the romances the same impression is given by the single Welsh

story of Arthur that survives in its entirety from the period before
Geoffrey, "Culhwch and Olwen." Culhwch is pronounced "Kil-
hooch," with the *ch* as in "loch." The story is in the *Mabinogion*.
In its present, eleventh-century form it is a product of many
years of enlargement, and has become a catchall. Its medley of
elements could not have been drawn from one narrowly defined
source. No known traces of Celtic myth, in Britain or Savoy, come
anywhere near to giving an adequate groundwork. Nor does any
bundle of anthropological motifs or any Nart saga explain it.
Moreover, all such speculations are swamped by the tale itself—
by its verve, color, and ferocity, its wild humor and occasional
beauty. "Culhwch and Olwen" shows how the Welsh Arthur had
developed in popular imagination shortly before Geoffrey. It also
shows, once again, that Geoffrey was not developing him further,
but recreating an Arthur closer to history with the aid of other
materials.

Culhwch's stepmother lays him under a curse. He cannot
marry unless he weds Olwen, the daughter of Ysbaddaden the
Chief Giant. Believing she will favor him, but foreseeing obstacles, he goes to ask help from Arthur, who is his cousin.

Off went the boy on a steed with light-grey head, four
winters old, with well-knit fork, shell-hoofed, and a gold
tubular bridle-bit in its mouth. And under him a pre-
cious gold saddle, and in his hand two whetted spears of
silver. A battle-axe in his hand, the forearm's length of a
full grown man from ridge to edge. It would draw blood
from the wind; it would be swifter than the swiftest
dew-drop from the stalk to the ground, when the dew
would be heaviest in the month of June. . . . And two
greyhounds, whitebreasted, brindled, in front of him,
with a collar of red gold about the neck of either, from
shoulder-swell to ear. The one that was on the left side
would be on the right, and the one that was on the right
side would be on the left, like two sea-swallows sporting
around him. . . . Never a hair-tip stirred upon him, so
exceeding light his steed's canter under him on his way
to the gate of Arthur's court.

The gatekeeper is Glewlwyd Mighty-grasp, the same who confronts Arthur in the dialogue poem, now in Arthur's service himself. He is unwilling to open. "Knife has gone into meat, and drink into horn, and a thronging in Arthur's hall. Save the son of a king of a rightful dominion, or a craftsman who brings his craft, none may enter." Culhwch, however, threatens him. "I will raise three shouts at the entrance of this gate, so that it shall not be less audible on the top of Pengwaedd in Cornwall and in the depths of Dinsel in the North, and in Esgeir Oerfel in Ireland. And every woman with child that is in this court shall miscarry." Glewlwyd goes off to tell Arthur, confessing that he has never seen such a fine fellow as the one at the gate; not in many years of travel in India, Africa, Corsica, and other surprising places, nor as Arthur's companion when he "conquered Greece unto the east" (a throwaway line—there are many). Arthur says Culhwch should not be left outside in the wind and rain. So the suitor gets in.

As usual, Arthur's status is uncertain. Culhwch salutes him as "sovereign prince of this Island," yet one reason why the prospect is doubtful is that he has no authority over Ysbaddaden. The giant, in fact, claims authority over Arthur. The storyteller gives a long list of members of the court. They are hard to count exactly, but a fair assessment would be 227 men and 29 named women. They include several familiar figures, such as Cai and Bedwyr again, and Gwenhwyvaer, "the first lady of this Island." They also include Gildas, the historian; Taliesin, the poet; Gwyn son of Nudd, "in whom God has set the spirit of the demons of Annwn lest this world be destroyed"; and Creiddylad daughter of Lludd, the proto-Cordelia. They also include Sgilti, who can run along the treetops; Sugyn, who can drink up a sea till three hundred ships lie stranded; Uchdryd, who can toss his red beard over the rafters of the hall; and Clust, who can hear an ant stirring fifty miles off. They also include three "kings of France"—we are a long way from historical fact. They do not include Tristan, or Lancelot, or Galahad, or Perceval. Snippets of information in passing refer to Arthur's Cornish home, Kelliwic, and to the future battle of Camlann.

Arthur promises his help. Some of the warriors accompany Culhwch to the giant's fortress, and a shepherd's wife persuades Olwen to come out.

> She came, with a robe of flame-red silk about her, and
> around the maiden's neck a torque of red gold, and
> precious pearls thereon and rubies. Yellower was her
> head than the flower of the broom, whiter was her flesh
> than the foam of the wave. . . . Whoso beheld her
> would be filled with love of her. Four white trefoils
> sprang up behind her wherever she went; and for that
> reason was she called Olwen.

(Because of the trail of magic flowers; Olwen is said to mean
"White Track.") Culhwch explains his errand, and she is compli-
ant. Her father is not. The giant is also under a spell, and doomed
to die when his daughter finds a husband. Several suitors have
vanished already. Culhwch visits him three times, and each time
the result is an altercation. Ysbaddaden throws a poisoned spear
at him, but without effect.

> Culhwch caught it and hurled it back, even as he
> wished, and pierced him through the ball of the eye, so
> that it came out through the nape of his neck. "Thou
> cursed savage son-in-law! So long as I am left alive, the
> sight of my eyes will be the worse. When I go against
> the wind they will water, a headache I shall have, and a
> giddiness each new moon."

Culhwch tries once more. The giant now agrees to the marriage in principle, but makes preposterous conditions meant to
avert it. To prepare the bread for the wedding feast, Culhwch
must clear away a wood, plough the soil, sow and reap, all in one
day. To boil the meat he must get the caldron of Diwrnach the
Irishman. To hold the milk he must get the bottles of Rhynnon
Stiff-beard in which no liquid ever turns sour. To dress Ysbaddaden's hair for the occasion he must fetch a comb and scissors
from between the ears of Twrch Trwyth, a King who was turned
into a boar for his sins. The list of things required for this wedding
goes on and on, and the chief labors involve subsidiary ones,
bringing the total up to forty.

Culhwch returns to the court, and Arthur and his followers
set to work. The story of the labors introduces more characters,
among them another giant, a witch, talking animals, and an un-

doubted god, Mabon, who is the Celtic deity Maponus. Arthur makes use of his ship *Prydwen*, the one he took to Annwn. The climax is the hunting of the boar Twrch Trwyth, the adventure mentioned in Nennius's "The Marvels of Britain." Twrch Trwyth is colossal, and inflicts heavy casualties on the hunters. He leads them a long chase and finally swims out to sea off Cornwall, but not before they have got the comb and scissors. Culhwch claims his bride, and an enemy chops the giant's head off.

8
Majesty

Arthur Rediscovered

As a country united under one sovereign, England grew from the early kingdom of Wessex, the realm of the West Saxons. The Wessex dynasty's founder was Cerdic, who dominated a few Saxon settlements near the Hampshire coast. His successors pushed slowly inland by way of Salisbury. The main West Saxon population, however, was in and around the Thames Valley. Through some unknown agreement the smaller body merged with the larger, and descendants of Cerdic reigned over the entire complex. Their kingdom gradually expanded till it stretched from Cornwall to Kent. Under Alfred the Great it just survived a Norse onslaught in the ninth century, and after him it advanced through the Midlands and farther, by consent more than conquest. Alfred's grandson Athelstan ruled the whole of the territory which the Anglo-Saxons had made their own. This was now properly called England.

In 1066 William, Duke of Normandy, took over the kingdom, and Normans moved in from their homeland across the Channel as a new governing and landowning caste. After a few decades they were less sharply distinct from the native English. For three centuries, nevertheless, England was to have a French-speaking nobility and kings with Continental domains. The Norman Conquest led to a migration of Bretons back to their ancestral island. They came over with the Normans and shared in the spoils. One by-product was that Breton minstrels brought tales of Arthur, and compared notes with the Cornish and Welsh. They may have brought the prophecy of his Second Coming, and their presence certainly helped to prepare the ground for his rediscovery. The Anglo-Saxons had never had any interest in him, since from their point of view he was an enemy. Wherever they were in charge, except in parts of the West Country, the memories of him had virtually expired. Now these began to flow in again from the Celtic fringe.

About 1125 the historian William of Malmesbury wrote an ably researched book, *The Acts of the Kings of the English.* He revised portions of it after visiting Glastonbury, where the monastic community, having existed without a break from pre-Saxon times, preserved traditions that were little known anywhere else. William mentions the mystery over Arthur's grave, and his predicted return, in a sentence already quoted. He also has a paragraph of Arthurian history. He is aware of the crucial fact which authors after him obliterate: that Ambrosius and Arthur were active at the same time, directly after Vortigern. There, however, his information gives out, and by a guess based on a few words of Nennius he allots the royal title to the wrong one. "Ambrosius, who was monarch of the realm after Vortigern, repressed the overweening barbarians through the distinguished achievement of the warlike Arthur." He accepts Arthur's personal role at Badon, despite the time problem. Conscious of the obscurities, he voices a hope that some other scholar will sort things out. "This is that Arthur of whom the trifling of the Britons [probably the Bretons] talks such nonsense even today: a man clearly worthy not to be dreamed of in fallacious fables, but to be proclaimed in veracious histories, as one who long sustained his tottering country."

William's suggestion was taken up halfheartedly by Caradoc of Llancarfan and Henry of Huntingdon. Caradoc wrote that life of Gildas which brings Arthur in, as a fifth-century High King displaced. (An earlier life of the same saint says nothing about him.) Henry inserted a mention of Arthur's battles in a narrative of the Saxon invasion, dating them only by a vague retrospect of "those times," stuck in at random between 527 and 530. Henry calls him "the leader of the soldiers and kings of Britain," which, by accident or design, is quite a good phrase. But the author who made the major response was of course Geoffrey of Monmouth. In a postscript to the *History of the Kings of Britain* he names the previous three—William, Caradoc, Henry—and tells them to leave those kings to him, because he alone has the "ancient book in the British language."

Of Geoffrey's aims and achievement in the *History,* little more needs to be said, and mostly by way of recapitulation and summing-up. He wanted to give the Welsh and Bretons a glorious past. He wanted to flatter the ruling Normans (or some of them) by making them inheritors of a splendid kingdom, with historic claims beyond England. Concerning Arthur himself he knew the Continental tradition, seemingly through Breton channels, and on to this he grafted Welsh material—chiefly battles, and characters already connected with Arthur, such as Kay and Bedevere. Like William of Malmesbury, he knew the correct dating, though on reflection he confused it. Generally he kept clear of the mythical and fairy-tale themes. Some of these were to find their way into romance all the same, notably the quest for a wonder-working vessel. Geoffrey himself turned to the marvelous later in his verse *Life of Merlin,* introducing legends which he had not known when he wrote the larger work.

Some of the romancers who came afterward retold parts of the *History,* but on the whole Geoffrey supplied the framework for romance rather than the main impulse. He gave substance to Arthur and the court. The Round Table, when first mentioned by his French adapter, Wace, is said to have been devised in this shape so that all places should be equal and there should be no wrangles about precedence among the knights. After Wace its story grows more elaborate. In the anonymous romance *The Quest of the Holy Grail* Merlin is stated to have designed it to symbolize the round universe. There is also a symbolism going back to the table of the Last Supper. As that one had a place for Judas of ill omen, so Arthur's has the Siège Perilous, a chair which no one can safely occupy except the knight destined to accomplish the Grail quest. Merlin made the table for Uther, Arthur's father. It passed into the possession of the father of Guinevere, and then to Arthur himself when he married her. Sometimes it is alleged to have seated 150 knights—a number which raises a problem about its size, and the resulting inaccessibility of most of its surface. One artist solves the problem by making it ring-shaped, with gaps for servitors to pass through.

Wace, in his adaptation of Geoffrey, also explained where the knightly adventures fitted in. The adventures themselves, however, were due to authors with other sources of inspiration. There may be one exception, a remarkable one. A few of the romances were written in Latin. Among them is *De Ortu Walwanii*, The Rise of Gawain. Its supposed author is Robert of Torigni, abbot of Mont-Saint-Michel from 1154 to 1186. Robert is the first person known to have had a copy of Geoffrey's *History*, which he showed to Henry of Huntingdon in 1139. He also wrote a continuation of that chronicle by Sigebert of Gembloux which Geoffrey may have taken hints from, and mentioned Geoffrey and his work in it. Robert's authorship of *De Ortu* has been denied, but Dr. Mildred Day, its editor and translator, defends it. If she is right, *De Ortu* is a unique hybrid, a romance inspired directly by Geoffrey and written by a historian.

The reason for taking special notice of it lies in what is hinted about the time of the action. The author expands a few words in the *History* telling how Gawain spent his youth in Rome. He says the boy was brought there soon after a sacking of the city by barbarians. After sundry adventures Gawain returns to Britain and becomes an honored member of Arthur's court. The conspicuous detail here is the sack of Rome, a historian's touch. It could be the Gothic sack in 410 or the Vandal sack in 455, implying in either case that the author saw the fifth century as the period Geoffrey indicates for the action. However, if the author was Robert, a man as well read as he would not have put the story as far back as 410, because it would not have harmonized with any workable date for Arthur. The sack of Rome has to be the Vandal one in 455, and several of the incidents can be neatly explained as based on real happenings during the years 455–70, perhaps even on Sigebert's record of them. *De Ortu Walwanii* may give us another glimpse of the chronicle tradition revealed by Professor Moorman, which assigned Arthur to that very stretch of time. It suggests that a scholar who knew Geoffrey's work, and may have met him, settled on this as the proper reading of the *History* and the proper dating of Arthur.

But whatever the truth about *De Ortu*, it remains an exception. During the twelfth century, tales of Arthur and his people were spreading everywhere, and usually from other sources than Geoffrey. One proof is a sculpture in the cathedral at Modena in Italy which portrays Arthurian characters and was carved not later than 1120, before the *History* was written. Much was due to minstrels and storytellers from Brittany, who spoke French as a necessity of their calling. Wace says he heard of the Round Table from Bretons, and also heard of the Breton forest of Brocéliande as a scene of legend. He went there himself, though he was disappointed: "A fool I returned, a fool I went; a fool I went, a fool I returned." Another source was Ireland. The Irish had nothing to say of Arthur, but their literature supplied Celtic motifs of a congenial sort, which were borrowed and rehandled.

Thus began what came to be called the Matter of Britain. Medieval storytellers recognized this as one of three main bodies of material, the others being the Matter of Rome and the Matter of France. The Matter of Rome meant classical legend and history, Greek as well as Roman—the siege of Troy, the wanderings of Aeneas, the founding and fortunes of Rome itself. The Matter of France meant the deeds of Charlemagne and his peers, headed by Roland, and their wars against the Saracens around the year 800. The Matter of Britain meant chiefly Arthur with all he implied. It was a complicated and powerful mixture, growing from the Celtic rediscovery, the flowing-back of traditions after a long effacement, their diffusion through Christendom. But these were combined with current interests—chivalry, love, religion. They were transformed and updated, and woven into tales of different provenance. Meanwhile, Geoffrey's *History*, both directly and through Wace, gave structure and conviction to what might otherwise have become a confusion.

Most of the early romance-writing was in French, which was the language of educated people in England, the English kings' possessions in France, and the French kingdom adjoining them. Arthurian tales were told, however, in English and German. In due course Italy, Spain, Portugal, Holland, and Scandinavia all made their contributions. The Welsh went further than they already had, producing not only imitations of French stories, but another based on their native material, *The Dream of Rhonabwy*, and chronicles based on Geoffrey. Crusaders and pilgrims spread the literature eastward. In the words of a commentator on Geoffrey, about 1170, even before most of the major works were written:

> What place is there within the bounds of the empire of Christendom to which the winged praise of Arthur the Briton has not extended? Who is there, I ask, who does not speak of Arthur the Briton, since he is but little less known to the peoples of Asia than to the Bretons, as we are informed by our palmers who return from the countries of the East? The Eastern peoples speak of him as do the Western, though separated by the breadth of the whole earth. Egypt speaks of him, and the Bosporus is not silent. Rome, queen of cities, sings his deeds, and his wars are not unknown to her former rival Carthage. Antioch, Armenia and Palestine celebrate his feats.

Growth of a Mystique

Royal sponsorship had its place in all this. Wace presented a copy of his poem to Eleanor of Aquitaine, wife to Louis VII of France and then Henry II of England, founder of the line of kings known as Angevins. Henry had already shown his approval, and he commissioned Wace to compose another work, a chronicle of the dukes of Normandy. Eleanor had a private court in Poitou in western France where poets and romancers were favored. It is just possible that, through her, fifth-century matter came from yet another source—communities in her own Aquitaine to the south, descended from Britons carried off as prisoners after the disaster of 470. A more active patron was Eleanor's daughter by her first marriage, the Countess Marie de Champagne. Under her aegis and direction the poet Chrétien de Troyes wrote a series of verse romances. These are the first known major presentations of some of the characters and themes: Lancelot, for instance, and the Grail. In the preface to one of them, Chrétien says: "It is my pleasure to relate a matter quite worthy of heed concerning the King whose fame was such that men still speak of him far and near; and I agree with the opinion of the Bretons that his name will live on for evermore."

Why the royal interest? One motive was political. When Henry II became King in 1154, his marriage to Eleanor placed a

THE ANGEVIN EMPIRE
AT HENRY II's DEATH, 1189

SCOTLAND

North
Sea

IRELAND

GWYNEDD
POWYS
WALES
ENGLAND
WELSH
EARLDOMS

LONDON

The Channel

NORMANDY   PARIS

BRITTANY   MAINE   DOMAINS
OF THE
ANJOU   FRENCH
KINGS
TOURAINE
NANTES

POITOU

Atlantic Ocean

AQUITAINE

GASCONY   TOULOUSE

Ty Grey

THE ANGEVIN EMPIRE AT HENRY II'S DEATH, 1189
This had continued to expand after his marriage to Eleanor. England,
southeastern Ireland, Normandy, Maine, Anjou, and Touraine formed
the basic kingdom. Wales, the rest of Ireland, Brittany, Nantes, Poitou,
Aquitaine (including Gascony) and Toulouse were dependencies.

huge Continental empire under the English Crown. Only a fraction of France was ruled by the King of France. Yet in spite of its
massive superiority, Henry's monarchy had a parvenu air. The
French King had a mystique behind him, being the heir of the
mighty Charlemagne more than three centuries earlier, whom
the Matter of France commemorated. For Henry and his successors the Matter of Britain came as a welcome retort. It made
them heirs of a greater sovereign earlier still—spiritually, if not
lineally. The realm they ruled had once been foremost in grandeur and civilization. King Arthur had presided over a chivalric
Utopia, and the romancers echoed Geoffrey (and, remotely, historical fact) in making him campaign and wield power on the
Continent. In 1187 the name Arthur was given to Henry's grandson, who could be expected to ascend the throne someday as
Arthur II. His uncle King John prevented it, and most of the
Continental empire was lost. Yet the Matter of Britain continued
to weave its spell.

It was richer in content than the Matter of France, and more
attractive to the age. Charlemagne's cycle had produced a single
great epic, the *Song of Roland.* This was martial, masculine,
unsubtle. Western Christendom in the later twelfth century
wanted more, because, in several respects, the atmosphere had
altered. The Crusades had opened up contact with the affluent
and civilized East. On the higher social levels women were gain-
ing slightly more influence. A rebirth of philosophic debate, and
also of heresy, was giving religion new dimensions.

One result of the literary explosion sounds like a paradox: it
reduced Arthur himself. Surveying it as a whole, we can see why.
With the shift of interest away from war and conquest came a
shift of focus away from the war leader and conqueror. The
Arthur of romance is still very much a special person, a creature
of magic, and more so than in Geoffrey. Merlin is responsible not
only for his existence but for the sword-in-the-stone test which
enthrones him, the Round Table, and the gift of Excalibur. But
the glory is vested in a group rather than an individual, in the
court of Camelot, which is his personal capital and is destroyed
after his passing. Arthur tends to become a chairman, while his
knights perform the exploits. Sometimes he is less than admirable
himself. A version of the birth of Modred takes shape in which
the traitor is not his nephew but secretly his son, begotten in

incest, unrecognized as such yet discreditable all the same. Arthur is not so much a monarch of noble qualities as a monarch who brings them out in others.

On the whole, Arthurian romance was an upper-class taste. The ballads of Robin Hood and his Merry Men were to some extent a retort, from lower down the social scale. As for the actual stories, one theme which the Matter of Britain advanced was love. Courtly love was a fashionable medieval topic. It was a cult with a set of rules, worked out, according to legend, at "courts of love" presided over by Eleanor of Aquitaine. Its stress on the extramarital is reflected in the famous Arthurian love stories, the Lancelot-Guinevere affair and the Tristan-Iseult affair. In both it is the woman who is unfaithful to a spouse. Both women are queens—Guinevere of Britain, Iseult of the subkingdom of Cornwall.

Guinevere's infidelity is a fixture of the Arthurian legend, but its nature varies. In Geoffrey's *History* she becomes Modred's mistress while Arthur is campaigning abroad, so that she shares in the betrayal. Later versions remove this guilt from her: she pretends that she will comply with the traitor's desires, but eludes him. In the mainstream of romance her great and genuine love affair is with Lancelot. At first their love is innocent, then it grows into a passionate and tragic adultery. Lancelot dares not be seen with her too often, and tries to keep his distance, for which she reproaches him. Always they come together again. Elaine, the Fair Maid of Astolat, falls in love with Lancelot and arouses the Queen's jealousy. He tells Elaine he can never marry and her heart is broken.

At last Modred forces the scandal into the open. Since the Queen's infidelity counts as treason, Arthur has to sentence her to be burned at the stake. Lancelot arrives with an armed band and rescues her, but the fighting between his followers and the King's is the beginning of the break-up of the Round Table. After Arthur has passed away, Guinevere retires to a convent at Amesbury, and Lancelot takes a grief-stricken leave of her and settles near Glastonbury as a hermit.

Professor Jean Markale thinks there is more here than medieval invention. The stories are based on genuine tradition of Celtic society, which, however, medieval minds could not handle. A Celtic Queen, free and equal, could take lovers. In the twelfth century such a person was not a comprehensible figure. To a male romancer a free and equal woman could only be a disloyal and insubordinate woman. Therefore, when the Lancelot-Guinevere affair passes beyond courtly adoration into a serious relationship, the Queen stands condemned and a public disclosure forces Arthur to execute her, or try to. Iseult is excused only by having accidentally drunk a magic love potion.

Whether or not the Celtic past peeps through in the love stories, it certainly does in the Quest of the Holy Grail. Pre-Christian things went into it—Arthur's voyage to the caldron of Annwn, the character Bran, and much else. The Grail made its entry into romance, with weird accompaniments, before anyone explained what it was. Toward the close of the twelfth century the poet Robert de Boron said it was a vessel used by Christ at the Last Supper, at which he instituted the Eucharist. This linked it with the sacrament of the altar, and Catholic belief in the real presence of Christ when the bread and wine are consecrated. The Grail had come into the hands of Joseph of Arimathea, the rich man who laid Christ's body in the tomb, and had eventually been brought to Britain. It was endowed with supernatural properties of a Christian kind. It was a source of healing and inspiration and visions, and its finding, or "achievement," was a transcendent mystical experience. That at least was the form given to its story by romancers who wrote in French. Details, however, varied widely. Sometimes it was a chalice, sometimes a bowl or dish. At first the principal Grail-seeking knight was Perceval. Gawain too attempted the quest. Then Lancelot was credited with a son named Galahad, whose purity of body and soul enabled him to achieve the Grail fully. But the German poet Wolfram von Eschenbach, taking up the Perceval tale in *Parzival*, presented the Grail quite differently, making it a wonder-working stone with celestial origins. Through all the main versions runs a strange, esoteric Christianity, drawing pagan imagery into a kind of initiation.

Behind the image of the Grail are pre-Christian beliefs about sacred or wonder-working vessels, Celtic and otherwise. Even when it is given its Christian guise the Grail is made out to be a source of fertility and bodily nourishment. But it becomes something higher also, a medium of divine revelation. Though a few of

Arthur's questing knights have glimpses of it, nearly all prove unworthy of the full vision.

The stories are mystical and symbolic, and do not present the Grail as if it were simply a holy relic like the many relics enshrined in churches. As a matter of fact, no one during the Middle Ages seems to have claimed seriously to possess the cup of the Last Supper. When relics were enormously popular, and far-fetched claims were made freely, this silence is curious. It hints that there may have been a real mystery. The misconception that the Grail *was* simply a relic has inspired modern fancies identifying it as some particular vessel. Such a claim has been made for a silver chalice from Antioch north of Lebanon, though this is centuries later than Christ, and for an old wooden bowl once at Nanteos in Wales.

In some way the theme was involved with Glastonbury. Robert de Boron speaks of the Grail being taken to the "Vales of Avalon," meaning not a mythical apple orchard but central Somerset. In another romance, *Perlesvaus,* the author claims to have learned "the whole story" at Glastonbury Abbey. The abbey said the Grail-keeper, Joseph of Arimathea, had been the builder of the first church on its site. Glastonbury had some sort of sacred character before Christianity. The Tor, the legend-haunted hill rising above, has a system of paths or terraces which have been interpreted as the remnants of a prehistoric maze. Geoffrey Russell, the first to expound this idea, argued that the Grail quest began as a ceremonial maze-threading, a pre-Christian ritual which was turned into a Christian myth. Archaeologists who have studied the Tor are willing to consider his maze; few serious students of the Grail theme have taken his further step. As for Glastonbury's Christian community, its undoubtedly early date made a growth of legend about its beginnings only natural, the more so as the original church on the site really was so old that no one knew who had built it. Joseph does not appear in the abbey's earliest accounts of itself. It is far from clear who thought of him first, or why.

In 1191 the monks had linked Glastonbury with Arthur by another route. They announced that they had found his grave in their burial ground. According to their report, a Welsh or Breton bard had divulged the long-kept secret to Henry II. Some years later the abbot ordered an excavation. Seven feet down the diggers unearthed a stone slab, with a cross of lead underneath. An inscription on the cross said HIC IACET SEPULTUS INCLITUS REX ARTURIUS IN INSULA AVALONIA, "Here lies buried the renowned King Arthur in the Isle of Avalon." This dismissed the mythical Avalon in favor of a literal location, as Robert de Boron did in his Grail story. Glastonbury was not far from being an island early in the Christian era, when the water level was different. Nine feet farther down the monks reached a rough coffin made from a hollowed-out log, like a dugout canoe. Inside were the bones of a tall man who had seemingly been killed by a blow on the head, because the skull was damaged. There were also some smaller bones and a lock of fair hair, which they decided were Guinevere's. The Welsh historian Gerald de Barri, otherwise Giraldus Cambrensis, visited the abbey and wrote two copious accounts of the find, in which he quotes the inscription from memory, getting it a little wrong.

Most modern authors (not all) reject the discovery as a fake. A few years before, they point out, the abbey had been largely burned down. Funds were needed for rebuilding, and Arthur's

grave can be explained as a publicity stunt. Another motive perhaps was to please the King by proving Arthur was dead—a
rebuttal of the Welsh, who kept up an intransigent stance in the
belief that he would come back to lead them.

However, the theory of a pure fake was refuted in 1963
when Ralegh Radford reexcavated the site. He proved not only
that the monks had dug where they said, but that they had got
down to a stratum of very early burials. There is no longer any
doubt as to the grave. The question is simply whose it was, and
this turns on the lead cross. It was lost in the eighteenth century
(a claim of its rediscovery in 1982 was exploded). But a copy of
one side of it, made by the antiquary William Camden, was published in 1607. Gerald says it named Guinevere as well as Arthur;
if it did, she was on the other side. The clumsy lettering does not
suggest the style of the twelfth century, and the Latin spelling
Arturius is an archaic form which was used five hundred years
earlier, but never—so far as anyone knows—between that time
and the exhumation. The problem is complex and has certainly
not been cleared up. The Arthur = Riothamus equation might be
thought adverse to the grave, on the ground that if he died
overseas, he would not have been buried at Glastonbury. Yet he
might have got back, or his bones might have been brought home
later, for reinterment with his wife's in a holy place of his own
country.

The monks' unscrupulosity, however real, had its limits.
They never produced the other obvious grave, that of Joseph of
Arimathea. A visionary named John Blome actually searched for
it, but without success. This second, negative result makes the
genuineness of the first a shade likelier. If the monks were willing
to fake Arthur's grave, nothing prevented them from faking Joseph's too, as a permanent attraction for pilgrims; yet they did
not. They continued to name him as their founder, and a fourteenth-century abbey chronicle by one of them, John of Glastonbury, adapted one or two episodes from the Grail stories. But the
borrowing was slight, and while the abbey claimed to possess
many holy relics, it never claimed to possess, or ever to have
possessed, the Holy Grail. It asserted instead that Joseph brought
two small "cruets," with drops of the blood and sweat of Christ.
These had been buried with him, wherever he was.

Glastonbury's rejection of the Grail is significant. It shows an attitude to the Matter of Britain which affected not only monastic chronicles but, little by little, the romances themselves. From a medieval Christian viewpoint several of the themes were suspect. The Quest of the Grail was orthodox, yet it was orthodox in an offbeat way. Pagan imagery bulked too large, and the quest was a private adventure, alien to the spirit of churchgoing Christianity. In the milieu of the time the Grail's bizarrerie could not last very long. Writers tended to drift on to the safer ground of allegory.

The element of magic changed also. Geoffrey had introduced both the principal magical characters. Merlin was in all his work, and the enchantress Morgen, later called Morgan le Fay, was in his *Life of Merlin.* In their background was that Celtic freedom from animosity toward the pre-Christian scheme of things, and both were benign figures. But the Christianity of the Middle Ages was less able to approve, and it tightened with the passage of time. Things were Christian or heathen, white or black. Magic was essentially heathen; therefore it was not good.

Merlin as portrayed by Geoffrey was the fatherless prophet in the legend of Vortigern and his soothsayers. However, Geoffrey also worked in traditions of a more or less historical bard named Myrddin, who lived in the North toward the end of the sixth century. Possibly he also worked in some myth about a demigod who set up Stonehenge, thus making the character not merely double but triple. At any rate, his Merlin stood between paganism and Christianity, and was strange without being sinister. In the romances, however, Merlin grew more ambiguous. His mother's spirit companion was now said to have been a devil, seeking to harm humanity by begetting an evil prophet. Her piety, it was explained, neutralized the evil, so that Merlin could play his role in Britain's affairs. Nonetheless he came to a bad end, shut in a living tomb through his own amorous foolishness, when a woman used his magic against him.

As for Morgen, she was one of the characters with a clearly divine origin, recognized even in the Middle Ages. She began as the Celtic goddess Matrona, who became Modron in Welsh. Touches of an Irish goddess were added to her, so that she too was a composite. Geoffrey made her a healer, heading a benevolent sisterhood, and nursing Arthur after his last battle. In romance, however, the hardening of orthodoxy gradually told. As an enchantress she simply could not be good. She became a malicious witch, ensnaring knights, and mischief-making at Arthur's court.

The Royal Theme

With the dubious elements expunged or revised, it was all the easier for monarchs to take the Matter of Britain seriously and exploit it for their own prestige. Edward I read the romances and paid a state visit to Glastonbury, where he and his Queen installed the bones of Arthur and Guinevere in a new tomb of black marble, in a place of honor before the high altar. Edward may have been responsible for a "Round Table" which is still on view at Winchester. He would have had it made for a Round Table entertainment, a form of aristocratic festival in which gatherings of nobles played Arthurian roles, jousted, and so forth. Edward is known to have held several, including a very splendid one to celebrate his second marriage in 1299. He also had an eye to the political aspect. In 1301, writing to the Pope about his claim to Scotland, he cited Geoffrey of Monmouth. Arthur had ruled Scotland, so he should too.

Edward III visited Glastonbury in 1331, and later took an interest in the search there for Joseph's grave. Though Joseph remained elusive, the abbey produced a pedigree showing that Arthur was descended from him, thereby linking the monarchy with Christ. This kind of exercise was not new: Grail romance had already given Lancelot an ancestry of the same kind. Edward III toyed with the notion of reviving the knighthood of the Round Table as an actual order of chivalry, though, in the end, he founded the Order of the Garter instead. All too probably Geoffrey's account of the Arthurian empire encouraged him to try conquering France. The project unleashed the Hundred Years' War and came near success. The English kings' French domains did not expire finally till 1453.

By then England was a well defined nation-state, with an English-speaking sovereign and nobility, and a population that blended Celtic, Anglo-Saxon, and Norman strains. Nationality now affected the Church. At ecclesiastical councils the bishops of different countries vied for precedence, and the English claimed it on the ground that the Church in their country was senior.

Joseph of Arimathea, they said, had got to Glastonbury before any Christians got to France or Spain.

The Matter of Britain was generally less creative after the thirteenth century. However, the finest of the poems composed in English, *Sir Gawain and the Green Knight,* belongs to the fourteenth. Its unknown author uses the alliterative verse of old Anglo-Saxon poetry, with each line having two or three words beginning with the same sound. Rhymes occur only at the end of sections of twenty lines or so. The story begins with Arthur's holding court at Camelot. A gigantic man enters, clad in green and carrying a great axe. He challenges any of Arthur's knights to strike a blow at him with the axe, on the understanding that the knight will allow him to strike a similar blow in return a year hence. Gawain volunteers, and cuts his head off, in the reasonable expectation that no return blow will ever be struck; but the Green Knight picks up his head, and leaves seemingly full of life. Gawain goes honorably to keep the tryst and undergoes trials at the hands of several mysterious people, coming through with almost complete credit, as a result of which the Green Knight spares him. Enchantment, here, is a test of Gawain's Christian virtue.

A fair sample is the passage describing Gawain's blow and its disconcerting sequel.

On the ground the Green Knight graciously stood,
With head slightly slanting to expose the flesh.
His long and lovely locks he laid over his crown,
Baring the naked neck for the business now due.
Gawain gripped his axe and gathered it on high,
Advanced the left foot before him on the ground,
And slashed swiftly down on the exposed part,
So that the sharp blade sheared through, shattering the bones,
Sank deep in the sleek flesh, split it in two,
And the scintillating steel struck the ground.
The fair head fell from the neck, struck the floor,
And people spurned it as it rolled around.
Blood spurted from the body, bright against the green,
Yet the fellow did not fall, nor falter one whit,
But stoutly sprang forward on legs still sturdy,
Roughly reached out among the ranks of the nobles,
Seized his splendid head and straightway lifted it.
Then he strode to his steed, snatched the bridle,

Stepped into the stirrup and swung aloft,
Holding his head in his hand by the hair.
He settled himself in the saddle as steadily
As if nothing had happened to him, though he had No head.
He twisted his trunk about,
That gruesome body that bled;
He caused much dread and doubt
By the time his say was said.

This astonishing fairy tale, however, is an offshoot from the main body of romance. The standard English form of the Arthurian legend is due to Sir Thomas Malory, who completed his prose cycle about 1469. He collected, translated, and adapted older romances, but he was far more than a collector, translator, or adapter. He gave the legend a new pattern and cohesion, with a freshness and literary power of his own, and a serious intent: to point a sad contrast between the Arthurian golden age and the reality of England in the Wars of the Roses, with rival kings scheming and fighting. The contrast is not confined to matters of state. It is also, as it were, social. Speaking in his own person, Malory makes some observations on that topic of love to which the romancers before him give pride of place. His English is not too distant from modern English and can be quoted more or less directly:

Like as May month flowereth and flourisheth in many gardens, so in likewise let every man of worship* flourish his heart in this world, first unto God, and next unto the joy of them that he promised his faith unto; for there was never worshipful man nor worshipful woman, but they loved one better than another; and worship in arms may never be foiled, but first reserve the honour to God, and secondly the quarrel must come of thy lady: and such love I call virtuous love.

But nowadays men cannot love seven night but they must have all their desires: that love may not endure by reason; for where they be soon accorded and hasty, heat soon it cooleth. Right so fareth love nowadays, soon hot soon cold: there is no stability. But the old love

* The word "worship" refers to honor and merit, not religion.

was not so; men and women could love together seven years, and no lecherous lusts were between them, and then was love, truth, and faithfulness: and lo, in likewise was used love in King Arthur's days.

He adds that Guinevere "was a true lover, and therefore she had a good end."

In 1485 the pioneer English printer Caxton published Malory's work in a much-revised form, calling it a "noble and joyous book," surely one of the finest phrases ever to appear in a publisher's blurb. Caxton's timing was excellent. In the same year the theme sprang to life again in a new monarchical myth. Henry Tudor defeated Richard III and became Henry VII. He was fractionally Welsh, claiming descent from Cadwallader, a much-revered King of Gwynedd whom Geoffrey makes out to have been the last sovereign in the British line. Henry marched to battle under the standard of the Red Dragon of Wales, which owed its origin to Geoffrey's account of Merlin and the pool with the dragons in it. His immediate title to the throne came via the House of Lancaster, and by marrying the heiress of the opposed House of York, he united the Roses. Tudor propagandists presented him not only as the healer of the long civil strife but, through his ancestry, as the restorer of a true "British" monarchy rooted in the Arthurian past. In effect he was fulfilling the dream of the Return. To clinch that pretension he named his firstborn son Arthur and had him baptized at Winchester, where Malory (usually) located Camelot. Unfortunately, the prince died young, and, as once before, a prospective reign of Arthur II faded away.

Nevertheless, under Elizabeth I the Tudor myth was revived and improved. In his vast allegorical poem *The Faerie Queene* Edmund Spenser versified Geoffrey, portrayed Arthur as an almost messianic hero, and extolled Elizabeth's England as his kingdom reinstated. That was the climax. Afterward the myth became entangled with politics in a narrower sense and the Stuart kings' notions of their divine right. Their opponents replied by exploding Geoffrey as a historian, thereby proving that there had never been an ancient British monarchy hallowed by heaven. With the discrediting of Geoffrey, Arthur himself seemed discredited. The theme ceased to inspire major authors, and in the eighteenth century it virtually faded out.

It came back with the poets of the Romantic movement. Blake, Wordsworth, and Scott rediscovered it, and a series of Victorians followed—Matthew Arnold, William Morris, Swinburne, and above all Tennyson. In his *Idylls of the King* Tennyson attempted a fairly complete new telling. As soon as Arthur resurfaced in his fullness he acquired, yet again, a contemporary royalist quality. Tennyson was poet laureate. He dedicated the *Idylls* to the memory of Prince Albert, the late consort, whom the "blameless" Arthur of his poetry grew to resemble; and he closed them with a loyal address to the Queen herself.

In Tennyson's treatment the Matter of Britain is allegory rather than history, though he has conscientiously read the historians. As he puts it to Victoria:

> But thou, my Queen,
> Not for itself, but thro' thy living love
> For one to whom I made it o'er his grave
> Sacred, accept this old imperfect tale,
> New-old, and shadowing Sense at war with Soul,
> Ideal manhood closed in real man,
> Rather than that gray king, whose name, a ghost,
> Streams like a cloud, man-shaped, from mountain peak,
> And cleaves to cairn and cromlech.

The *Idylls* are about a spiritually inspired monarchy, embodying the highest in human nature, triumphant over the baser promptings. Arthur as *Restitutor* in Britain, where he masters the barbarians and "makes a realm and reigns," symbolizes the human soul in its noblest aspiration. When portraying a court influenced by his ideals Tennyson stresses holy matrimony rather than love affairs, going distinctly beyond Malory. This change gives Guinevere's infidelity a clearer function in the scheme. The rebellion of the unruly flesh, the baser nature, becomes a fatal example, and at the end everything falls apart in cynicism and despair. All is lost, yet with no implication that the experiment was misguided to start with. Spiritually inspired monarchy is still an ideal worth cherishing. Tennyson's main difficulty is that his plan makes the Lancelot-Guinevere adultery central, together with its pendant the Tristan-Iseult adultery, yet, writing for Victoria in the moral atmosphere of her reign, he can never go into detail. The sins on which the catastrophe turns have to be handled by allusions and flashbacks.

Tennyson was a truly popular poet, a bestseller on a grand scale, and his Arthurian daydream may have had more influence than anyone realized. He happened to be writing during England's last serious upsurge of republican feeling, caused by Victoria's neglect of her duties in mourning for Albert. The movement foundered in 1872, smashed by public rejoicings when the Prince of Wales recovered from typhoid. Tennyson mentions them in the epilogue to the *Idylls*, which first came out in a collected edition soon afterward. The publication was as timely as Caxton's publication of Malory. Everything was now ready for the Crown to renew its glamor, and, through the poet laureate, Arthur played his part.

9

The Modern Quest

The New Matter of Britain

Arthur's changing fame in our own time dates from 1927. That
was the year of E. K. Chambers's book *Arthur of Britain,* which
started the academic pursuit of the "historical Arthur." It was
also the year of a work of poetry, John Masefield's *Midsummer
Night,* which was the first attempt by a major English poet to get
behind the medieval romance and make full use of the older
Welsh tradition.

Those who followed Chambers in their various ways—Collingwood, Jackson, Alcock, Morris, and others—showed that the
realities, if any, did lie in the post-Roman Britain where Geoffrey
put them. Meanwhile, the archaeologists built up knowledge of
that Britain. They were not looking for Arthur, and it is most
unlikely that any archaeologist ever will. To find anything with
his name on it would be an almost incredible stroke of luck, not a
possibility justifying costly work. Excavation, however, did shed
light on the milieu of legend and the context of the hypothetical
hero. At Cadbury it did somewhat more. Even there the pre-
Roman material heavily outweighed the post-Roman, but
Cadbury was inevitably linked with the great name. For a time it
brought a welcome convergence in Arthurian studies, as special-
ists in different fields learned to talk to each other.

A complaint heard before and during the Cadbury period
was spectacularly refuted by events. This might be called the

literary objection. It ran roughly thus: "We have the Arthurian stories, which are immortal literature. Looking for historical facts behind them is a mistake. At best it is sterile and irrelevant, at worst it spoils the stories by contrasting them with a smaller and meaner reality." In the words of T. H. White, author of *The Once and Future King* and last of the 100 percent conservatives, Arthur was not a "distressed Briton hopping about in a suit of woad in the fifth century."

One would have thought that the search for truth was a worthwhile activity in itself. But even on literary grounds, White's sneer was misguided. Even his fellow conservative John Steinbeck, who experimented with retelling Malory, took an interest in Cadbury and was planning a visit to the excavations at the time of his death. Quite simply, the trends which were inaugurated in the same year by Chambers and Masefield eventually converged. The serious quest enlarged and enriched the mythos. It inspired a whole series of creative writers, following in the path Masefield pioneered, but with new knowledge gleaned from scholarship.

These writers have combined the themes of romance with what is known or guessed about Arthur's time, or bypassed the romances entirely and tried to resurrect the Arthurian age. Alongside novels, plays, and films quarried from the old Matter of Britain, a new Matter of Britain has taken shape, which in no way detracts from it, and is a quest in its own right—a quest by way of imagination.

In 1938 and 1944 Charles Williams published *Taliessin through Logres* and *The Region of the Summer Stars,* together composing a cycle of complex poems based not only on the Grail and other medieval motifs but on the modern attempts to reconstruct the history. In 1955 R. C. Sherriff portrayed a purely fifth-century Arthur in a play, *The Long Sunset.* Another dramatic essay was John Arden's *The Island of the Mighty,* performed in 1972, an amazing amalgam of facts and legends by a brilliant playwright. This evoked an Arthurian Britain resembling a postcolonial country in Asia or Africa, with Arthur standing for order in the old imperial sense, and succumbing to resurgent Celticism and tribalism.

Rosemary Sutcliff, Mary Stewart, and Marion Bradley are gifted and popular novelists in a list which runs to more than a

dozen. Rosemary Sutcliff's *Sword at Sunset* is a story of Arthur as
commander in chief. Mary Stewart's trilogy *The Crystal Cave,
The Hollow Hills,* and *The Last Enchantment* is the life of Merlin
told from his own point of view. Marion Bradley's *The Mists of
Avalon* is a feminine and pagan version. All these novelists have
felicitous touches bringing together history, legend, and imagination. Outstanding is Mary Stewart's interpretation of the sword
which Arthur must take up to prove his kingship. It becomes the
sword of Maximus, the Emperor proclaimed in Britain whose
daughter Vortigern is said to have married, and who passes into
Welsh genealogy and romance as a kind of honorary Briton. The
Emperor's sword, in a secret chapel, is a token of the right to rule
in the island. Through Merlin's eyes the scene in which Arthur
takes it up before an assemblage of nobles, establishing himself as
High King, is a weird blend of supernatural manifestations and
vivid reality.

> The chapel swam with colour and the glint of jewels
> and gold. The air smelled cold and fragrant, of pines
> and water and scented smoke. The rustle and murmur-
> ing of the throng filled the air and sounded like the
> rustle of flames licking through a pile of fuel, taking
> hold. . . .
> Flames from the nine lamps, flaring and then dying;
> flames licking up the stone of the altar; flames running
> along the blade of the sword until it glowed white hot. I
> stretched my hands out over it, palms flat. The fire
> licked my robe, blazing white from sleeve and finger,
> but where it touched, it did not even singe. It was the
> ice-cold fire, the fire called by a word out of the dark,
> with the searing heat at its heart, where the sword lay.
> The sword lay in its flames as a jewel lies embedded in
> white wool. *Whoso taketh this sword.* . . . The runes
> danced along the metal: the emeralds burned. The
> chapel was a dark globe with a centre of fire. The blaze
> from the altar threw my shadow upwards, gigantic, into
> the vaulted roof. I heard my own voice, ringing hollow
> from the vault like a voice in a dream.
> "Take up the sword, he who dares." . . .
> Arthur came slowly forward. Behind him the place

was dim, the crowd shrunk back into darkness, the shuffle and murmur of their presence not more than the breeze in the forest trees outside. . . . He waited, not doubtful, not blindly trusting; waiting only.

"Come," I said gently. "It is yours."

He put his hand through the white blaze of fire and the hilt slid cool into the grip for which, a hundred and a hundred years before, it had been made.

Possibilities

To have hit on Arthur-Riothamus is not to have found the whole solution. Once again, what he does is transform the debate. Inconclusive attempts to prove that Arthur existed can cease. The man called Riothamus undoubtedly did exist. The question is whether the legend originated from him, whether he was the "real Arthur" (so far as anyone was), whatever later heroes may have been incorporated into the figure of the King. While many facts point already to an affirmative answer, further progress may well be hoped for.

One promising result of these findings is the opening up of a field on the Continent. From Chambers to Morris the search for origins was bedeviled by the assumption that Arthur's presence in Gaul was pure fantasy. The dogma diverted attention from evidence which was there all along, in Sidonius and Jordanes and Gregory of Tours, and also in the *Goeznovius* preface, with its Arthur whose identity shows up clearly as soon as other testimonies are properly read. As we have amply seen, dropping the dogma is a major step forward. It means, first, that Geoffrey's tale of the Gallic warfare becomes worth sifting, not for facts which he doesn't give, but for clues which he does. His triple reference to the Emperor Leo stands out at once, as the only chronological fix for Arthur. This leads to the neglected texts, to the identity they reveal for him, and thence to the chronicles indicating the same period.

However, inquiry does not have to halt there. Continental matter could go further. It need not even be a question of disinterring new records, since, so far, everything has been done by looking at known records with new eyes. Is there anything more in Berry or Burgundy or in Brittany itself? Breton genealogies include forms of Riothamus, perhaps used as a title, perhaps as a name. Who were the men so called, have they any significance? Again, there is a curious little fact which shows how an account of Arthur-Riothamus might have reached Breton historians. Gildas is said to have gone to Brittany and founded a monastery at Rhuys near the coast. Whether it was founded by him or not, the monastery was real. Early in the tenth century the monks fled from the Norse and traveled inland to central France—to Berry, in fact. Ebbon, the seigneur of the town of Déols, made them welcome and they settled nearby. When the danger was past they returned to Brittany. Déols was the site of Arthur-Riothamus's battle against the Goths. Did the monks' patron, Ebbon, show them some obscure chronicle while they were living in the neighborhood?

There may be scope in the study of place names and local legends. Thus, do French places named in the romances suggest a geographic pattern, as the "Arthur" places in Britain do? Are any tales told in Berry or Burgundy? And, once again, could any unlocated Arthurian battles be pinned down by name on the Continent, as perhaps Agned can? And what about archaeology? Early traces of Britons in Armorica are pushing back the earliest colonization to the fourth century, where the Maximus legend, and Geoffrey, always did put it. The settlements would have been small, not amounting to a true beginning of Brittany, but they existed. Are there traces of Britons up the Loire, or in central Gaul?

Back in the island, meanwhile, the possibilities are far from exhausted. For instance, Nennius's battle list now makes better sense. The two fairly sure locations, Celidon and Chester, fall into place in terms of date. The association of the firmly located battles with a firmly attested leader could open the way to a new understanding of the list. And the leader's title, or honorific, suggests a further approach. The British High Kingship which it expresses was a short-lived institution, lasting only from about 425 to 470. During that time the Britons had two confirmed high kings, Vortigern and Arthur-Riothamus, plus maybe one pretender, Vortimer. Still, they were ruled for a while somewhat as the Irish were, and the High Kingship in Ireland, which is far better recorded, might shed an indirect light on its British counterpart.

With archaeology in Britain, apart from chance finds, indirect illumination is the best thing to hope for. The great legendary sites have already been worked upon. They may still harbor more than is known. But the notion that the only way to make progress would be to go on digging at "Arthurian" sites is quite erroneous. Alcock's reappraisal of Cadbury, in 1982, was due almost entirely to comparison with other hill forts which had been explored after it. Work on the reoccupation of these strongholds in the fifth and sixth centuries has a long way to go yet. It may never disclose anything more about Arthur-Riothamus, but as it builds up a more detailed picture of the period, his place in it may grow clearer. As the network of power and population is mapped, some of the riddles of the Welsh triads may unravel. The capital of the kings of Gwynedd, at Aberffraw in Anglesey, has come to light through excavation after many years of abortive guessing.

The Golden Age

Why the spell? Why the rebirth, four or five times throughout the centuries?

A conspicuous feature of Arthur's rebirth today is the interest in British legend in the United States. Arthurian novels are American bestsellers; Arthurian tours are sponsored by American universities. The International Arthurian Society, the academic body in this field, has hundreds of American members, and America supports a newsletter of Arthurian studies and a quarterly magazine. Hence, the modern vogue is more than a postimperial British nostalgia. Nor can it be explained as the medieval vogue might be. In the Middle Ages the romances had an array of attractions which nothing else could compete with: war and love, magic and tournaments, chivalry and questing, and religion-with-a-difference. There was something for every taste—upper-class taste, at all events. But on the face of it, a modern novelist who works in the same field has nothing to offer which is not offered by other novelists.

Americans speak of "roots." I doubt if this is the whole answer, since most Americans are not British-descended. Yet there is a thought here, a half-realized one. Realized fully, it does help in understanding the revival, and earlier revivals too. Oddly, it was best realized in the past by that not very engaging person Henry Tudor, who became Henry VII.

During the Cadbury excavation, for which part of the money was raised by public appeals, some criticism was leveled at the project on the ground that it was a deception. To the public, it was argued, Camelot meant only the Camelot of romance, which was obviously not there. When people grasped that it wasn't, they would feel cheated, and fund-raising for other excavations would then be harder. This was plausible, yet it turned out to be utterly wrong. The public appeals brought in increasing sums year by year. When guiding parties of visitors I was often surprised by the degree of their acceptance. They saw only trenches and postholes, pottery shards and corroded knives, tumbledown bits of wall. Yet, generally speaking, these were enough to evoke the spell. For at least a very large number of people it seemed not to depend on any particular imagery. As in the literary field, the quest was neither irrelevant nor destructive. The trenches, postholes, and so forth simply became part of the mythos.

Arthur of course is a shape-shifter, passing through transformations. To diagnose the spell of his legend we must ask what is the constant, the active ingredient in all versions. I would define it as *the long-lost glory or promise which is not truly lost.*

Arthur's kingdom embodies the notion of a far-away golden age. That does not imply an impossible prosperity and contentment. It does imply a time when individuals who deserved admiration were at the center of things; a time of greatness, even if it was the greatness of a minority; a time of hope, even if it was a tenuous hope. A fragment of our past—something in the nature of "roots," if you will—is viewed in a certain way. Arthur's legend began as a memory of a *Restitutor,* of civilization endangered and beset, and of Britons headed by their King staging a brave, temporarily successful renewal. The Welsh lost interest in the civilization as Roman and alien, but they remembered the bravery. They made Arthur the mightiest man of the Island of the Mighty, in a heroic age of Celtic warriors, Celtic saints, Celtic marvels. The romancers drew inspiration from several sources, and transposed all they took into medieval terms, making Arthur's realm a chivalric Utopia retrieved from anarchy, giving scope for the ideals of their audience. Modern authors have reverted to the earlier levels. A few are iconoclasts, but even they acknowledge the magnificent image by trying to break it.

However—and this is the second part of the pattern—the golden age is a doomed one. Historically, the High Kingship came to grief through treachery in Gaul. The Welsh gave Arthur a domestic downfall at Camlann, and introduced his destroyer Modred. Medieval authors restored the motif of treachery and made Modred a nemesis. Caxton's edition of Malory summed up the inherent tragedy in its title, *Morte d'Arthur,* Death of Arthur. And I know of no modern writer, however venturesome, who has dared to give Arthur's career a happy ending.

The end, however, is not actually the end. He who "restored" once lives on, with inherent power to "restore" again, to reinstate his golden age. Arthur-Riothamus vanished in Burgundy, but there is no certainty what became of him. The Welsh learned from the Bretons to insist that Arthur was still alive, in his cave or his enchanted island. The belief spread wider, and Malory echoed it: "Men say in many parts of England that King Arthur is not dead, but had by the will of Our Lord Jesu into another place; and men say that he shall come again." Though Malory mentioned the tomb at Glastonbury, with its implied disproof, he quoted what he said was inscribed on it: HIC IACET ARTHURUS, REX QUONDAM REXQUE FUTURUS, "Here lies Arthur, King that was, King that shall be." Even when Arthur could no longer be expected to return literally, he could return symbolically through a spiritual heir and a restoration of the values he stood for. Henry Tudor pretended to have brought this about, and despite the death of his son, the intended Arthur II, the pretense stood up for more than a century.

Through insight or accident, Henry touched a deep chord in human nature. He exploited a British myth to harness a universal impulse. Greater revolutions than his have been powered by it. In the recurrent vision a long-lost glory or promise can be reinstated for a fresh start, with intervening corruption swept away. There can be a "return."* We can see the impulse at work in the sixteenth-century Christian reformers, who professed to be restoring the lost purity of the Church as the apostles knew it; in the

---

* I have gone into this in detail in another place. See *Camelot and the Vision of Albion.*

eighteenth-century French revolutionaries, who proposed to bring back the natural goodness of humanity by destroying the institutions which had corrupted it; in the twentieth-century Indian activists led by Gandhi, who roused the masses with talk of a buried India of sages and village communes and cottage industry, and preached self-rule through its rebirth in a village resurrection. These historic movements, and others, show apocalyptic energies being unleashed by a mode of thinking which the Return of Arthur symbolizes. This is not the place to discuss why such visions have the power to stir human hearts, or whether the leaders of the movements were right or deluded. The facts are the facts.

Arthur's immortality means that the golden age of his kingship is still somehow "there" and recoverable—like the pristine apostolic Church, like unspoiled humanity, like Gandhi's ideal India. Which is one reason at least why the spell can still take hold at subconscious levels. He can return, after a fashion, through research and the works of imagination. His Britain can resurface, after a fashion, through archaeology.

Does anything lie beyond that? Could anything happen which would seem to fulfil the prophecy, and reinstate the Arthurian reign? The question sounds absurd. Yet, while the Camelot mystique of the Kennedy presidency was only a fanciful transfer of the image, it proved how potent the image could be, even in politics. Henry VII posed successfully as the King through whom the prophecy would be fulfilled, and an Arthurian movement might be possible today if its chiefs could hit on a formula—witness the Nazi use of Wagner and the Siegfried mythology. It is easy to conjure up an alarming picture of a latter-day leader being proclaimed as a new Arthur, even as Arthur reincarnate, and attracting influential and sinister mystics promising their own brand of golden age.

I believe, though, that the facts are less disturbing. By opening up the deeper layers, the modern quest has ruled various notions out. Arthur could not be invoked, not on a large scale, as a patron saint of neofascist medievalism or elitist nostalgia. No party could annex the mystique without a monstrous falsification. Perhaps that last thought is the key one. Here is a spellbinding, indestructible theme, national, yet transcending nationality. For better or worse it has affected the history of the country where it began. It has survived eclipses and demolitions, and Britain cannot be thought of without it. Yet no conceivable movement or government could entrap it in a program. That is a comment on the limitations of movements and governments. The undying King is a strangely powerful reminder that there is Something Else. By nurturing that awareness, and a questing spirit, his fame may have its effect on human thinking. It may influence history again, outside movements and governments; and not only in Britain.

Appendix
The Blood Royal: A Fancy

Neither the medieval kings nor the Tudor kings claimed to be literally descended from Arthur. The royal inheritance from him was collective; English monarchs were the successors to his kingdom. Yet those who promoted this view may have missed the most glorious connection of all. Here the usual course of events is reversed. We do not confront a legend which scholarship refutes. We confront a possibility, unknown to legend, which scholarship reveals—a speculation, but an alluring one.

Sir Iain Moncreiffe of that Ilk, the eminent genealogist, moves toward it when discussing the ancestry of Prince Charles's son William. In his book *Royal Highness* he refers to "British high kings of the fifth century" who were very possibly related to present royalty, "among them probably King Arthur." Sir Iain is thinking of the royal family's Welsh line of ancestry, which goes back through the Tudors to King Maelgwn of Gwynedd and through him to Cunedda, overlord of Wales in the early fifth century. Cunedda's descendants are said to have included various princes and princesses who would have been cousins of Maelgwn. One family tree credits him with a daughter Gwen, and Gwen with a daughter Ygerna, who was Arthur's mother. Even if this is right, of course, it fails to bring Arthur close to the royal line traced through Maelgwn. As an ancestor of the House of Windsor, he looks very collateral indeed. What might be asked is whether he had issue himself, from whom another line might be traced, making Elizabeth II a direct descendant.

The signs that Riothamus was an alternative label for Arthur draw attention to Breton genealogies in which a Riothamus appears as an early ancestor. Is it the King? The question is difficult because a wealthy Briton named John, who went over to Armor-

ica and founded a local dynasty, seems also to have been called
Riothamus. He may have assumed it as a title. The indications are
that John flourished some decades after the title's original holder,
but he confuses the matter; Morris, in fact, thought John and the
original Riothamus were the same, though Fleuriot rules that
out. At any rate, someone in Brittany known as Riothamus is said
to have had a son Daniel, who had a son Budic, and he at least
could be the Riothamus identified with Arthur. His grandson
Budic lived as an exile in Britain for a while, and it has been
suggested that a study of Breton genealogies might show a link
with Welsh ones, thereby following through from Arthur-Riothamus to Welsh kings and thence to present-day English royalty.

Even if this is totally wrong, it draws attention to a curious
point about Arthur in Britain. The telling of his story betrays a
gap in tradition, as if something had dropped out. A query over-
hangs the succession and is ignored and unaccounted for. In
Geoffrey's *History* Arthur has neither son nor daughter. His
cousin Constantine succeeds him. Sons are mentioned in other
places, but bafflingly. Llacheu is scarcely more than a name, and
Amr, in Nennius's "The Marvels of Britain," is killed by Arthur
himself with no explanation given. Some romancers make Modred a son of Arthur, but also make him a bastard of shameful
origin. It is strange to find a King with an amply described family
and several male offspring, yet none with whom the question of
inheritance is so much as raised. Was his heir a senior son whose
memory the Welsh chose to suppress?

There are hints that Arthur was married more than once,
and that the Welsh nearly did suppress his earlier marriage. Gerald, the author who describes the Glastonbury cross, says it called
Guinevere his *second* wife. The statement cannot be checked, for
the reason given—that Camden, whose drawing of the cross is all
that preserves its appearance for us, drew only one side of it and
any mention of Guinevere was presumably on the other. But
Gerald did see it, and while his memory is inaccurate, he would
hardly have made up such an unlikely touch. Was Arthur's heir a
son by a first wife whom storytellers eliminated?

Suppose we approach this question of lineage from the present-day end. The United Kingdom of Great Britain and Northern
Ireland grew around England, which grew around Wessex, and
the House of Windsor is still descended from the West Saxon

kings, through all interminglings of Scandinavians, Normans, Welsh, Scots, and Germans. Elizabeth II's first Wessex ancestor is Cerdic, who landed on the shore of Southampton Water with a grown-up son and five shiploads of followers. So says the *Anglo-Saxon Chronicle,* putting the event in 495. In other words, the Queen's pedigree goes back to someone whose life overlapped Arthur's.

As history the *Chronicle's* early West Saxon entries carry even less weight than most, and the early line of West Saxon kings is dubious. But the founder, Cerdic, is certainly real, because no Saxon court genealogist would have invented him. His name is not Saxon at all but British. It appears in various forms, one of them being Ceredig, the name borne by the Clyde ruler, so that it was definitely a royal name among fifth-century Britons. Cerdic of Wessex may have had Saxon blood, seeing that Saxons accepted him as a leader; but he seems to have reckoned himself a Briton, because he gave his son a Celtic name too, Cynric.

Guesswork and fiction have tried to connect him with the battle of Badon, but the evidence is all against it. A more interesting question is where he came from. Professor James Campbell has echoed a suggestion I made in 1960, that we should look for the beginnings of Cerdic's enterprise in the Loire country. Not all the Saxons left after the defeat at Angers, and in the later fifth century, Britons and Saxons were still living close together. A Briton might have recruited Saxon warriors there as the Frankish King Childeric did earlier. With a combined force Cerdic could have sailed to Britain to make his bid. He made it, moreover, not as a mere freebooter but as something more legitimate, which he already was. The *Chronicle* speaks of him and his son as *ealdormen,* "princes," when they land in Britain. Founders of other Saxon dynasties are not honored thus. Whether or not Cerdic raised his following in the Breton borderlands, it is reasonable to press the query as to his background and rank.

A clue may lie in a word which is mysteriously repeated. When the West Saxon kingdom coalesced, its people were sometimes called the *Gewisse.* This means "Allies" or "Confederates." It was supposed, however, to mean "Gewis's Folk," Gewis being a mythical ancestor; and Geoffrey calls Vortigern "ruler of the Gewissei." Geoffrey knows nothing about Cerdic, but it looks as if somebody he read did know about him—somebody who believed that he inherited the lordship of the Gewisse from Vortigern, and inferred that Vortigern too was lord of them. He wasn't, but the belief in a connection and an inherited title could have been correct.

The *Chronicle* gives Cerdic a Saxon pedigree which is clearly bogus. It comes down to a father called Elesa. A real fifth-century Saxon father would never have given his son a British name, so Elesa can be discounted; he and his forebears have been grafted on to Cerdic to give him desirable ancestors. Cerdic's actual parentage is an open question. Timewise, he works quite well as a grandson of Vortigern via the offspring of a second marriage in 430 or thereabouts—perhaps even the marriage to a Saxon woman which legend makes so much of.

Who would that offspring have been? Not a son. Vortigern's sons were apparently by his first marriage, and nothing suggests that any of them fathered a Cerdic. But Nennius also has a wildly confused story about a daughter with whom, he says, Vortigern had an incestuous relationship. In one place she is made out to have been the mother of the bishop Faustus, who was born early in the fifth century, though she could not then have been old enough; in another the relationship is put near Vortigern's death, forty years or so later. The incest motif is part of the blackening of Vortigern's character. But behind it, very possibly, is a statement in some lost record that he had a daughter who "bore a son to the High King," and this was ignorantly taken to mean the High King Vortigern himself. It could have meant Arthur-Riothamus.

We now have an acceptable story. Vortigern, let us say, married his Saxon round about 430, and they had a daughter. In the 450s Arthur-Riothamus married her. This was part of whatever arrangement made him High King, just as Vortigern's first marriage, to a daughter of the Emperor Maximus, had been part of whatever arrangement made *him* High King. Cerdic, born in the 450s, was Arthur-Riothamus's son, three-quarters British and one-quarter Saxon. Celtic custom allowed him to inherit some sort of title from Vortigern via his mother. He went to Armorica and became the father of Cynric in the 470s. Planning a return to Britain, he exploited his fractional Saxon blood to attract Saxons to his cause. In 495, when Cynric was adult and an effective partner, he led his expedition across and established a little domain on the Hampshire coast. The fractional Saxon blood continued to be exploitable and helpful, as other Saxons trickled into the area.

If the Riothamus of the Breton genealogy was indeed Arthur, his alleged son Daniel would have been a younger one. An extraordinary thing is said about Daniel—that he became "king of the Alamanni." These were a Germanic people, some of whom became involved with Saxons and Franks in complications which there is no need to go into. A few may have emigrated to Britain. The point is that whatever Daniel's kingship of the Alamanni may imply, it hints that the family of Riothamus did dominate Germanic groups on the Continent, exactly as Cerdic would have had to do.

Obviously, if Cerdic was Arthur's true heir, this was a matter which the Welsh would have preferred to forget. From their point of view Vortigern was an arch-villain, his daughter was the product of a traitorous marriage, Arthur should have known better than to marry her, and their son was a renegade. All the same, Cerdic the prince did establish himself in Hampshire; and English royalty is descended from Arthur-Riothamus.

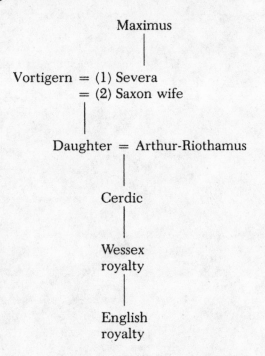

Maximus

Vortigern = (1) Severa
= (2) Saxon wife

Daughter = Arthur-Riothamus

Cerdic

Wessex
royalty

English
royalty

Prince Charles's son, whose ancestry Sir Iain Moncreiffe examined, is named William. But his second name is Arthur, and he could elect to use it instead. Appropriately?

Notes

The page numbers in the headings refer to related passages in the main text, which are supplemented here.

Pages 19–20

For the mystique of the later Roman Empire, see especially two books: Ernest Barker, *From Alexander to Constantine,* and Hans Lietzmann, *From Constantine to Julian.*

Page 39

The Valle Crucis pillar says Vortigern married Maximus's daughter Severa (spelled Sevira). Geoffrey of Monmouth does not mention her, except to the extent of indicating a marriage before the Saxon one. However, he does say that before Vortigern became King he was the "ruler of the Gewissei." Only one other person in Geoffrey's *History* is so described, a certain Octavius, the father of Maximus's supposedly British wife (page 39). There could be a notion here of a title transmitted to Vortigern in the female line, from Octavius to his daughter who married Maximus, and thence in some way to Vortigern. The natural inference is that the second link was supplied by Vortigern's marrying a daughter of Maximus, and this is exactly what the inscription says he did. Severa would probably have been older than her husband. Hence, it is quite plausible that she should have died early enough to allow his second, Saxon marriage, which looms so large in Geoffrey's story.

Page 53

James Campbell's comment on the King is in *The Anglo-Saxons,* page 37.

Page 59

On Geoffrey's knowledge, see also pages 78-80. Another interesting aspect of his book is slowly becoming apparent. His general picture of Roman and post-Roman Britain does have a sort of ghostly rightness. Throughout the period historians used to reduce the Britons to near nullity. The pre-Roman age was followed by "Roman Britain," in which the conquerors counted for everything and the Celtic people sank to the status of anonymous natives. Then, almost without a break, the Saxons were supposed to have poured in, slaughtering most of the natives and driving the remnant into Wales and Cornwall. While a fantasy like this has persisted in some schoolbooks, the facts as they are partly emerging belie it.

No one would follow Geoffrey in imagining Britain as self-governing through the Roman period. But there is more willingness today to see its Celtic society as carrying on and preserving a character of its own. The Roman regime was an intrusion—tremendous, creative, and lasting in some of its effects—yet the basic Britain was never extinguished or replaced. Afterward, Celtic culture resurfaced in art and life-styles.

It is clear too that the spell of real independence after 410 was more than a mere blink between conquests. Geoffrey is—after his fashion—right, not only in telling of British rulers then, but in portraying phases of British-Saxon coexistence. Thus, while Vortigern may not have married Hengist's daughter, there is at least one hint that such interdynastic marriages occurred (the case of Cerdic, discussed on pages 197–98). Again, Geoffrey speaks of the intermingling of Saxons with British women. Here too he is not as utterly misguided as historians formerly implied. Archaeology suggests that many of the new people lived at peace in their settlements, and were perfectly good neighbors.

Even when they moved forward much of the advance probably happened quietly and without local opposition. In parts of the country Saxon pressure and British counterattacks did produce serious fighting, yet the armed clashes were sporadic. The old notion of total enmity, with exterminatory warfare raging all the time, was due mainly to the habits of minstrels and chroniclers, who stressed battles and had less to say about the absence of battles.

Page 66

Gildas is the Briton quoted on page 43. His vital and neglected testimony to the Saxon withdrawal is in his Chapter 25 ("After a time, when the cruel plunderers had gone home . . ."). His statement about the date of Badon is confusing. In the text as we have it, the meaning is usually taken to be that the victory was won in the year of his own birth and that he is writing in the forty-fourth year after it. Bede, however, adapts the passage and seems to have read a copy of Gildas which was different, because he puts the battle in the forty-fourth year after the advent of the Saxons. Since he brings the Saxons to Britain around the middle of the fifth century (too late), he puts Badon, by implication, in the 490s. There is even a third possibility, based on a different reading of the Gildas text as we have it—that the battle happened in the forty-fourth year of the struggle initiated by Ambrosius's counteraction, that is, somewhat after 500. This was always a minority view and has gone largely out of favor. The basic problem is that the passage is highly compressed and convoluted, and it is not certain from what starting-point the "forty-fourth year" is reckoned. However, no interpretation will shift Badon very far from 500.

Page 72

Nennius has also been faulted on the ground that he describes Arthur as carrying an image of the Virgin Mary, whereas devotion to the Virgin was not known so early among British Christians. However, it was already popular in many parts of the fifth-century Roman world—certainly as far west as Italy—and Gildas has a passage indicating a Marian shrine in Britain which was at least very early. See my book *Avalonian Quest*, pages 142–43.

Page 77

The Camboglanna favored as Camlann by the northern school is the Roman fort at Birdoswald. It overlooks the River Irthing, which winds below in a valley and has the crooked bank which etymology appears to call for. Camboglanna would have evolved into Camlann in Welsh, but it would have taken a long time to pass through the change. Even if the *Annales* chronicler has picked up a reference to this fort, the reference must be centuries later than the battle, so that quite likely all we are getting is one of the many legends that came to associate Arthur with a medley of places up and down Britain. See also pages 84 and 120–21.

Page 84

David Dumville's attack on Alcock and Morris was in an article entitled "Sub-Roman Britain: History and Legend" (see Bibliography).

Page 85

The chronological fix for Vortigern is in some notes appended to Nennius. He is stated to have achieved power in the consulship of Theodosius and Valentinian. This was a normal Roman method of dating, and the year which is defined corresponds to 425.

Page 93

Geoffrey throws the early part of the fifth century into disarray by putting the Britons' appeal to Aëtius, which was in 446, before the reign of Constantine. He calls the Roman "Agicius," which implies that he is following Gildas, who spells the name Agitius. Probably Geoffrey did not realize who "Agitius" was. He has the further excuse that Gildas himself gives the appeal out of sequence, before the settlement of the Saxon federates. Bede would have put Geoffrey right about the name, but apparently he missed Bede's correction.

Page 95

Geoffrey's method of filling the gap between Arthur and the mission to Kent, led by St. Augustine of Canterbury, is rather interesting. He does it chiefly by a violent rehandling of Gildas. Gildas denounces several British kings by name, all of them regional despots living in his own time, the 540s. Geoffrey takes four of them and turns them into kings of Britain reigning successively. In this way he contrives four consecutive reigns. The first is the Constantine whom he makes Arthur's successor. Then come Aurelius Conanus, Vortiporius, and "Malgo" (Maelgwn). The four reigns are still not enough to satisfy him. He adds a fifth, followed by the Saxon triumph and an indefinite but eventful "long time" before he gets to the mission. However vague about dates he may have been, his basic thinking plainly demanded a long interval between Arthur and Augustine.

This is not quite the end of the matter: see page 205.

Page 97

If Geoffrey had Riothamus in mind, in this part of the story at least, and looked for him in the aforementioned chronicle by Sigebert of Gembloux, he would have found him in the entry for 470. That same entry would have given him the Emperor "Lucerius." The previous entry, for 469, is the other one that mentions "Lucerius," and it also mentions Childeric.

Pages 98–99

Gildas gives the essential clue to the British High Kingship when he speaks of the Britons having a *superbus tyrannus,* "preeminent ruler." In the form Vortigern the syllable *vor* means "over," the rest is "king" or "chieftain." Vortigern was the overking. While historians accept him as real, his son Vortimer, whom Geoffrey portrays as briefly taking his place, is viewed with more skepticism. Vortimer may not have been Vortigern's son, but etymology gives him a certain plausibility. The British original of Vortimer would have been Vortamorix. The *vor* is the same syllable as before, meaning "over"; *tamo* is the superlative suffix like the English "-est"; and *rix,* akin to the Latin *rex,* is another word for "king." So Vortimer means the "over-most" or "highest" king. It is a different expression of the same paramountcy.

Riothamus, therefore, is the third in a series. The first syllable of its British form Rigotamos is the same as the last syllable of Vortamorix. The rest, after the linking vowel, is the same as the *tamo* part of it. Hence Rigotamos is "king-most" or, if taken adjectivally, "supremely royal." With Vortigern, Vortimer, and Riothamus, there is a plain transition from one designation to another: Vortigern, Vor-tamo-rix, Rigo-tamos. The third fits into a slot created by the first and second. The appearance of the same style in three forms might have been due to the unstable conditions. Possibly Vortimer actually was proclaimed as a rival in Vortigern's lifetime, adopted the altered and more grandiloquent title, and was then killed or otherwise removed. Riothamus reigned afterward as one of the pro-Romans who were coming to the fore, and rearranged Vortamorix to dissociate himself from his predecessors.

Plutarch, in his *Life of Theseus* (Chapter 16), gives a Greek word which is exactly equivalent to Rigotamos—i.e., Basileutatos, made up of "king" plus a superlative suffix. It is definitely not a name, but a term of honor applied to Minos of Crete.

Page 99

When Geoffrey changes the Romans from allies to enemies, he may be taking a hint from the Roman failure to support Riothamus. But he is capable of inversions like this without any hint at all. The one which he contrives earlier in the *History* is in his version of Carausius's revolt and the Roman reconquest (see page 28). He turns one of the Romans' successful generals, Asclepiodotus, into a British King who fights against them. In this way he makes Asclepiodotus's victory a British victory and a Roman defeat!

Page 100

The present A.D. system of dating—*Anno Domini*, "in the year of Our Lord"—reckons from the year of Christ's birth, the Incarnation, or rather from a year inaccurately allotted to it in 525 by a monk named Dionysius. *Anno Domini* dating became the general norm during the sixth century, though it was later in reaching the British Isles. There was a previous Christian method, based on the work of a certain Victorius, which counted not from Christ's birth but from his death, the Passion, and put this event in the year which we now call A.D. 28. After *Anno Domini* became standard, scribes sometimes copied out dates computed by the old method without making the adjustment, or even without realizing that it had to be made. Thus they passed on a twenty-eight-year error.

The date 428 for the arrival of the Saxons (page 41) occurs in a note to Nennius which actually says 400; other particulars make it clear that the error has slipped in, and 428 is meant. This is one reason for giving it credence: the note must go back to an earlier record, written when the old method of dating was still in use.

While 442 as a supposedly A.D. date would be too early for the passing of Arthur, there are signs that Geoffrey may not have miscorrected it immediately, and that a vanished first edition of the *History*—suspected on other grounds—actually had it. Two early chroniclers in France, who manifestly knew his work, got the notion that Arthur flourished in the 420s and 430s. This is so absurd as to suggest that they felt themselves compelled by an apparently very precise and positive date. They may have seen a copy with 442 in it. One of them has Arthur reigning in 421, and compounds the absurdity by having Gildas born in the same year. This has a certain interest. Gildas was born in the year of Badon, and to judge from the *Annales Cambriae*, those who credited Arthur with that victory supposed his passing to have occurred twenty-one years after it. The chronicler, therefore, may have been counting back from a "passing" assigned to 442.

If Geoffrey's final 542 is due to his making a misguided hundred-year correction, he was perhaps not quite unaware of the havoc he was causing, and not quite indifferent. As observed (page 203), he had already contrived bogus reigns and other events to bridge the wide gap between Arthur and St. Augustine of Canterbury. But the "corrected" date reduced this to fifty-five years, 542–97. As a further afterthought—it rather appears—he made two of his intermediate kings die young. That, at any rate, is what they do in the *History* as we now have it.

Page 104

For the proof that the *Goeznovius* preface is not derived from Geoffrey, whatever its date, see pages 305–6 of my article "A Certain Very Ancient Book" (see Bibliography).

Pages 106–7

Guesswork about sources is bound to be fanciful. However, there does need to
have been a document we no longer possess, somewhere in the background of
Goeznovius and Geoffrey. It would have been a text composed on the Continent, giving an account of Riothamus in Gaul; doubtless many other things too,
but certainly that. The known early authors—Jordanes, Sidonius, Gregory of
Tours—supply facts, but these are scattered through hundreds of pages and
only make a story when assembled in their historical setting. Someone, at the
very least, had to do the assembling. But the assembler had other information in
any case. None of the early authors supply such details as the place name
Avallon.

If, as suggested, Geoffrey's 542 is a double error with the older Christian
chronology underlying it, the original text can scarcely have been much later
than the sixth century. After that, *Anno Domini* dating was the Continental
norm, the date would simply have been given as 470, and no error would have
occurred. Such an early original would have been in Latin. Geoffrey's "ancient
book in the British language," if real, could have been a Breton translation or
adaptation of it, but would have had to be appreciably later, because, in the
sixth century, Breton was not a written language.

A Latin original could explain still another feature of Geoffrey's story, the
transfer of the treachery theme from Arvandus, the deputy of the Emperor, to
Modred, presented as the deputy of Arthur himself. The Latin word *imperator*,
"emperor," could be applied to a High King, as Irish usage proves. So a Latin
phrase about "the treason of the emperor's deputy" could have been read as
meaning a deputy of the High King. A Breton adapter might have passed this on
to Geoffrey as an honest misunderstanding.

Simply as a study in possibilities, consider the following paragraph:

> When Leo reigned at Constantinople, and Simplicius was pope, the
> Romans still laid claim to Gaul. Parts of it were held by the Britons, and
> by nations which had come out of Germany. At that time a fleet arrived
> with the army of the king of the Britons. These were warriors against
> the Saxons. In the island of Britain the Saxons had drawn back after
> great devastation. The king and his men passed successfully through
> the northern part of Gaul and advanced into the country neighbouring
> the Burgundians, who were allied to the Romans. The Britons' strength
> was brought to nothing by the treason of the deputy of the emperor
> *[imperator]*, who had dealings with barbarians. Because of this a hostile
> army was raised and a battle was fought in which many Britons per-
> ished. It was the year 442. Their leader departed into the region where
> the place called Avallon is. No one tells of his end.

None of this is fiction. It is history throughout, with every statement based
on accepted records, including the date, as counted from the Passion. Such a
synthetic paragraph proves nothing; the possibility of composing it proves
something. The facts about the Riothamus affair could have been stated in a way

which would have supplied groundwork for both *Goeznovius* and Geoffrey. In other words, the hypothetical source text behind them both is a credible thing. Given the simple understanding—implied in *Goeznovius*—that this "king of the Britons" whom two writers call Riothamus had the personal name Arthur, the rest would follow. William and Geoffrey would both have needed more, but they could have found more, and fitted it in. William perhaps recognized the method of dating, and mentally made the correct adjustment; Geoffrey did not, and "emended" the date to 542.

Page 108

The "Two eccentrics": see page 205.

Page 115

As Alcock has pointed out, when Gildas mentions the Britons' appeal to Aëtius and calls him "Agitius," it looks as if he has confused him with Aegidius. This could be due to Gildas's having heard or read some account of British refugees in Armorica seeking help from Aegidius.

Page 116

The pre-Roman finds at Cadbury have no direct bearing on its "Arthur" phase, but they suggest a possibility as to why a martial High King might have chosen it for his citadel. They show that the life of the British village on the plateau went on without a break after the Roman invasion in A.D. 43, and ended only with an assault and capture an appreciable time later. Cadbury, perhaps, was a center of anti-Roman activity during the revolt led by Boudicca, which started in 60 and went on into 61. The episode is puzzling, since historians say nothing of any action so far west. But the Romans certainly stormed the place, and afterward, taking no chances, moved the surviving inhabitants to the foot of the hill outside the fortifications. While they ruled, the summit area was deserted, though a small temple may have been built during the fourth-century pagan revival. Cadbury-Camelot seems to emerge as a sort of parallel to Masada, the last stronghold of the Jewish rebels a few years later, holding out when the territory all around was under Roman control. It could have been invested with symbolic value, disposing the High King to reoccupy and restore it.

Page 117

On Lucius Artorius Castus, and the possibility that he was remembered, see my book *Kings and Queens of Early Britain,* pages 42–43.

Page 118

As remarked, guesswork about sources is bound to be speculative. To suggest that Geoffrey's "ancient book" gave the substance of a Latin poem is not to exclude the suggestion on page 206 that it gave the substance of a piece of straight history. It could have done both. Nennius does both in his own field, since his sketch of Arthur's wars seems to be based on a poem, whereas other parts of his book are undoubtedly based on prose sources.

The idea that Artorius could have been a nickname raises another possibility, not to be taken too seriously, but at least amusing. It depends on a sort of word play. In the extant copies of Sidonius's letter, Riothamus is spelled as here, with the *h* in the middle. But the early copyists were Frankish scribes, who sometimes modified spellings. In the fifth century a likelier Latin form would have been Riotamus without the *h*. Artorius is almost an anagram of this. An order, medallion, or whatever saying RIOTAMUS R., the *R* standing for *rex (Britonum)*, King of the Britons, would have supplied all the letters for ARTORIUS with only the *M* left over; and anagrams made up in antiquity were not always perfect. There are Jewish instances of names and phrases involving such rearrangements, and a more recent and famous one, reputedly, is Voltaire.

Page 121

Patrick's immense age is by no means unparalleled among the saints. Quite a number of Celtic holy men are made out to have been implausibly long-lived. A biographer may (for example) have wanted to persuade his readers that the saint was a disciple of some other distinguished person, so that he had to be born earlier; or that some other distinguished person was a disciple of his, so that he had to die later.

The *Anglo-Saxon Chronicle* supplies two cases of life-prolongation very close to Arthur. It says that the founder of the West Saxon dynasty, Cerdic, brought his expedition to land in 495 with his son Cynric. Both are called *ealdormen*, "princes." Cynric would hardly have been mentioned if he had been a child, and by implication he is adult. Cerdic, therefore, is likely to have been in his forties and was certainly not much younger. Yet in 530 he is named as chief conqueror of the Isle of Wight, therefore still an active warrior, and he lives on till 534. Cynric, born probably in the 470s, is still fighting in 556 and does not die till 560. These lives of a father and son are theoretically possible, but under early Saxon conditions they are beyond reasonable belief. The motive may have been to forge genealogical links, or to associate the first chiefs with famous victories.

Page 124

The two ways of designating the High King resemble the two ways of designating the hero who comes closest to being a Spanish Arthur-figure. He is known to history as Ruy Díaz de Bivar, to epic and romance as el Cid Campeador, "the Lord Champion." Spanish records are fuller and have prevented his identity from getting confused. The earliest epic of the Cid mentions the name as well. But it has long stretches where Ruy Díaz never occurs. If it had survived only as scrappily as the early Arthur material, poets might have taken up the tale of the Cid without knowing who he was. The name and title are the other way round, but the principle is the same.

Pages 174–76

On Glastonbury, see my *Avalonian Quest*, where the statements made here are made at greater length and substantiated.

Page 197

Vortigern's alleged status as "ruler of the Gewissei" has a further ramification mentioned on page 201. The hint at transmission of a title in the female line has its relevance to Cerdic, or at least to the speculation about his parentage which is offered here.

Bibliography

Alcock, Leslie. *Arthur's Britain*. London: Allen Lane the Penguin Press, 1971.
———. *"By South Cadbury Is That Camelot . . ."* (short title, *Cadbury-Camelot*). London: Thames, 1972.
———. "Cadbury-Camelot: A Fifteen-Year Perspective," *Proceedings of the British Academy* 68 (1982): 355–88.

Anglo-Saxon Chronicle. Edited and translated by G. N. Garmonsway. London: Dent, 1953; New York: Dutton, 1953.

Annales Cambriae, see Nennius.

Ashe, Geoffrey. *Avalonian Quest*. London: Methuen, 1982; London: Collins, Fontana, 1984.
———. *Camelot and the Vision of Albion*. London: Heinemann, 1971; New York: St. Martin's, 1971.
———. "A Certain Very Ancient Book," *Speculum*, April 1981, 301–23.
———. *From Caesar to Arthur*. London: Collins, 1960.
———. *A Guidebook to Arthurian Britain*. London: Longmans, 1980; London: Aquarian Press, 1983.
———. *Kings and Queens of Early Britain*. London: Methuen, 1982.
———, ed. *The Quest for Arthur's Britain*. London: Pall Mall, 1968; New York: Praeger, 1968; Paladin Press, 1971 and 1982.

Baring-Gould, S., and Fisher, John. *The Lives of the British Saints*. 4 vols. London: Cymmrodorion Society, 1907–13.

Barker, Ernest. *From Alexander to Constantine*. London: Oxford, Clarendon Press, 1956.

Bede. *A History of the English Church and People*. Translated by Leo Sherley-Price. London: Penguin, 1955.

Blair, Peter Hunter. *An Introduction to Anglo-Saxon England*. 2d ed. London: Cambridge, 1977.

Brinkley, Roberta F. *Arthurian Legend in the Seventeenth Century*. Baltimore and London: Johns Hopkins Press, 1932; new edition: New York: Octagon Press, 1966.

Bromwich, Rachel. *Trioedd Ynys Prydein*. The Welsh triads, with translation and notes. Cardiff: University of Wales Press, 1961.

Brown, Peter. *The World of Late Antiquity*. London: Thames, 1971.

Campbell, James, ed. *The Anglo-Saxons*. Ithaca, N.Y.: Cornell University Press, 1982.

Cavendish, Richard. *King Arthur and the Grail*. London: Weidenfeld, 1978.

Chadwick, H. M., and Chadwick, N. K. *The Growth of Literature*. Vol. 1, *The Ancient Literature of Europe*. London: Cambridge, 1932; New York: Macmillan, 1932.

Chadwick, N. K. "The Colonization of Brittany from Celtic Britain," *Proceedings of the British Academy* 51 (1966): 235–99.
———. *Early Brittany*. Cardiff: University of Wales Press, 1969.
———, ed. *Studies in Early British History*. London: Cambridge, 1954.

Chambers, E. K. *Arthur of Britain*. London: Sidgwick, 1927; New York: Barnes & Noble, 1964; reissue of British edition, 1966.

Chrétien de Troyes. *Arthurian Romances*. Translated by W. W. Comfort. London: Dent, 1955; New York: Dutton, 1955.

Clancy, Joseph P. *The Earliest Welsh Poetry*. London: Macmillan, 1970.

Collingwood, R. G., and Myres, J. N. L. *Roman Britain and the English Settlements*. 2d ed. London and New York: Oxford, 1937.

Darrah, John. *The Real Camelot*. London: Thames, 1981.

Ditmas, E. M. R. *Breton Settlers in Cornwall After the Norman Conquest*. Cymmrodorion Society, 1978.
———. "A Reappraisal of Geoffrey of Monmouth's Allusions to Cornwall," *Speculum*, July 1973, 510–24.
———. *Tristan and Iseult in Cornwall*. Gloucester: Forrester Roberts, 1969.

Dumville, David. "Sub-Roman Britain: History and Legend," *History* 62 (1977): 173–91.

Eadie, John W. "The Development of Roman Mailed Cavalry," *Journal of Roman Studies* 57 (1967): 161–73.

Eschenbach, Wolfram von. *Parzival*. Translated by Helen M. Mustard and Charles E. Passage. New York: Knopf, 1961.

Ferguson, John. *Pelagius*. Cambridge: Heffer, 1956.

Finberg, H. P. R. *The Formation of England, 550–1042*. St. Albans: Hart-Davis, MacGibbon, 1974.

Fleuriot, Léon. *Les Origines de la Bretagne*. Paris: Payot, 1980.

Frere, Sheppard. *Britannia*. London: Routledge, 1967.

Geoffrey of Monmouth. *The History of the Kings of Britain*. Translated by Lewis Thorpe. London: Penguin, 1966.

———. *Vita Merlini (The Life of Merlin)*. Edited and translated by J. J. Parry. Urbana: University of Illinois Press, 1925.

Gerould, G. H. "King Arthur and Politics," *Speculum,* January 1927, 33–51.

Gildas. In *History from the Sources*. Vol. 7, *The Ruin of Britain*. Edited and translated by Michael Winterbottom. Chichester: Phillimore, 1978.

Gododdin, see Clancy.

Gougaud, Louis. *Christianity in Celtic Lands*. London: Sheed & Ward, 1932.

Greenlaw, Edwin. *Studies in Spenser's Historical Allegory*. London: Oxford 1932; Baltimore: Johns Hopkins Press, 1932; new edition: New York: Octagon Press, 1966.

Gregory of Tours. *The History of the Franks*. Translated by Lewis Thorpe. London: Penguin, 1974.

Hoare, F. R., ed. and trans., *The Western Fathers* (containing the *Life of St. Germanus)*. London and New York: Sheed, 1954; new edition: New York: Harper, 1965.

Jackson, Kenneth H. *Language and History in Early Britain*. Edinburgh: Edinburgh University Press, 1953; Cambridge: Harvard University Press, 1954. See also the first two chapters of Loomis, *Arthurian Literature in the Middle Ages*.

Jerrold, Douglas. *An Introduction to the History of England*. London: Collins, 1949.

John of Glastonbury. *Chronicle*. Edited by T. Hearne. Oxford, 1726.

Jones, A. H. M. *Constantine and the Conversion of Europe*. London: English Universities, 1948.

Jordanes. *The Gothic History*. Translated by C. C. Mierow. Princeton: Princeton University Press, 1915.

Knowles, David. *The Monastic Order in England*. London: Cambridge, 1950.

Lagorio, Valerie M. "The Evolving Legend of St Joseph of Glastonbury," *Speculum,* April 1971, 209–31.

Legend of St. Goeznovius, see Ashe, "A Certain Very Ancient Book"; Chambers, *Arthur of Britain;* and Fleuriot, *Les Origines de la Bretagne*.

Leland, John. *Itinerary*. Edited by Lucy Toulmin Smith. Arundel: Centaur Press, 1964; Carbondale: Southern Illinois University Press, 1965.

Lietzmann, Hans. *From Constantine to Julian*. London: Lutterworth, 1953.

Littleton, C. Scott, and Thomas, Ann C. "The Sarmatian Connection," *Journal of American Folklore* 91 (1978): 513–27.

Lloyd, John Edward. *A History of Wales*. 2 vols. London: Longmans, 1939.

Loomis, R. S., ed. *Arthurian Literature in the Middle Ages*. London: Oxford, Clarendon Press, 1959; New York: Oxford, 1959.

Mabinogion. Translated by Gwyn Jones and Thomas Jones. London: Dent, 1949; New York: Dutton, 1949.

Malory, Sir Thomas. *Le Morte d'Arthur*. Caxton's text edited with modernized spelling by Janet Cowan. 2 vols. Harmondsworth: Penguin, 1969.
————. *Works*. Edited by E. Vinaver. London: Oxford, Clarendon Press, 1948; New York: Oxford, 1947.

Markale, Jean. *King Arthur: King of Kings*. Translated by Christine Hauch. London: Gordon & Cremonesi, 1977.

Mason, Eugene, trans. *Arthurian Chronicles* (including the Arthurian portion of Wace). London: Dent, 1962.

Millar, Ronald. *Will the Real King Arthur Please Stand Up?* London: Cassell, 1978.

Moncreiffe of That Ilk, Sir Iain. *Royal Highness*. London: H. Hamilton, 1982.

Morris, John. *The Age of Arthur*. London: Weidenfeld, 1973.

Nennius. In *History from the Sources*. Vol. 8, *British History* (including the *Annales Cambriae*). Edited and translated by John Morris. Chichester: Phillimore, 1980.

Padel, O. J. "Tintagel: An alternative view." In *A Provisional List of Imported Pottery in Post-Roman Western Britain and Ireland*, edited by Charles Thomas. Redruth: Institute of Cornish Studies, 1981.

Perlesvaus. Translated by Nigel Bryant. Cambridge: D. S. Brewer, 1978.

Piggott, Stuart. *The Druids*. London: Penguin, 1974.

Procopius. *History of the Wars*. Translated by H. B. Dewing. 7 vols. London: Heinemann, 1914–40; New York: Macmillan, 1914–40.

The Quest of the Holy Grail. Translated by P. M. Matarosso. London: Penguin, 1969.

Radford, C. A. *The Pillar of Eliseg* (i.e., the Valle Crucis monument). Edinburgh: H.M. Stationery Office, 1980. See also contributions to Ashe, *The Quest for Arthur's Britain*.

Rahtz, Philip. See contribution to Ashe, *The Quest for Arthur's Britain*.

Rees, Alwyn, and Rees, Brinley. *Celtic Heritage*. London: Thames, 1961.

Robinson, Joseph Armitage. *Somerset Historical Essays*. London: British Academy, 1921.
————. *Two Glastonbury Legends*. London: Cambridge, 1926.

Ross, Anne. *Pagan Celtic Britain*. London: Routledge, 1967; London: Sphere, Cardinal, 1974.

Scott, John. *The Early History of Glastonbury*. Woodbridge: Boydell & Brewer, 1981.

Sheldon, Gilbert. *The Transition from Roman Britain to Christian England.* London: Macmillan, 1932.

Sidonius Apollinaris. *Poems and Letters.* Edited and translated by W. B. Anderson. 2 vols. London: Heinemann, 1936 and 1965; Cambridge: Harvard University Press, 1936 and 1965.

Sigebert of Gembloux. *Chronicle,* in vol. 160 of *Patrologia Latina.* Edited by J. P. Migne. Paris, 1844–55.

Sir Gawain and the Green Knight. Translated by Brian Stone. London: Penguin, 1974.

Slover, Clark H. "Glastonbury Abbey and the Fusing of English Literary Culture," *Speculum,* April 1935, 147–60.

Stenton, F. M. *Anglo-Saxon England.* London: Oxford, 1943; New York: Oxford, 1947.

Stevens, C. E. *Sidonius Apollinaris and His Age.* London: Oxford, Clarendon Press, 1933.

Tatlock, J.S.P. *The Legendary History of Britain.* Berkeley and Los Angeles: University of California Press, 1950.

Treharne, R. F. *The Glastonbury Legends.* London: Cresset, 1967.

Wace, see Mason.

Wilhelm, James J., and Gross, Laila Zamuelis, eds. *The Romance of Arthur.* New York: Garland, 1984.

William of Malmesbury. *The Acts of the Kings of the English.* Translated as *William of Malmesbury's Chronicle* by John Sharpe; revised by J. A. Giles. London: Bohn, 1847.

Williams, Charles. *Arthurian Torso.* A fragment edited by C. S. Lewis. London: Oxford, 1948.

Index